HILARY MANTEL is the author of eleven novels, a collection of short stories, and a memoir, *Giving Up the Ghost.* She writes both historical and contemporary fiction, and her settings range from a South African township under apartheid to Paris during the French Revolution, from a city in twentieth-century Saudi Arabia to rural Ireland in the eighteenth century.

Her novel *Wolf Hall* is about Thomas Cromwell, chief minister to Henry VIII. It won the 2009 Man Booker Prize, the inaugural Walter Scott Prize, and in the United States won the National Book Critics Circle Award. *Bring Up the Bodies* won the 2012 Man Booker Prize and the Costa Book Award. Taken together, *Wolf Hall* and *Bring Up the Bodies* have sold more than three million copies and have been translated into thirty-six languages. She is working on *The Mirror and the Light,* the third book in her Thomas Cromwell trilogy.

D1206873

MIKE POULTON's recent adaptations and translations for the stage include Chekhov's *Uncle Vanya* (directed by Lucy Bailey at The Print Room, London); Schiller's *Luise Miller* (directed by Michael Grandage for the Donmar Warehouse, London); *Anjin: The English Samurai* (directed by Gregory Doran for Hripro in Tokyo); Malory's *Morte d'Arthur* (directed by Gregory Doran for the Royal Shakespeare Company); Schiller's *Wallenstein* (directed by Angus Jackson at Chichester Festival Theatre); Schiller's *Mary Stuart* (directed by Terry Hands at Clwyd Theatr Cymru); Ibsen's *The Lady from the Sea* (directed by Lucy Bailey at Birmingham Repertory Theatre); Chekhov's *The Cherry Orchard* (directed by Philip Franks at Chichester Festival Theatre, and Terry Hands at Clwyd Theatr Cymru); Ibsen's *Rosmersholm* (directed by Anthony Page at the Almeida Theatre, London); Strindberg's *The Father* (directed by Simon Coury at the Samuel Beckett Theatre, Dublin); and a two-part adaptation of Chaucer's *Canterbury Tales* (directed by Gregory Doran for the Royal Shakespeare Company, and performed at the Swan Theatre, Stratford-upon-Avon, in the West End, and on tour of the U.S. and Spain).

His acclaimed version of Schiller's *Don Carlos* premiered at the Sheffield Crucible in a production directed by Michael Grandage with Derek Jacobi as King Philip II of Spain. It has since been widely performed, including by Rough Magic Theatre Company in Dublin (directed by Lynne Parker), and at the Goteborgs Stadsteater (directed by Eva Bergman). Other productions include Ibsen's *Hedda Gabler* (West Yorkshire Playhouse/Liverpool Playhouse); Turgenev's *Fortune's Fool* (directed by Arthur Penn at the Music Box Theater, Broadway; nominated for a Tony Award for Best Play, and winner of seven major awards including the Tony Awards for Best Actor for Alan Bates and Best Featured Actor for Frank Langella); *Uncle Vanya* (directed by Bill Bryden at the Birmingham Rep; with Charles Dance); *Ghosts* (Theatre Royal Plymouth); *The Seagull, Three Sisters, The Dance of Death,* and an adaptation of Euripides, *Ion* (all directed by David Hunt at the Mercury Theatre, Colchester).

WOLF HALL

and

BRING UP
THE BODIES

The Stage Adaptation

Adapted by
Mike Poulton

From the novels by
Hilary Mantel

*With an introduction by Mike Poulton
and character notes by Hilary Mantel*

PICADOR • NEW YORK

www.picadorusa.com • picadorbookroom.tumblr.com
www.twitter.com/picadorusa • www.facebook.com/picadorusa

Picador® is a U.S. registered trademark and is used by St. Martin's Press under license from Pan Books Limited.

For book club information, please visit www.facebook.com/picadorbookclub or e-mail marketing@picadorusa.com.

Amateur Performing Rights: Applications for performance, including readings and excerpts, by amateurs in the English language throughout the world (excluding the Unites States of America and Canada) should be made before rehearsals begin to the Performing Rights Manager, Nick Hern Books, The Glasshouse, 49a Goldhawk Road, LondonW12 8QP, *telephone* +44 (0)20 8749 4953, *e-mail* info@nickhernbooks.co.uk, except as follows:
Australia: Dominie Drama, 8 Cross Street, Brookvale 2100, *fax* (2) 9938 8695, *e-mail* drama@dominie.com.au
New Zealand: Play Bureau, PO Box 9013, St Clair, Dunedin 9047, *telephone* (3) 455 9959, *e-mail* play.bureau.nz@xtra.co.nz
South Africa: DALRO (pty) Ltd, PO Box 31627, 2017 Braamfontein, *telephone* (11) 712 8000, fax (11) 403 9094, *e-mail* theatricals@dalro.co.za
United States of America and Canada: Alan Brodie Representation Ltd., see details below:

Professional Performing Rights: Applications for translation and for performance by professionals in any medium (and by stock and amateur companies in the United States of America and Canada) should be addressed to Alan Brodie Representation Ltd., Paddock Suite, The Courtyard, 55 Charterhouse Street, London EC1M 6HA, *fax* +44 (0)20 7183 7999, *Web site* www.alanbrodie.com.
No performance of any kind may be given unless a license has been obtained. Applications should be made before rehearsals begin. Publication of these plays does not necessarily indicate their availability for performance.

The Library of Congress Cataloging-in-Publication Data is available upon request.

ISBN 978-1-250-06417-2 (trade paperback)
ISBN 978-1-250-06418-9 (e-book)

Picador books may be purchased for educational, business, or promotional use. For information on bulk purchases, please contact the Macmillan Corporate and Premium Sales Department at 1-800-221-7945, extension 5442, or write to specialmarkets@macmillan.com.

The stage adaptation of *Wolf Hall* and *Bring Up the Bodies* was originally published in Great Britain by Fourth Estate, an imprint of HarperCollins Publishers, and Nick Hern Books

First U.S. Edition: March 2015

10 9 8 7 6 5 4 3 2 1

Wolf Hall and *Bring Up the Bodies* were originally commissioned by Playful Productions and were first produced by the Royal Shakespeare Company at the Swan Theatre, Stratford-upon-Avon, on 11 December 2013. These productions transferred to the Aldwych Theatre, London on 1 May 2014, presented by Matthew Byam Shaw, Nia Janis and Nick Salmon for Playful Productions and the Royal Shakespeare Company, Bartner/Tulchin Productions and Georgia Gatti for Playful Productions.

The Royal Shakespeare Company's productions of *Wolf Hall* and *Bring Up the Bodies* were subsequently produced on Broadway at the Winter Garden Theatre, New York, on 20 March 2015, by Jeffrey Richards, Jerry Frankel, Matthew Byam Shaw, Nia Janis and Nick Salmon for Playful Productions, Carole Shorenstein Hays, Jam Theatricals, Ron Kastner, Kyodo Tokyo, Inc., Tulchin Bartner Productions, Scott M. Delman, Dominion Pictures, Rebecca Gold, Just for Laughs Theatricals, Kit Seidel, Georgia Gatti for Playful Productions, Jessica Genick, Will Trice and the Shubert Organization.

MARK SMEATON	**Joey Batey**
CHARLES BRANDON, DUKE OF SUFFOLK	**Nicholas Boulton**
KATHERINE OF ARAGON/ JANE BOLEYN, LADY ROCHFORD	**Lucy Briers**
JANE SEYMOUR/ PRINCESS MARY/ LADY WORCESTER	**Leah Brotherhead**
MARY BOLEYN/ LIZZIE WYKYS/ MARY SHELTON	**Olivia Darnley**
THOMAS HOWARD, DUKE OF NORFOLK	**Nicholas Day**
ENSEMBLE	**Mathew Foster**
GREGORY CROMWELL	**Daniel Fraser**

GEORGE BOLEYN, LORD ROCHFORD/ EDWARD SEYMOUR	**Edward Harrison**
BARGE-MASTER/ WOLSEY'S SERVANT	**Benedict Hastings**
LADY IN WAITING/MAID/ MARGERY SEYMOUR	**Madeleine Hyland**
CARDINAL WOLSEY/ SIR JOHN SEYMOUR/ SIR WILLIAM KINGSTON/ ARCHBISHOP WARHAM	**Paul Jesson**
ANNE BOLEYN	**Lydia Leonard**
ENSEMBLE	**Robert MacPherson**
THOMAS CROMWELL	**Ben Miles**
CHRISTOPHE/ FRANCIS WESTON	**Pierro Niél Mee**
KING HENRY VIII	**Nathaniel Parker**
STEPHEN GARDINER/ EUSTACHE CHAPUYS	**Matthew Pidgeon**
THOMAS MORE/ HENRY NORRIS	**John Ramm**
HARRY PERCY/ WILLIAM BRERETON	**Nicholas Shaw**
RAFE SADLER	**Joshua Silver**
THOMAS CRANMER/ THOMAS BOLEYN/ FRENCH AMBASSADOR	**Giles Taylor**
THOMAS WYATT/HEADSMAN	**Jay Taylor**

All other parts played by members of the Company.

Novelist	**Hilary Mantel**
Adapted by	**Mike Poulton**
Directed by	**Jeremy Herrin**
Set and Costumes Designed by	**Christopher Oram**
Wolf Hall Lighting Designed by	**Paule Constable**
Bring Up the Bodies Lighting Designed by	**David Plater**
Music by	**Stephen Warbeck**
Sound by	**Nick Powell**
Movement by	**Siân Williams**
Casting by	**Helena Palmer CDG**

This text may differ from the play as performed.

WOLF HALL

and

BRING UP THE BODIES

Adapted for the stage by Mike Poulton

From the novels by Hilary Mantel

Contents

Adapting *Wolf Hall* and *Bring Up the Bodies*
Mike Poulton

Over three years ago I was asked if it might be possible to adapt Hilary Mantel's *Wolf Hall* for the stage. At the time of asking, *Bring Up the Bodies* did not exist. I'd read *Wolf Hall* and been gripped by it – from the first page to the last – page 653. It's an extraordinary read. To call it a historical novel diminishes it – for me it's a deeply serious piece of literature that happens to be set in and around the Court of Henry VIII. I can think of no other contemporary work of period fiction that comes near it. It's that rare thing – a novel that richly deserved its fame and the accolades and prizes heaped upon it. I knew that Hilary was at work on a sequel and I was counting the days. I read *Wolf Hall* again. I said that I thought it could be made into a play if the right adapter could be found. 'Might you be the right adapter?' I was asked.

I had never worked with a living author. Earlier collaborators, Schiller, Chekhov, Turgenev, Chaucer, Malory, were all long dead. Hilary is very much alive, and I knew that for the project to work she and I would have to get on together, and agree about how best to engineer the transformation. I imagined it would be like taking apart a Rolls-Royce and reassembling the parts as a light aircraft. After three years together I can say that our collaboration has proved to be, for me at any rate, the most rewarding part of the experience. I have learned so much. Hilary has been generous and committed in every way with advice, with time, with invention, with challenges – all coming out of a deep knowledge of her subject, and easy familiarity with the complex minds of the characters she has created. Fortunately, she also has a love and instinctive understanding of the workings of theatre. Above all it's been fun – a lot of fun. Her attitude from the first was that she had brought Cromwell and company to life, and I was free, within the limits of the story and the requirements of historical accuracy, to move them about on the stage as I saw fit. Though on many occasions she has had to pull me out of holes into

which I've dug myself. I've never had that sort of help from
Friedrich von Schiller.

So what were the problems we faced at the outset? I felt that,
in terms of staging – in order to create a workable dramatic
framework – we had to get to the death of Anne Boleyn. If we
could do that, we'd have a strong tragic arc – the ascendancy of
Anne followed by her rapid decline. If Thomas Cromwell's rise
from obscurity was to be the story of the play, the Court of
Henry VIII must be the stage upon which he acts, and the rise
and fall of Anne Boleyn the engine that drives the action. I
knew Hilary was working on a sequel to *Wolf Hall*, to be called
The Mirror and the Light. Could she take me as far as Anne's
execution? Yes, of course she could. But by the time she
reached the summer of 1536 we had another book, *Bring Up the
Bodies*, and so much tempting new material that the original
play was rapidly becoming two plays. Since that time the only
heartbreak in the process has been deciding what to set aside.

Structurally, the new material was exactly what was needed.
Wolf Hall would take us to Anne's coronation, and *Bring Up the
Bodies* to her execution. But the growing scale of the project
and size of the cast meant that we needed a new partner and a
new home. The Royal Shakespeare Company, under its brightly
shining, new-minted Artistic Director, Gregory Doran,
welcomed us in. This was a turning point. I'd worked five times
with Greg, and I knew that from the RSC we'd get the
expertise, support and resources the plays needed and deserved.
We have not been disappointed.

It might be thought that the sheer length of the two books
would present problems. I never thought so. The way a novel is
structured cannot be reproduced on the stage – there could be
no question of simply putting two whole novels on their feet.
They had to be completely re-imagined as plays. The immediate
questions were what would be lost, and what, if anything,
would be gained in the stage versions? We set out to convert our
difficulties into opportunities.

The content of the books cannot be condensed. You can't
repaint the jewel-like miniature scenes of the original with
broad brushstrokes. You can't ask an actor to play a summary of
events – actors need detail. Adaptation is the process of
choosing vital and dramatic details from the novels and re-
laying them like stepping stones along a clear route from a

beginning, through a middle, and then in a headlong rush to the end. Pace is everything. To falter on stepping stones is to end up in the river.

Losses and gains? Strong characters are the life of Hilary's books. So in terms of character, nothing could be changed. I wanted Cromwell, Wolsey, Anne and Henry – and all the other powerful characters we've included – to leap alive and fully formed from the pages of the books onto the stage of the Swan. If this could be accomplished, I felt the spirit of the book would remain intact. Incident has been lost. Obviously, we can't reproduce every scene and every conversation we read in the original work, so we've had to be highly selective. There's no doubt that readers will have favourite scenes that are not shown in the plays. But the story should gain a different sort of pace and drive in the playing. In the novels it's as if we're standing at Cromwell's shoulder observing what he observes and sharing his thoughts. Seeing events through Cromwell's eyes was the prime requirement of the adaptation. Sometimes what works perfectly in a novel won't read in a live performance. Some of the most memorable images in the books are formed in Cromwell's head: his reflections, his plotting, his private anguish, and, most of all, his barely contained laughter. Cromwell is very often on the point of dissolving into mirth. We decided at an early stage not to indulge in 'pieces to camera' – monologues delivered chorus-like by Cromwell to the audience. So in working with RSC actors through the drafts – there have been nine – we decided to give Cromwell two confidants, one from his household, one from Court, with whom he can share his thoughts: Rafe Sadler and Thomas Wyatt. And we have also provided him with a few completely new scenes which have no equivalent in the books.

Once the characters were comfortable, and sure-footed, on stage, it became possible to give them their heads in order to drive the plotting forward. There are many fewer characters in the plays than in the novels – a cast of one hundred and thirty would overcrowd the intimate playing space of the Swan – but other characters have risen to prominence and have been given more to do in the telling of the story. Christophe, for example, in some ways a model of Cromwell's younger self, seems to be everywhere, and is usually up to mischief.

Our choice of theatre – the Swan is always my first choice – suggested, or rather insisted upon, a particular tone and style for our two plays. It's a small space with a deep thrust stage. Wherever you sit, you feel you're part of the action. Instead of looking over Cromwell's shoulder, as in the books, throughout the plays you're on stage with him. And he is on stage all the time. There's spectacle – masques at Court, dances, courts of inquiry, even a coronation and a deer hunt. There's detail – quiet scenes at home in Austin Friars, a fire in the Queen's chambers in the middle of the night, scenes of intrigue and interrogation, and ghostly visitations. But there are no elaborate stage tricks – no revolves, lifts, nor clever-clever scene changes – everything has to be accomplished by the actors. They have their voices, their costumes, music, lighting, props, and an infinitely flexible playing space that can carry us in seconds from King Henry's bedchamber, where he huddles for warmth over a fire, to a cold night on a boat in the middle of the River Thames. The Swan is the perfect theatre for storytelling. I'd previously worked through the twenty and more stories of *The Canterbury Tales* there, and there were valuable lessons to be learned from that experience. As I re-read *Wolf Hall*, and later *Bring Up the Bodies*, many more times, I tried to gear scenes to what I knew would work well in the Swan. And I knew – from touring *Canterbury Tales* – that if a play works in the Swan, it will play well in other theatres.

In bringing these two great novels to the stage, I have tried to replace the private pleasure of reading with the communal excitement of live theatre. When you read *Wolf Hall*, Cromwell and company get inside your head – they look as much through your eyes as you look through theirs. When you watch *Wolf Hall*, I hope we're offering you a completely different experience – it should be like stepping into the world of *Wolf Hall* and *Bring Up the Bodies* – being rowed down the Thames with a dejected Wolsey, sitting at dinner with the King, chasing rats with Christophe, being in the Tower with Thomas More, or waiting to take a turn at swinging the headsman's sword.

8

Notes on Characters
Hilary Mantel

THOMAS CROMWELL

You are the man with the slow resting heartbeat, the calmest person in any room, the best man in a crisis. You are a robust, confident, centred man, and your confidence comes from the power you have in reserve: your Putney self, ready to be unleashed, like an invisible pit bull. No one knows where you have been, or who you know, or what you can do, and these areas of mystery, on which you cast no light, are the source of your power. When you are angry, which is rare, you are terrifying.

Your date of birth is unknown (nobody noticed) but you are in your forties during the action of these plays and about fifty at the time of Anne Boleyn's fall. Your father was a blacksmith and brewer, the neighbour from Hell to the townsfolk of Putney, a heavy drinker and prone to violence. Your mother's name is unknown. You don't say much about your past, but you tell Thomas Cranmer, 'I was a ruffian in my youth.' Whatever this statement reveals or conceals, you have a lifelong sympathy with young men who have veered off-course.

At about the age of fifteen you vanish abroad. You join the French Army and speak French. You go into the household of a Florentine banker and speak Italian. You set up in the wool trade in Antwerp and speak Flemish and also Spanish, the language of the occupying power. You come home to London: and who are you? You're a man who speaks the language of the occupying power. Traces of the blacksmith's boy are almost invisible. The rough diamond is polished. You have seen at least one battle at close quarters, a calamitous defeat for your side; it's enough to turn you against war. You have seen childhood poverty and modest prosperity and you know all about what money can buy. You have learned from every situation you have been in. You are flexible, pragmatic and shrewd, with a streak of sardonic humour. You are widely read, understand poetry and art. Somewhere on the road you found God. Your exact views (like much about you) remain unknown. But you are a reformer and your religious feelings are strong and genuine.

On the other hand… you're quite prepared to torture someone, if reasons of State demand it and the King agrees. (You probably don't torture Mark Smeaton.) You are a natural arbitrator and negotiator, preferring a settlement to a fight, but if pushed – as you are by the Boleyns in 1536 – you are ingenious and ruthless.

You marry Elizabeth Wykys, a prosperous widow with connection in the wool trade. You have three children. You take up the law and go to work for Cardinal Wolsey, looking after his business affairs. You help him raise the funds for Cardinal College (which is now Christchurch) by closing or amalgamating a group of small monasteries, work which equips you for the mighty programme of Church reorganisation you will soon undertake for Henry.

You and Wolsey are close. When he falls from favour, you are the only person who remains completely loyal. Much about you is equivocal, but this is not. You get yourself a seat in the Commons, and through his long winter in exile at Esher you attend every sitting, trying to talk out the charges that have been brought against him. You expend effort and your own money. When he goes north, you remain in London looking after his interests. You warn him that the way to survive is to retire into private life. But, though he listens to you on most matters, in this instance he doesn't. His loss is devastating to you. Ten years later, you are still defending his good name: though Wolsey, a corrupt papist, ought to have been everything you hate.

You first come to Henry's notice when Wolsey's empire has to be pulled apart. Henry does not think he has many true friends and is touched by your loyalty to the Cardinal. You become his unofficial adviser long before you are sworn in to the Council. Your promotion causes predictable outrage, not just because of your humble background but because you are still known as the Cardinal's man. To save everyone embarrassment, it is proposed you adopt a coat of arms from another, more respectable family called Cromwell. But you refuse. You are not ashamed of your background; you don't talk about it, but you don't conceal it either. In fact, you never apologise, and never explain. (And when you get your own coat of arms, you incorporate a motif from Wolsey's arms, so that it flies in the faces of his old enemies for years to come.)

When your wife (and two little daughters) die, you do not marry again. This, for the time, is unusual. We don't know your reasons. You have women friends; this is not understood, for example, by the Duke of Norfolk, who tells you that he never had a conversation with his own daughter until she was about twenty years of age, and was perplexed to find that she had 'a good wit.'

Your household at Austin Friars, as you progress in the King's service, is transformed, extended, rebuilt, into a great ministerial household, a power centre, cosmopolitan and full of young men who are there to gain promotion. You take on the people written off elsewhere, the wild boys who are on everybody's wrong side, and make them into useful workers. You are an administrative genius, able to plan and accomplish in weeks what would take other people years. You are good at delegating and your instructions are so precise that it's difficult to make a mistake. You extend the secretary's role so that it covers most of the business of State; you know what happens in every department of Government. Your ideas are startlingly radical, but mostly they are beaten off by a conservative Parliament. At the centre of a vast network of patronage, you have a steady tendency to grow rich. You are generous with your money, a patron of artists, writers and scholars, and of your own troupe of actors, 'Lord Cromwell's Men'. The kitchen at Austin Friars feeds two hundred poor Londoners daily. All the same, you are a focus of resentment. The aristocracy don't like you on principle, and the ordinary people don't like you either. In the opinion of the era, there's something unnatural about what you've achieved. In the north they think you're a sorcerer.

Much of your myth is ill-founded. You do not control a vast spy network. You do not throw elderly monks into the road; in fact, you give them pensions. You are not the dour man of Holbein's portrait but (witnesses say) lively, witty and eloquent. You have a remarkable memory, and are credited with knowing the entire New Testament by heart. Your particular distinction is this: you are a big-picture man who also sees and takes care of every detail.

Apart from your intellectual ability, your greatest asset is that you manage to get on with the most unlikely people. You are affable, gregarious, and amazingly plausible. You easily convince people you are on their side, when common sense should suggest different. You tie people to you by favours rather than by fear, and so they don't easily see what a grip you've taken. People open their hearts to you. They tell you all sorts of things. But you tell them nothing.

What do you really think of Henry? No one knows. You don't seem to feel the warmth towards him that Wolsey did, but you respect his abilities and you serve him because he is the focus of good order and keeps the country together. Dealing with him on a day-to-day basis needs tact and patience. You are optimistic and resilient, and believe there's hope even for the bigoted and the terminally stubborn. Those who are on the inside track with you have their interests protected, and you take trouble to help out those in difficulties. But those who cross you are likely to find that you have been out by night and silently dug a deep pit beneath their career plans.

Your weakness is that you do not head up a faction or an interest group and have no power base of your own; you depend completely on the King's favour. You are resented by the old nobility, and you are destroyed when your two implacable enemies, Norfolk and Gardiner, manage to make common cause. But by then, you have reshaped England, and even the reign of the furiously papist Mary can't undo your work; you have given too many people a stake in your remodelled society.

ELIZABETH CROMWELL

You were the daughter of Henry Wykys, a prosperous wool trader, and were first married to Thomas Williams, a yeoman of the guard, and then to Cromwell. Your family were connected to Putney and may have been Welsh in origin. You have three children, Gregory, Anne and Grace. You die in one of the epidemics of 'sweating sickness' that sweep the country in the late 1520s, and your daughters follow you. You are a member of a close family and your sister, mother and brother-in-law continue to live at Austin Friars for many years.

We know nothing about you, so we can only say, 'women like you'. City wives were usually literate, numerate and businesslike, used to managing a household and a family business in cooperation with their husbands. In *Wolf Hall* I make you a 'silk woman', with your own business, like the wife of Cromwell's friend Stephen Vaughan, who supplied Anne Boleyn's household with small but valuable articles made of silk braid: cauls for the hair, ties for garments. Cromwell watches you weave one of these braids, fingers moving so fast that he can't follow the action. He asks you to slow down and show him how it's done. You say that if you slowed down and stopped to think you wouldn't be able to do it. He remembers this when he is deep into the coup against Anne Boleyn.

CARDINAL ARCHBISHOP THOMAS WOLSEY

You are, arguably, Europe's greatest statesman and greatest fraud. You are also a kind man, tolerant and patient in an age when these qualities are not necessarily thought virtues.

You are not quite the enormous scarlet cardinal of the (posthumous) portrait. You are more splendid than stout, a man of iron constitution who has survived the 'sweating sickness' six times. You are a cultured Renaissance prince, as grand and worldly as any Italian cardinal. Renowned for the speed at which you travel, you are capable of an unbroken twelve-hour stint at your desk, 'all which season my lord never rose once to piss, nor yet to eat any meat, but continually wrote his letters with his own hands…' Your household observes you with awe, as does the known world. You hope you might be Pope one day, but think it would be more convenient if you could bring the papacy to Whitehall; you wouldn't want to give up your palaces or your place next to your own monarch, and anyway you could probably run Christendom in your spare time.

You are the son of a prosperous butcher and grazier, and your family seem to have known how extraordinary you were, because they sent you to Oxford, where you took your first degree at fifteen and where you were known as 'the boy bachelor'. The Church is the route to advancement for the poor boy. And your route is paved with gold. You acquire influential patrons and enter the service of Henry VII.

When Henry VIII came to the throne you were ready to take much of the burden off the young back, and the Prince was glad to let you carry it. You have real esteem and affection for the young Henry, and he loves you for your personal warmth as well as your unique abilities. You are not only Lord Chancellor but the Pope's permanent legate in England. So your concentration of power, foreign and domestic, lay and clerical, is probably greater than that wielded by any individual in English history, kings and queens excepted. You are more than the King's minister, you are the 'alternative king', ostentatious and very rich; suave, authoritative, calm; an ironist, worldly-wise, unencumbered by too much ideology. You never simply walk, you process: your life is a spectacle, a huge performance mounted for the benefit of courtiers and kings. You are acting, particularly, when you're angry: after the performance, you shrug and laugh.

Until the point where this story starts, you have been able to solve almost every problem that's faced you. You are so sure of yourself, that your unravelling is total and unexpected and tragic.

When Henry first asks for an annulment of his marriage, you are confident that you will be able to secure it. But the politics of Europe turn against you, and you find yourself trapped, faced with an impatient, angry monarch, and between two women who hate you: Katherine of Aragon, who has always been jealous of your influence with the King, and Anne Boleyn, who resents you because, before the King set his heart on her, you frustrated the good marriage she intended to make. You are astonished by the extent of the enmity you have aroused (or at least, you say you are) and, like everyone else, you are baffled by the King's conduct; he wants you banished, then he offers to make peace, then he wants you banished.

For a year your enemies at Court are nervous that the King will reinstate you. No one is capable of assuming your role in Government, and Henry quickly learns this. When you are packed off to the north of England, you do not behave like a man in disgrace. You draw both the gentry and the ordinary people into your orbit, and soon you are living like a great prince again, and writing to the powers of Europe to ask them to help you regain your status. When these letters are intercepted, you are arrested and set out to London to face treason charges.

Soon after your arrest you have what sounds like a heart attack, followed by an intestinal crisis which leads to catastrophic bleeding. There are rumours that you have poisoned yourself. You are forced to continue the journey, and die at Leicester Abbey. Your body is shown to the town worthies so that no one can claim that you have survived and escaped, to set up opposition to Henry in Europe. It is the kind of precaution usually taken for a prince. Even dead, you spook your opponents. Your tomb – which you have been designing for twenty years, with the help of Florentine artists – is taken apart bit by bit and elements find their way all over Europe. At St Paul's, Lord Nelson occupies your marble sarcophagus, rattling around like a dried pea.

KING HENRY VIII

Let's think of you astrologically, because your contemporaries did. You are a native of Cancer the Crab and so never walk a straight line. You go sideways to your target, but when you have reached it your claws take a grip. You are both callous and vulnerable, hard-shelled and inwardly soft.

You are a charmer and you have been charming people since you were a baby, long before anyone knew you were going to be King. You were less than four years old when your father showed you off to the Londoners, perched alone on the saddle of a warhorse as you paraded through the streets.

Even as a child you behaved more like a king than your elder brother did. Arthur was dutiful and reserved, always with your father, whereas you were left with the women, a bonny, boisterous child, able to command attention. You were only ten when your brother married the Spanish Princess Katherine, but when you danced at the wedding, all eyes were on you.

At Arthur's sudden death, your mother and father are plunged into deep grief and dynastic panic. It's by no means sure that, were your father also to die now, you would come to the throne as the second Tudor; no one wants rule by a child. But your father battles on for a few more years, and you step into Arthur's role gladly, an understudy who will play the part much better than the original cast member. Later, do you feel some guilt about this?

You are eighteen when you become King, a 'virtuous prince', seemingly a model for kingship; you are intellectually gifted, pious, a linguist, a brilliant sportsman, able to write a love song or compose a mass. Almost at once, you marry your brother's widow and you execute your father's closest advisers. The latter action is a naked bid for popularity, and it ought to give warning of the seriousness of your intent. Still, early in your reign you put more effort into hunting and jousting than to governing, with a bit of light warfare thrown in. You prefer to look like a king than be a king, which is why you let Thomas Wolsey run the country for you.

You are sexually inexperienced and will always be sexually shy; you don't like dirty jokes. You have a few liaisons, but they are low-key and discreet. You never embarrass Katherine, who is too grand to display any jealousy, though she is too much in love with you not to care. However, you cosset and promote your illegitimate son, Henry Fitzroy (a son you can acknowledge, as his mother was unmarried). Fitzroy has his own household, so is not part of the daily life of the Court, but is loaded with honours.

You are approaching forty when this story starts, five years younger than Thomas Cromwell. You are not ageing particularly well; still trim, still good-looking, you remain a superb athlete and jouster, but in an effort to hang on to your youth you have taken to collecting friends who are a generation younger than you, lively young courtiers like Francis Weston.

Your manner is relaxed, rather than domineering. You are highly intelligent, quick to grasp the possibilities of any situation. You expect to get your own way, not just because you are a king but because you are that sort of man. When you are thwarted, your charm vanishes. You are capable of a carpet-chewing rage, which throws people because it is so unexpected, and because you will turn on the people closest to you. But most of the time you like to be liked; you have no fear of confronting men, though you don't seek confrontation, but you will not confront a woman, so you are run ragged between Katherine and Anne, trying to placate one and please the other. Unlike most men of your era, you truly believe in romantic love (though, of course, not in monogamy). It is an ideal for you. You were in love with Katherine when you married her and when you fall in love with Anne Boleyn you feel you must shape your life around her. Likewise, when Jane Seymour comes along…

When you ask Katherine for an annulment, you are not (in the view of your advisers) asking for anything outrageous. The Pope is usually keen to please royalty, and there are recent precedents in both your families. The timing is what's wrong; the troops of Katherine's nephew the Emperor march into Rome and the Pope is no longer free to decide. You are outraged when Katherine resists you and Wolsey fails you. You believe in your own case; you are a keen amateur theologian, and you think you know what God wants.

You are highly emotional. You are religious, superstitious, vulnerable to panic. Because you are so afraid of dying without an heir you've become a hypochondriac, and gradually a sort of self-pity has corrupted your character. You are so different from Cromwell that there's probably little natural sympathy between you; you get your brotherly love from Archbishop Cranmer. But

you need Cromwell as a stabilising force. You can carry on
being loved by your people, as long as he will carry your sins
for you. He begins by amusing and impressing you, proceeds by
making you rich, and ends by frightening you. When, in 1540,
you are told by Cromwell's enemies that he intends to turn you
out and become King himself, you completely believe it. For a
few weeks, anyway. Then, as soon as his head is off, you want
him back. It's the Wolsey story over again. Who is to blame?
Definitely not you.

ANNE BOLEYN

You do not have six fingers. The extra digit is added long after
your death by Jesuit propaganda. But in your lifetime you are
the focus of every lurid story that the imagination of Europe can
dream up. From the moment you enter public consciousness,
you carry the projections of everyone who is afraid of sex or
ashamed of it. You will never be loved by the English people,
who want a proper, royal Queen like Katherine, and who don't
like change of any sort. Does that matter? Not really. What
Henry's inner circle thinks of you matters far more. But do you
realise this? Reputation management is not your strong point.
Charm only thinly disguises your will to win.

You are the most sophisticated woman at Henry's Court, with
polished manners and just the suggestion of a French accent.
Unlike your sister Mary, you have kept your name clean. You are
elegant, reserved, self-controlled, cerebral, calculating and
astute. But you are (especially as the story progresses) inclined
to frayed nerves and shaking hands. You are quick-tempered
and, like anyone under pressure, you can be highly irrational.
You look at people to see what use can be got out of them, and
you immediately see the use of Thomas Cromwell.

You come to the English Court in your early twenties, but
you are in your late twenties before you catch Henry's attention,
and ours in the plays. Your contemporaries did not think you
were pretty because they admired pink-and-white blonde
beauty, and you (judging by their descriptions) were dark and
slender. This difference becomes part of your distinction. It's
your vitality that draws the eye. You sing beautifully and dance
whenever you can. You are the leader of fashion at the Court,
before you become Queen.

When you are first at Court you become involved with Harry
Percy, the heir to the Earldom of Northumberland. In the strictly
regulated hierarchy of Court marriages, he is 'above' you, and is
already promised to the daughter of the Earl of Shrewsbury.
Cardinal Wolsey steps in and makes Harry Percy go ahead with
the Shrewsbury marriage. It's at this point, your detractors will
say, that you start to hate Wolsey and look for revenge. As far as
the Cardinal is concerned, it's nothing personal. But it wouldn't
be surprising if you took it personally. Harry Percy will later
claim you had made a promise of marriage before witnesses,
which would count as binding. At the time you are silent about
the business. Whether you had feelings for Harry Percy, or were
acting out of ambition, is not clear.

When the King makes his first approaches you are wary
because you don't intend to be a discarded mistress, like your
sister Mary. You make him keep his distance and work hard for
a smile. To think that you, a knight's daughter, could replace the
Queen of England is an idea so audacious that it takes a while
for the rest of Europe to catch up with it. It's assumed that, once
Henry's divorce comes through, he will marry a French
princess. You are Wolsey's downfall; for a long time, though he
remembers you exist, he doesn't know you're important to the
King. As far as he is concerned, he has finished his dealings
with you when he makes Harry Percy reject you. There was a
time when the King told Wolsey everything. But since you
came along, that age has passed.

Your campaign to be Queen is fought with patience and
cunning. Saying 'no' to Henry is a profitable business and you
are made Marquise of Pembroke. There is a point when, after
you feel Henry has committed himself to you, you'd probably
be willing to go to bed with him; but by that time, he's intent on
remaining apart until you are married. He says you have
promised him a son, and he wants to be right with his
conscience and with God. Any child you have must be born
within your marriage. You marry secretly in Calais, at the end
of 1532, and a few weeks later, with no fuss, on English soil.
Elizabeth is born the September following. Though Henry is
disappointed not to have a boy, he doesn't (as myth suggests)
turn against you. He is glad to have a healthy child after losing
so many, and confident of a boy next time.

Are you really a religious woman, a convinced reformer? No
one will ever know. It's probable that you picked up your ideas

at the French Court, where the intellectual as well as the moral climate is freer. There's nothing to gain for you in being a faithful daughter of Rome. The texts you put Henry's way are self-serving, in that they suggest the subject should be obedient to the secular ruler, not to the Pope. But you go to some trouble to protect and promote evangelicals. 'My bishops', as you call them, are your war leaders against the old order.

Your family – your father, Thomas Boleyn, and your uncle the Duke of Norfolk – expect that, if they back you as Henry's second wife, it will be to the family's advantage, and they will be your advisers and indeed controllers. They are shocked to find that, once Queen, you consider yourself the head of the family. They begin to distance themselves from you as you 'fail' Henry by not providing a son, but your brother George is close to you and always loyal. Your sister Mary has a shrewd idea of what is going on; after the first blaze of triumph, you are unhappy.

You expected to be Henry's confidante and adviser, as Katherine was in the early days of the first marriage. But Henry is less open now, and his problems (many of them caused by your marriage) are new and seem intractable. Gradually you realise that Cromwell, whom you regarded as your servant, is accreting more and more power and that he has his own agenda and his own interests.

Meanwhile, you are locked into an unwinnable contest with Henry's teenage daughter Mary. She will never acknowledge you as Queen, even after her mother is dead. From time to time your temper makes you threaten her. No one knows whether you mean your threats, but it's widely believed you would harm her if you could.

After Elizabeth's birth you miscarry at least one, maybe two children. Henry feels he has staked everything on a marriage that, despite his best efforts, no one in Europe recognises. You start to quarrel. Ambassador Chapuys gleefully retails each public row in dispatches. Cromwell warns the Ambassador not to make too much of it; you have always quarrelled and made up. But, unlike Katherine, you don't take it quietly when Henry looks at other women. That he would become interested in someone as mousy as Jane Seymour seems like an insult.

Besides, you are bored. You were always cooler than the King and perhaps irritated by his adoration. He is not a good lover. You collect around you a group of admiring men who are good for your ego. You don't see the danger in what becomes an explosive situation. Or perhaps you do see it, but still you crave the excitement.

Meanwhile, nothing good is happening to your looks. Ambassador Chapuys describes you as 'a thin old woman' at thirty-five. There is only one attested contemporary portrait, a medallion, not a picture. In it you can clearly see a swelling in your throat, which was noticed by your contemporaries, who also called you 'a goggle-eyed whore'. To our mind, this suggests a hyperthyroid condition. You are nervous and jittery, outside and inside. There's something feverish and desperate about your energy. You can't control it and you are wearing yourself out.

At some point on the summer progress of 1535 you become pregnant again. At the end of January, on the day of Katherine's funeral, you lose the child, a boy. (Contrary to the myth that's taken hold, there is no evidence that the child was abnormal.) In the opinion of Ambassador Chapuys: 'She has miscarried of her saviour.' You celebrated when you heard of Katherine's death, but it is not really good news for you. In the eyes of Catholic Europe, the King is now a widower, and free.

You are now in trouble. You are right in thinking you are surrounded by enemies. Nothing you could do would ever reconcile the old nobility to your status, and the tactless and noisy rise of your family has cut across many established interests. Katherine's old friends and supporters are beginning to conspire in corners, and make overtures to Cromwell. Will he support the restoration of the Princess Mary to the succession, if they back him in a coup against you?

When Henry decides he wants to be free, the idea is to nullify the marriage, not to kill you. The canon lawyers go into a huddle with Cromwell. Then the whole business is accelerated and becomes public, because in late April 1536 you quarrel with Henry Norris; and afterwards you visibly panic, giving the impression of a woman who has something to hide. Everything you say is keenly noted and carried to the King, who immediately concludes you have been unfaithful to him. Cromwell is talking to your ladies-in-waiting. It's possible that, even at this stage, he is not sure how he will bring the matter to a crisis. But when you are arrested you break down and talk wildly, supplying yourself the material for the charges against you.

By the time of your trial and your death you have collected yourself and are, according to Cromwell, 'brave as a lion'.

KATHERINE OF ARAGON

Thomas Cromwell: 'If she had been a man, she would have been a greater hero than all the generals of antiquity.'

You are the daughter of two reigning monarchs, Ferdinand of Aragon and Isabella of Castile. Your father was known for his political cunning and your mother for her unfeminine fighting spirit. When you are told that you have failed, because you have only given Henry a daughter, and a woman can't reign, there must be a part of you that asks, 'Why not?' Another part of you understands; though you are highly educated, you are conventional and accept what your religion tells you: that women, after God, must obey men. This is a conflict that will run through your life.

You have known since you were a small child that you were destined for an English alliance, and even in your nursery you were addressed as 'the Princess of Wales'. You are an object of prestige for the Tudors, who are a new and struggling dynasty with a weak claim to England. At fifteen you come to England to marry Prince Arthur. You are beautiful and much admired, tiny, fair-skinned, auburn-haired. You are sent to Ludlow to hold court as Prince and Princess of Wales. Within a few weeks, Arthur is dead. You will always say that your marriage was never consummated. Some of your contemporaries, and some historians, don't believe you. Perhaps you are not above a strategic lie. Your parents would have told one and not blinked.

Now you enter a bleak period of widowhood. King Henry VII doesn't want you to go back to Spain. You're his prize, and he wants to keep your dowry. After he is widowed, he thinks of marrying you himself, a project your family firmly veto. You remain in London, without enough money, uncertain of your status, on the very fringe of the Court. Your salvation comes when Arthur's seventeen-year-old brother succeeds to the throne. It's like all the fairytales rolled into one. After a period of seven years, the handsome prince rescues you. He loves you madly. You adore him.

And you always will. Whatever happens, it's not really Henry's fault. It's always someone else, someone misleading him, someone betraying him. It's Wolsey, it's Cromwell, it's Anne Boleyn.

You look like an Englishwoman and, as Queen, an Englishwoman is what you set out to become. When Henry goes to France for a little war, he has such faith in you that he leaves you as Regent. All the same, the King's advisers suspect your intentions. You act as an unofficial ambassador for your country, and are ruthless in pushing the interests of Spain, a great power which at this time also rules the Netherlands. Your nephew, Charles V of Spain, becomes Holy Roman Emperor, making him overlord to the German princes, in territories where new religious ideas are taking a hold. You are not responsive to these ideas. You come from a land where the Inquisition is flourishing, and though your parents have reformed Spain's administration, they have done it in a way that consolidates royal power. Probably you never understand why Henry has to listen to Parliament, or why he might want popular support.

At first you are Henry's great friend as well as his lover. Then politics sours the relationship; Henry and Wolsey have to move adroitly between the two great power blocs of France and Spain, making sure they never ally and crush English interests. And your babies die. There are six pregnancies at least, possibly several more; the Tudors didn't announce royal pregnancies, still less miscarriages, if they could be hidden. They only announced the happy results: a live, healthy child. You have only one of these, your daughter Mary.

You are older than Henry by seven years. And the pregnancies take their toll on your body. You become a stout little person, but you are always magnificently dressed and bejewelled; a queen must act like a queen. You are watched for signs that your fertile years are over. When Henry decides he must marry again, the intrigues develop behind your back. You are not at first aware, and nor is anyone else, that Henry has a woman in mind and that woman is Anne Boleyn. You believe he wants to replace you with a French princess, for diplomatic advantage, and you blame Wolsey, who you have always seen as your enemy; for years he has been your rival for influence with the King. You think you understand Henry. But for years he's been drifting away from you, the boy with his sunny nature becoming a more complex and unhappy man.

Once the divorce plan is out in the open, no notion of feminine obedience or meekness constrains you. You fight untiringly and with every weapon you can find, legal and moral. The King says that Scripture forbids marriage with a brother's wife. You insist that you were never Prince Arthur's wife, that you lay in bed together as two good children, saying your prayers. You also believe that even if you and Arthur had

consummated your marriage, you are still legally married to
Henry; the Pope's dispensation covered both cases.

No settlement is in sight. You are offered the option of
retiring to a convent; if you were to become a nun, your
marriage would be annulled in canon law, and, given that you
are deeply religious, Henry hopes that might suit you. But as far
as you are concerned, your vocation is to be Queen of England,
and that is the estate to which God has called you, and you and
God will make no concessions. You are always dignified, but
you will not negotiate and you will concede nothing.

You are sent to a series of country houses: not shabby or
unhealthy, as the legend insists, but remote, well away from any
seaports. You are separated from your daughter, which agonises
you, because she is in frail health and also you fear that she will
be pressured into accepting that she is illegitimate. Though you
are provided with a household to fit your status, you live in
virtual isolation because you will not answer to your new style
of 'Dowager Princess of Wales' and insist on being addressed as
Queen. Soon you have confined yourself to one room, and your
trusted maids cook for you over the fire. Henry sends Norfolk
and Suffolk to bully you, without result. Finally you are
divorced in your absence. You die in January 1536, after an
illness of several months' duration, probably a cancer. The
rumours are, of course, that Anne Boleyn has poisoned you.

Cromwell's admiration for you is on the record: even though
his life would have been made simpler if you had just vanished,
he admired your sense of battle tactics and your stamina in
fighting a war you could not win. His approach is pragmatic and
rational; he's not a hater. You understand this. You may think, as
much of Catholic Europe does, that he is the Antichrist. But you
write to him in Spanish, addressing him as your friend.

PRINCESS MARY

Born seven years into your parents' marriage, you are the only
surviving child. You are in your mid-teens when you appear in
this story. You are small, plain, pious and fragile: very clever,
very brave, very stubborn. You hate Anne Boleyn, and revere
your father, following your mother's line in believing that he is
misled. When you are separated from Katherine, and kept under
house arrest, you are physically ill and suffer emotional
desolation. You believe when Anne is executed that all your

troubles are over. You are stunned to find that your father still requires you to acknowledge your illegitimacy and to recognise him as Head of the Church. You resist to the point of danger. Thomas Cromwell talks you back from the brink. Your dazed, ambivalent relation with him begins in these plays.

STEPHEN GARDINER
Cambridge academic, Master of Trinity Hall, you are in your late thirties as this story begins, and secretary to Cardinal Wolsey, who admires your first-class mind, finds you extremely useful, and has little idea of the grievances you are accumulating. Tactless and bruisingly confrontational, you are physically and intellectually intimidating, and your subordinates and your peers are equally afraid of you. But you suspect Thomas Cromwell laughs at you, and you are possibly right. You can only stare with uncomprehending hostility as he talks his way into the highest favour with Wolsey first and then the King. Cromwell is at his ease in any situation. You are the opposite, constantly bristling and tense.

Your origins are a mystery. You are brought up by respectable but humble parents, who are possibly your foster-parents. The rumour is that you are of Tudor descent through an illegitimate line, and so you are the King's cousin. This may be why you get on in life; or it may be you are valued for your intellect; your personality is always in your way, and you seem helpless to do anything about it.

As you are politically astute and unhampered by gratitude, you begin to distance yourself from the Cardinal some months before his fall, and become secretary to the King. You are promoted to the bishopric of Winchester, the richest diocese in England. You are conservative in your own religious beliefs, but you are an authoritarian and a loyalist who will always back Henry, so you work hard for the divorce from Katherine, and you are all in favour of the King's supremacy in Church and State. But Henry finds your company wearing; you always want to have an argument. And he likes people who can read his mood and respond to it.

So once again the pattern repeats; you are pushed out of the King's favour by Cromwell, and have to watch him grow the secretary's post into the most important job in the country (after king). Cromwell is generally so plausible that even Norfolk sometimes forgets to hate him. But you never forget.

During the years of his supremacy, Cromwell will keep you abroad as much as possible, as an ambassador. When you finally make common cause with the Duke of Norfolk, his other great enemy, you will be able to destroy him.

Cromwell suspects, and he's right, that underneath all, you are a papist, and that, given a chance, a swing of political fortune, you would take England straight back to Rome. This proves true; in the reign of Mary Tudor, you grab your chance, become Lord Chancellor and start burning heretics.

WILLIAM WARHAM, ARCHBISHOP OF CANTERBURY

You are over eighty years old and are a man of immense dignity, when awake. You have been Archbishop for almost thirty years. A former Lord Chancellor, you were pushed out of that role by Wolsey. Your favourite saying is, 'The wrath of the King is death.' So you do not oppose Henry's divorce or the early stages of the Reformation, but at the very end of your life, as in your scene here, you find the unexpected courage to disagree with the King. So your rebuke carries weight.

THOMAS CRANMER, INCOMING ARCHBISHOP OF CANTERBURY

You are the introvert to Cromwell's extrovert. You act so much in concert that some less well-informed European politicians think you are one person: Dr Chramuel. When you and your other self are with Henry, you go smoothly into action, able to communicate everything to each other with a glance or a breath.

You are a reserved Cambridge don, leading a quiet life, when you chip in an idea about Henry's divorce: why doesn't he poll the European universities, to give his case some extra gravitas? The King likes this idea and soon you are at the heart of the struggle, a family chaplain to the Boleyns, guiding them, cautiously, towards reformed religion, and hoping to take Henry the same way. You must be wary of Cromwell, with his reputation as Wolsey's bully boy. But once you begin to work together, you instinctively understand each other and become friends.

Intellectually rigorous, you are not the cold fish you may
appear. As a young man, not yet a priest, you made an
impulsive marriage. This meant you had to give up your
fellowship at Jesus College, and try to find work as a clerk or
tutor; your father is a gentleman, but you have no money from
him, and Joan was just a servant when you met her. Within a
year you lose your wife in childbirth. The child dies too. Jesus
College takes you back. You are ordained. Perhaps nothing else
will ever happen to you?

Your promotion to Archbishop is something you could never
have imagined, even a year or two before it happened. Though
you can appear cerebral and withdrawn, you are in tune with the
emotions of others; you are a gentle person, who tends to calm
situations. You are psychological balm to Henry and to Anne,
both of them restless and irritable people. Henry loves you, and
(as Cromwell said) you can get away with anything, including
your increasingly Protestant convictions, and the second mad
marriage you make. You fall in love when you are on mission in
Germany, and smuggle your wife back. Henry is fiercely
opposed to married clergy; he must know about Grete, but he
closes his eyes.

You are possibly the only person in England without a bad
word to say about Anne Boleyn. You are swept up in the
terrifying process of her ruin, with hardly a chance to protest.
You turn this way and that: how can these allegations be true?
But if they were not true, would a man so good as Henry make
them? You do believe in his goodness, which is what he needs.
You go on trying to believe it, against all the accumulating
evidence. In many ways as the years go on, your role as
Archbishop becomes a torture to you. Though Henry makes
many concessions to reform, he remains stuck in the Catholic
mindset of his youth. You and Cromwell have to stand by while
he persecutes 'heretics' who share your own beliefs. Henry
thinks you are a hopeless politician, and likes you all the better
for it. But you are wiser than he thinks. You never pointlessly
antagonise him, but prudently and patiently salvage what you
can from each little wreckage he makes.

When Cromwell falls, you will go as far to save him as your
natural timidity allows. You will beg the King to think again,
and ask him pointedly, 'Who will Your Grace trust hereafter, if
you cannot trust him?' You are not naturally brave but you are

wise, humane and sincere, and eventually in Mary's reign you will die horribly for your beliefs.

THOMAS MORE

You would keep a tribe of Freudian analysts in business for life. They would hold conferences devoted just to you. An absent-minded professor with a sideline in torture, you turn on a sixpence, from threatening to cajoling to whimsicality. Ill-at-ease in your skin, self-hating, you show your inner confusion by your relationship with your clothes; you look as if you are wearing someone else's, and got dressed in the dark. This disarrayed outside makes you seem vulnerable, even harmless; but inside, your barriers are rigid and your core is frozen.

You have a father to live up to: good old Sir John More, stalwart of the London law courts, a man with a fund of anecdotes that you will be telling for the rest of your life. You follow him into the law. You think you should become a monk, but you fail. You decide you can't live without sex; and you don't want to be a bad monk. Perhaps, also, you want the warmth of family life. You can't do without people. You can't detach, as a religious man should. The realisation causes you anguish. The inner conflict, the consciousness of sin, is so painful you have to flagellate yourself as a distraction. You wear a hair shirt. Not figuratively, literally.

Yet you are one of the showpieces of Henry's Court: an intellectual, to vie with those good-quality ones they have abroad. You seem so modern, if we ignore the hair shirt. You are a scholar and a wit, a great communicator, a man attentive to your own legend; if you lived now, you would write a column for one of the weekend papers, all about the hilarious ups and downs of family life in Chelsea. You are a member of several Parliaments and serve as Speaker. You keep amicable relations with Wolsey while he is in power, but are ferocious at his fall. For all your urbanity, you are an excellent hater. When you write about Luther or other evangelicals, your detestation comes spilling out in an uncontrollable flood of scatological language. It's as if you have a poisoned spring inside you. Unluckily, the times allow you to release your violence, instead of forcing you to suppress it. You have a busy legal practice but your real vocation is persecuting heretics.

Posterity will excuse you, saying, 'It's what they did; those were not tolerant times.' But Cardinal Wolsey was loyal to Rome, and he managed his long tenure as Lord Chancellor without burning anybody. You preside over a handful of executions, but you damage the lives of many, imprisoning suspects until they are mortally ill or their businesses fail. You are not apologetic. You are proud of your record, and you want it mentioned in your epitaph, which, of course, you have written in advance.

You have been in Henry's life since he was a boy, and he looks up to you, and you are confident that you can influence him for the better. So when he asks you to take over as Lord Chancellor, you agree, as long as you don't have to work on his divorce. Within a short time your position becomes untenable, and it's obvious that the King is listening to Cromwell, not you. Your path has crossed Cromwell's many times. Your raid on his house, in these plays, is a convenient fiction, shorthand for the hostility between you, and modelled on your raids on Cromwell's friends. Probably you wouldn't care to confront him so directly, even after Wolsey's protection is withdrawn. Besides, you don't know where to place Cromwell; you're never sure whose side he's on. You suspect he might be solely motivated by money. You never imagine he's a man of conviction. Perhaps your failing, as a political animal, is that you don't give your opponents credit; you don't believe they are as clever or determined as you are. You think the King is still a boy who can be led. Quite possibly, you think Cromwell is overconfident and will come unstuck. He doesn't explain himself. Neither do you. You are a master of ambiguity and soon you need all your skills to keep you alive.

Henry permits you to retire into private life. You go home to Chelsea and live quietly. The country is seething with plots, but you keep your hands clean and you do not talk about your views. You refuse the invitation to Anne Boleyn's coronation, which is a mistake. It suggests to Henry and Anne that you remain hostile to their marriage, though you've never made any public objection. When you are required to take an oath to recognise Henry as Head of the Church, and Anne's daughter Elizabeth as heir, you refuse. But you won't say why. So you sit in the Tower of London for a year, while your family and friends try to talk you into a compromise, and Cromwell negotiates. Sometimes he pushes you and sometimes he gives you, you say, the good advice you'd get from a friend. Perhaps Henry will forget you? But he won't, because he's furious that a man he admired has turned against him.

You are not ill-treated. There is no question of physical force, but there is intense mental pressure, and there is fear and loneliness. Finally, you entrap yourself, in conversation with Richard Riche, a young lawyer you despise; you knew he was Cromwell's man, but you couldn't resist chatting away, 'putting cases' as if you were still a student. Riche reports your 'treason' and Cromwell hauls you into court. It's a failure on his part; victory would have been to break your spirit, and not to have the embarrassment of executing a famous opponent of the regime. You are not a martyr for freedom of conscience, as recent legend suggests. You are the old-fashioned kind of martyr, dying for your faith, or, as Cromwell sees it, for your belief that England should be ruled from Rome.

RAFE SADLER

You are twenty-one when this story begins, and as seasoned and steady as a man twice your age. You are brought up by Thomas Cromwell, but by the time you are in your late twenties you have become his father, and tell him off when you think he's being frivolous. You are a quietly admirable character, and you manage to do something very difficult: you last the distance in politics, and keep your integrity.

Your own father is a gentleman and minor official, caught up in the great dragnet of Wolsey patronage. He somehow spots Cromwell as the man to watch, though at the time he is only a young London lawyer. You grow up in his increasingly lively household, as close as a son, and by the time of the Cardinal's fall you are his chief clerk. Henry likes you, and in 1536 promotes you to a position in his own household, so you act as daily liaison for Cromwell. You are utterly loyal to him, hardworking, sober and shrewd. You're cautious by nature, practical, steady, very able, and seldom put a foot wrong. Thankfully, you do one silly thing in your life: instead of marrying for career advantage or money, you marry a poor girl with whom you've fallen in love. Whoever else might see this as a problem, Cromwell doesn't. He has your future in hand anyway.

You build yourself a shiny new country house at Hackney, the garden adjoining one of Cromwell's properties. Later you acquire a country estate. You and Helen have a whole tribe of children, the eldest called Thomas. Though you can't bear to be apart, you can never take Helen to Court, and you are mostly at Court as you are increasingly necessary to Henry. When, in 1539, Cromwell, staggering under the burden of work, finally parts with the post of Mr Secretary, the job is split between you and Thomas Wriothesley. At Cromwell's fall, you cannot save him but you behave with dignity and courage. You carry his last letter to Henry. Read it, Henry says. You do so. Read it again. And a third time: read it. You can see the King has tears in his eyes. But he doesn't speak; there's no reprieve. It is you who carries Cromwell's portrait from the wreck of Austin Friars, as his opponents loot it.

After Cromwell, you are beaten out of the top jobs by the unscrupulous Wriothesley, but make your name as an envoy to Scotland, a hardship posting which sometimes involves dodging musket balls. You are a little man, with no pretentions to military prowess, and no interest in sports other than hawking. But, at the age of forty, caught up in the Scots wars, you will ride into battle under Edward Seymour, and behave with such valour that you are knighted on the battlefield. Pent-up aggression, probably, from all those years of being discreet.

You serve three sovereigns (retiring from public life under Mary). You are a Privy Councillor for fifty years, and are still working for Elizabeth I at the age of eighty. You're too precious to be let go; you know where the bodies are buried. The Cromwellian ability to make money has rubbed off, and you die the richest commoner in England.

HARRY PERCY, EARL OF NORTHUMBERLAND

You are in your early twenties when you first become involved with Anne Boleyn and in your mid-thirties when these plays end. You were brought up in Wolsey's household and he had a poor opinion of your abilities. As the Earl of Northumberland's heir, you contracted a mountain of debt, and when your father came to Court to tell you off about your involvement with Anne Boleyn, he called you 'a very unthrift waster'. You seem to be a muddle-headed, emotional, unreliable young man, with poor judgement; not a man to dislike, not a cowardly man, but a confused one, frequently out of his depth.

Under protest, you give up Anne and contract the marriage arranged for you, with Mary Talbot, daughter of the Earl of Shrewsbury. Your only child with her does not survive and the marriage is miserable. When you inherit the earldom, you begin alienating land to pay your debts, prejudicing the holdings of your younger brothers. A complex of family quarrels and financial disasters adds to your unhappiness, though you are not frozen out by the King at this stage; your family name decrees that you should be made a Knight of the Garter, and the geography of your land holdings makes you important in defence against the Scots.

When you are sent to arrest Wolsey in Yorkshire, you are reported to be shaking with fear. He laughs at you and refuses to credit your authority, though he agrees to be taken into custody by the officials with you.

From about 1529 you are ill and convinced you will die early. Perhaps this makes you reckless. You refuse to live with your wife and, in the hope of obtaining her freedom, she tells her father that you have always claimed to be married to Anne Boleyn. Anne is on the point of marrying the King and insists on an investigation. Under pressure, you swear on the blessed sacrament that you never contracted a marriage with her. All the same, rumours persist.

In 1536 you are asked by Cromwell to retract your oath and say that you were, after all, married to Anne. This would give the King an easy and bloodless exit from his marriage. You refuse to do so. You are perhaps afraid of the consequences for your soul, and by now you resent and detest the Boleyns. (Chapuys has seen you as a candidate to join an aristocratic conspiracy against the King, but has been told you are 'light' and untrustworthy.)

You are one of the peers who sit in judgment at Anne's trial. You concur in the guilty verdict and then collapse.

You die in 1537, your lands taken over by the Crown. There is no new Earl until 1557.

CHRISTOPHE

On one of Cardinal Wolsey's State visits to France, he was
systematically robbed of his gold plate by a small boy who went
up and down the stairs unnoticed, passing the loot to a gang
outside. In the world of *Wolf Hall*, you are the small boy. So
you are a fiction, with a shadow-self in the historical record.

Thomas Cromwell is ignorant of your earlier life and
previous names when he runs into you in Calais in 1532. You
are the waiter in a backstreet inn, where he is entertaining a
cabal of elderly and impoverished alchemists from whom he
hopes to obtain a working model of the human soul. He has
time to notice that you are a cheeky, dirty, violent little youth,
who reminds him irresistibly of his younger self. Deciding he is
a great milord, you follow him to his lodgings and announce
you mean to 'take service' with him and see the world.

At Austin Friars you are an all-purpose dogsbody. With
difficulty, you make yourself fit to be seen with a gentleman.
You find good behaviour a great strain. The legacy of your
former life is that you are always hungry.

THOMAS HOWARD, DUKE OF NORFOLK

'I have never read the Scripture, nor will read it. It was merry in
England before the new learning came up: yea, I would that all
things were as hath been in times past.'

You are almost sixty when this story begins, with the vigour
of a man half your age; you run on rage. Your grandfather was
on the wrong side at the Battle of Bosworth, and your family
lost the dukedom. Your father regained the favour of Henry VII,
annihilated the Scots at the Battle of Flodden, and got the title
back. And you expect a battle every day, and are always armed
for one, visibly or not. You never forget what damage a king's
displeasure can do. To his face, you are creepingly servile to
Henry Tudor. In private, you probably regard him as a parvenu,
and a bit of a girly as well.

With the exception of Henry's illegitimate son, you are
England's premier nobleman, an old-style magnate who holds a
magnificent court in East Anglia. Your courtier's veneer is
paper-thin. You prefer warfare. But you are not without
diplomatic weapons, as you will lie to anyone.

You hate Wolsey: in your view, he is common, greedy and
pretentious. You are also frightened of him, as you think he has

the power to put a curse on you. You are one of the main agents of his fall, and you threaten that if he does not make speed to the north, away from Court, 'I will come where he is and tear him with my teeth.' You are supremely valiant at kicking a man when he's down.

You beat your wife, or at least she tells Cromwell that you do; she also complains that your in-house mistress knocked her down and sat on her. She tells Cromwell everything, *and* she sends him presents. Cromwell is everywhere you look, in your face, and once you accept it you approach him with a gruesomely false bonhomie, teeth gritted.

You back the efforts of your niece, Anne Boleyn, to become Queen, because you think it will be good for the family, but you turn against her when you realise that she has no intention of obeying her uncle. Presiding over her trial, you have no hesitation in sentencing her to death, and a few years later will do the same for another niece, Katherine Howard. Though you are innately conservative and papist, you say yes to anything Henry wants, and when Cromwell begins to dissolve the monasteries, you are first in line for the spoils. Your fortunes rise and fall through Henry's reign. You come into your own in the autumn of 1536, when rebellion breaks out in the north; you suppress it with ferocity and relish. You are triumphant when you finally see off Cromwell, but that triumph doesn't last; you are disgraced by the Katherine Howard affair, and later by the dynastic ambitions of your son, the Earl of Surrey. Though you are sentenced to death in 1546, you have a long wait in the Tower, and Henry dies the night before your scheduled execution. Unlike so many of your friends and enemies, you die in your bed in the reign of Queen Mary, in an England you don't really recognise any more.

CHARLES BRANDON, DUKE OF SUFFOLK

A blundering hearty, a big man with a big beard. Six or seven years older than Henry, you are one of the tiltyard stars he looks up to when he is a young lad just taking up dangerous sports. Your relationship with him is warm and brotherly.

Your father, who was well-connected but 'only' a gentleman, died at Bosworth fighting for the Tudors, and you are brought to Court young, so grow up in an arena where you can shine. You fight with Henry in his small French war of 1531. You are considered the King's principal favourite, are given offices and lands, and, five years into his reign, receive an enormous promotion to Duke of Suffolk. You are a good soldier, but considered over-promoted, a product of Henry's enthusiasm, and more use in war than peace.

Then you mess everything up in the most spectacular way. You are sent to France for the marriage celebrations of Henry's youngest sister, Mary, to the King of France. Louis XII is elderly and unattractive, Mary is a beauty of eighteen, and she has a crush on you; she marries under protest. Three months later, while you are still in France, Louis dies. Mary claims that Henry promised that if she would oblige him with the French alliance, she could choose her next husband herself. She chooses you. You think this is all a bit risky, but marry her because 'I never saw woman weepe so.' You then have to go back to England together and face Henry, who is so furious that there is a real possibility you will lose your head.

Wolsey intervenes and talks Henry around. An enormous fine is substituted for any other penalty. Most years Wolsey 'forgets' to collect it. You are wealthy because of the large pension Mary is given by the French, but the downside is that, for years, they treat you as their hired man at Henry's Court.

You are an irrepressible man. You are soon back in Henry's favour, though he sulks at you from time to time and falls out with you. As a politician, you are much less nimble than Norfolk, your East Anglian rival. Henry gives you nasty jobs, like trying to talk Katherine into compliance. You don't get on with the Boleyns, and are offended by the family's rise in the world. The rumour is that at some point before Henry's marriage to Anne, you go to him and tell him that Anne has had an affair with Thomas Wyatt; you're trying to save him from himself. At this point it's the last thing Henry wishes to hear, and he kicks you out. You're soon back at Court and happily blundering along. You love Henry, in spite of all.

You are baffled by Cromwell. But you find it best generally to do as he says.

After Mary Tudor's death in 1533, you marry a fourteen-year-old heiress who was intended for your son. She grows up to be a witty and strong-willed religious reformer who keeps a small dog called Gardiner, which she shouts at in public: it's the most successful joke of the English Reformation.

You remain rich. You remain honoured. You are a thread that connects Henry to his young self and to the England he inherited. You die in your bed, 1545. Henry pays for a magnificent funeral.

EUSTACHE CHAPUYS

You are born in Savoy, to a respectable but not wealthy family. You are a lawyer with university training, a meritocrat, able to make your way in the vast field of opportunity offered by service to the Holy Roman Emperor. You are in your late thirties (but, a fragile man, you seem older) when you come to London in 1529 to represent your master and to act as councillor and comforter to the embattled Queen Katherine. You will stay until 1545, with a brief intermission when diplomatic relations are broken off. That fact in itself is a testament to your endurance, and the faith placed in you by your distant boss.

You are a cultured man with a humorous turn of phrase. You are astute and subtle, but also passionately engaged in Katherine's cause, and you give wholehearted commitment to her, and then to her daughter Mary. For you, this is not just a matter of duty, it's personal. You labour under certain disadvantages; you don't speak English. But who does, in the Europe of the 1530s? (How much English you understand is a matter of debate.) Visiting Henry's Court, you never know what to expect. You have to swallow insults and threats, being snubbed and ignored. You are bobbing about in a sea of barbarians. Really, the only thing that makes life bearable is your regular suppers with Thomas Cromwell.

With Cromwell you can rattle along in colloquial French, your native tongue. You can pick up all the gossip. It may not be accurate, and you are aware that he may be teasing and misleading you, and yes, you know he's the Antichrist. But you can't help but like him, you tell the Emperor. He's so generous and so entertaining and neighbourly. You do believe he's on the Emperor's side, if only he could be brought to say so.

It takes all your courage to face Henry. Luckily you have a lot. You will not only face him but needle him, probing the areas of vulnerability. Perhaps, you say, he will never have a son: God has his reasons. Henry bellows at you: 'Am I not a man like other men? Am I not? Am I not?'

Your problem is this: your confidants are the old aristocratic families who support Katherine and Mary, and because you listen to them you misperceive the situation; you report to the Emperor several times that the English are ready to revolt and replace Henry, and you urge him to invade; in fact, the families you are involved with have little popular support. It is difficult for you to understand that the power structure is changing from below. There's something you're persistently not grasping. Perhaps it's Cromwell. One day when you are deep in conversation, he starts to smile and can't stop. You tell the Emperor that he has the grace to cover his mouth with his hand.

You are an arch-conspirator doomed to ineffectuality, a brave man on a failing mission. When the Emperor finally allows you to retire, on grounds of ill-health, you limp to the low countries and found a college for young men from your own country of Savoy. And you die peacefully, 1556: having made more of a mark on the history of England than you could ever have believed possible when you were sent among the savages.

SIR HENRY NORRIS

You are known as 'gentle Norris' the perfect courtier: emollient, but also, it seems, a man of genuine tact and kindness. You are chief of the King's Privy Chamber, and Henry's close friend; almost a brother: the man he wakes up to talk to, when he can't sleep. Your closeness to him makes your friendship invaluable to other courtiers. You are at the centre of a network of patronage and favours. You are very powerful because you can control who is admitted to the King's presence, and what he signs, and when. You grow discreetly rich. Like William Brereton, you are one of the 'marcher lords', with lands on the Welsh borders.

You are roughly Henry's contemporary, and like him a star jouster, but you are also clever enough to take on a role in the management of his finances which is deliberately impenetrable: you are in charge of the 'secret funds'.

This may be your undoing. When Thomas Cromwell comes marauding along, he doesn't want secrets; he wants complete charge of the revenue and what happens to it. You may take a certain amount of pleasure in thwarting him. As long as you and your friends control how the King lives day to day, you can limit Cromwell's access. It's a setback when he is given rooms

at Greenwich that communicate directly with Henry's. But the
Privy Chamber's mandarin workings are very hard to challenge.

You are also aware that Cromwell is involved in a clean-up of
border jurisdiction, and is intent on reforming the ineffectual
government of Wales. You're not stopping him. But you're not
exactly helping him either. The present situation suits you nicely.

You have an area of weakness; though you're not a child,
like Francis Weston, and you should know better, you've
become too close to Anne Boleyn.

You are a widower, and you are considered engaged to Mary
Shelton, Anne's cousin and lady-in-waiting. You'd better hurry
up, because Mary is being hotly pursued as a lover, not least by
Weston. But you don't hurry: why is that? Anne puts the question
in public, on 30th April 1536. Tormented, you quarrel with her,
and are overheard. It sounds as if you and Anne plan to marry, in
the event of the King's premature death. This is dangerous; it's a
short step from saying 'the King might die' to saying 'the King
will die.' Preparing for a tournament at Greenwich, you are
ignorant of the construction being placed on the quarrel.

On the day of the joust, Henry is in the spectator's stands.
You're having a bad day; your horse acts up and won't enter the
lists, and Henry offers you one of his own standby string of
mounts. But before the sport gets underway, Cromwell's
nephew, the irritatingly confident Richard, strides up to Henry
and whispers something to him: a nasty piece of news. Henry
rises from his place. He will ride back to London. You are
commanded to ride with him.

On the journey he tells you that you are an adulterer. You
have slept with his wife. You are shocked; and probably, you are
also innocent. Confess, he says, and I'll be good to you. There
can be mercy.

You don't believe it. It's an escalating horror. Back in
Whitehall you are interrogated by Master Treasurer, William
Fitzwilliam, one of Cromwell's wingmen. You admit
something. Perhaps that, yes, you are in love with Anne. You
immediately retract what you have said. You don't admit
adultery. But you seem resigned to what follows. You make no
inelegant protest. Perhaps you have too much experience to
think you can fight off Cromwell. You must wonder why the
King has so abruptly turned against you. Possibly you know the
one secret Henry tries to keep from the world; he's sometimes

impotent. Perhaps Anne told you. But perhaps it was Henry
himself, in an outbreak of late-night confidence: later regretted,
and with fatal consequences. Perhaps he thought you were
laughing at him, together with his wife: that's the one thing he
can't forgive.

SIR WILLIAM BRERETON

You come from a powerful Cheshire family and, like your
friend Norris, you are a marcher lord, with lands on the
disturbed and contentious Welsh border. You are a member of
Henry's Privy Chamber, one of his inner circle, but when you
are arrested and named as one of the Queen's lovers, there is a
certain amount of incredulity. No one thinks you are particularly
close to Anne. Thomas Wyatt, after your death, has trouble
writing a farewell verse about you. He says he hardly knows
you and, frankly, not too many people are complaining about
your demise.

Thomas Cromwell believes in economy of means. He's
looking for 'lovers', and you're standing about. Alas for
romance, it's all about Welsh government. In 1534, you execute,
illegally, a Welshman called Eyton, who had killed one of your
servants in a fight, but who has been acquitted by a London
jury. This is what Cromwell has set his face against: the
arbitrary 'justice' meted out by little lords. He marks your card.
But you're too arrogant to notice.

On the scaffold you seem free from illusion: 'I have
deserved the death.' You can hardly complain and, to your
credit, you don't. You have to learn the new, Cromwellian
system of weights and measures: one English courtier, in high
favour with the King and from a powerful family, is worth no
more than one obscure and friendless Welshman.

MARK SMEATON

You are about twenty-three at your death, but your origins are
not known; they are humble. You are a talented musician
brought up from teenage years in Wolsey's household, and
transferring to the Court at Wolsey's fall. You are part of George
Boleyn's coterie and by 1535 you are suspiciously well-dressed
and living beyond your official means. Where are you getting
the money?

You appear to have become obsessed with the Queen. You lurk outside her rooms, looking lovelorn, in the hope of a word from her. She explains to you, 'You cannot look to have me speak to you as if you were a gentleman, because you be an inferior person.' You sigh, 'A look suffices.' You turn your back and melt away. And so you glide towards disaster.

At the end of April 1536, the Court is alive with rumour but you do not suspect anything when you are invited to Thomas Cromwell's house in Stepney. You think you're going to provide entertainment, but don't guess as to its nature. By the time you leave the following day, en route to the Tower, you have confessed to being the Queen's lover and have implicated several other men. There are rumours that you were tortured at Cromwell's house and racked at the Tower. Torture is illegal in England without a royal warrant and it would not be like Cromwell to step outside the law. It's most likely that you are terrorised or tricked or both. If you had been racked at the Tower you would probably have been unable to walk to your impending execution. As a sign of favour, because you've been so helpful, you are allowed a gentleman's death by the axe instead of the common man's demise at the end of a rope.

GEORGE BOLEYN, LORD ROCHFORD
The younger brother of Anne and Mary, you are recognised in your lifetime as an accomplished and attractive young man, but there is a curious blank in history where you should be. You were a busy Court poet but your verses are lost. You were said to be handsome but no picture remains. You were committed to religious reform but your only religious writings are translations. You are oddly insubstantial and so, in these plays, you are your clothes: flamboyant, expensive and a bit silly.

You were brought to Court by your father when you were ten, for the Christmas celebrations, and stayed on to become one of the King's pages. You receive an excellent humanist education, speak some Italian as well as Latin and French, and are considered gifted. As you grow up you hardly know your sisters. This is quite usual for the time. But when you meet as adults, you and Anne become very close.

By the age of twenty, you are part of the King's Privy Chamber. Wolsey threw you out in 1525 when he reorganised the King's personal staff. But with both sisters, at one time or another, in the King's bed, your success is assured. You really know nothing except Court life. As Anne and the King move towards marriage, you are sent on several embassies to France. Your inexperience is not appreciated but you don't create any disasters. You're a good talker, which Henry likes. Ambassador Chapuys finds you personable and a civilised young man to deal with, but says you are always starting arguments about religion.

You do not like your wife and are said to be a great womaniser. When Anne becomes Queen you become Lord Rochford and acquire several offices of State. Your path inevitably crosses and re-crosses the path of Thomas Cromwell. You have nuisance value to him and when you are made Warden of the Cinque Ports, an important security post, he steps in and countermands your orders. You protest, but it's like spitting at a mountain in the hope you'll flatten it. At thirty-two, you have not acquired the gravitas your status suggests. The centre of your own little world, surrounded by flatterers, trivial people like the musician Mark Smeaton, you may not know that the King suspects your circle of gossiping about him and laughing at him. You are probably astonished to find yourself on trial for treason, and in addition accused of incest. You speak intelligently at your trial, Cromwell says, but it's too late; you are said to have spread rumours of the King's impotence, and in doing so you have put in jeopardy the status of the Princess Elizabeth. Because if the King is impotent, whose child is she? Possibly yours. You are dead before you can blink.

FRANCIS WESTON
You are a golden boy, son of a rich Surrey family. You are a page at Court, then a member of the Privy Chamber. You are a good athlete and musician, you show off and run up big debts, you gamble, you fall in love and have affairs with the ladies-in-waiting. You are just the kind of young man Henry loved to be with when he was twenty, and now he's forty you remind him of the good old days.

You are close to George Boleyn, and one of the young men who is always in and out of the Queen's rooms. You are married, with a young son. In April 1536, Anne Boleyn teases you, saying you do not love your wife but love Anne's cousin, Mary Shelton. You reply 'There is one I love better than these.' The Queen asks, 'Who?' You reply, 'It is yourself.'

So, if the fall of Anne is a Cromwellian plot, you are an obvious person to scoop up. You are not a player on the political scene, but you are part of the sweep-out of the Privy Chamber Cromwell wants to engineer. Your family offer the King a colossal sum of money if he will pardon you. There is no response and Cromwell refuses to meet your family.

In the Tower, Anne says she 'most fears Weston'. Presumably because you know things she doesn't want known and she does not think you would stand up to pressure, or perhaps because she knows that you don't like Norris and might implicate him.

On the scaffold you say that you'd intended to commit sins for twenty or thirty years, to 'live in abomination', and repent when you were a bit older. The transparent sincerity of this sentiment suggests you were not very bright.

Your wife remarries immediately.

SIR THOMAS BOLEYN

You are fifty when the action of the plays begin, a prominent courtier. On your mother's side you have ancient royal blood, but your wealthy paternal grandfather was Lord Mayor of London; hence the jibe that your people are 'in trade'. You are clever, well-connected, cultured, smooth and able; exactly the sort of man who gets on in the reign of Henry VIII.

You marry into the powerful Howard family, and so enhance your status, but you have a large number of children, so that you struggle financially for a number of years. Three children survive: Mary, Anne and George. You speak notably elegant French, and serve Henry on several high-profile diplomatic missions. You place your son at the English Court and your two daughters at Court in Burgundy and then France. Through your mother you have a claim on estates in Ireland, and when you bring Anne home, when she's twenty or twenty-one, it's with the intention of marrying her to one of your Irish connections. Anne has her own ideas, and you are probably dismayed that she has involved herself with the Earl of Northumberland's heir. If her initiative can be made to work, you will back it, but it probably can't. You know Harry Percy is already spoken for and you are afraid to cross Wolsey. You are ambitious but you are not a man of conspicuous moral courage.

However, when the King makes known his feelings for

Anne, you see the opportunities unfolding before you. At the French Court, being the King's official mistress is a lucrative and prestigious option; Mary did not take proper advantage of her situation, but Anne might. You begin to collect offices, titles and perquisites. After Wolsey's fall, you are appointed Lord Privy Seal. Once Anne is Queen, and you are Earl of Wiltshire, you position yourself as her *éminence grise*, and adopt the special title 'Monseigneur'. Soon, like Uncle Norfolk, you find your actual power with Anne is less than you expect.

You regard your daughter Mary as undeserving of your attention or money. After she is widowed, you make no effort to find her a second husband. When she runs off with William Stafford, you cut her off, and are, Mary says, 'cruel'.

When the King turns against Anne, and she and your son George are arrested, you appear to do nothing whatever to help them. You probably count yourself lucky not to be implicated. You take care to be helpful to Cromwell (who takes over your post as Lord Privy Seal) and you creep back to Court two years after Anne's fall, dying quietly in 1539.

THOMAS WYATT

You are a turbulent spirit.

We think of you as the greatest poet of your era, but your contemporaries don't see you that way; every gentleman pens verse. To your peers, you are one of the King's gang of young gentlemen, his regular tennis partner, more volatile and risk-taking than most, with apparently no sense of self-preservation. You get into debt. You are involved in an affray where a man is killed. You fall out with the powerful Duke of Suffolk, who will be trying to ruin you for the rest of your life. No one would be surprised if you were killed in a street fight or broke your neck in the tiltyard. You are in your late twenties when this story starts and it's time you grew up.

Your poetry is not published in your lifetime. It's circulated privately among the courtiers, coded and ambiguous; your friends think they understand it but probably don't. Because it's never been taken to the printer, it's flexible. It can be smudged out, rewritten: like the story of your life so far. Is Anne Boleyn your dark lady? No one can be sure. In the Tower in 1536, Anne will speculate on whether the men imprisoned with her are writing ballads, but will add, 'Only Wyatt can do it.'

Perhaps you spend your life searching for a purpose because your father, Henry Wyatt, is a hard man to live up to. As a known supporter of the future Henry VII, he was imprisoned and tortured under Richard III, and left in a dungeon to starve. He still carries the marks of his torture, a reminder of the old era of civil war. Prominent in the new order, he is a diligent and much-admired public servant. He is a friend of Wolsey and has a high opinion of Cromwell, appointing him one of his executors. When ill-health forces him into retirement, he hands you over to Cromwell, telling you to do exactly as he says. I've told my son, he writes to Cromwell, 'in every point to take and repute you as me.'

One miscalculation your father made; he married you off at seventeen to the daughter of a well-connected neighbour in Kent. Your wife was quickly and notoriously unfaithful. Is that why you are so touchy about your honour, about proving your manhood? Why you are so quickly angered, and why your expectations of human conduct are low? You are cynical about love. It makes a fool of you and it doesn't last. You expect to be betrayed.

Anne Boleyn is your damnation and Thomas Cromwell is your salvation. No one knows whether you and Anne were lovers. Only you know. No one is surprised that you are arrested with Anne's 'lovers'. You have been talked about for years and, to most people, you are the obvious suspect. What's more remarkable is that you escape execution. Soon after your arrest, Cromwell assures your father that you will be coming home safely. He is confident of his ability to save you. But he must be confident you will give him something in return: evidence against Anne, which he will use if he has to. No such evidence emerges in court, as it is not needed. But you emerge into your future, not only free but with financial compensation.

There is no emotional compensation. You write 'These bloody days have broke my heart.' In the years after Anne's death, England is an uncomfortable place for you. Cromwell sees you as a very clever man, but a man who feels too much. He sends you abroad on diplomatic missions, all of them uncomfortable and some of them dangerous. When you are away he looks after your business affairs. You come back to find yourself solvent and your papers in order. Soon you are in debt and disorder again.

When Cromwell walks to execution, you stand by the scaffold. He takes your hand and begs you to stop crying. You are the last person he speaks to. You go home and write a poem about it.

You are broken, disillusioned and worn out. You are dead before you're forty.

GREGORY CROMWELL

You are in your late teens as this story unfolds. You are Thomas Cromwell's only surviving child, and you are brought up as if you were a prince. You will be known to your contemporaries as 'the gentle and virtuous Gregory'. Implacably sweet-natured, you seem to be bowed under the weight of all that is invested in you.

You spent your first years away from home under the indulgent care of a Benedictine nun, who lobbied for you to stay with her until you were twelve. But at some stage your father decided you had to grow up and learn proper Latin, and everything else his son was going to need to know. A distracting series of tutors follow. You are being prepared for a career in public life. You are really only interested in hunting and going out with your dogs.

Your father ascends the career ladder and you have to turn into a courtier. You are surprisingly good at this, a perfect young gentleman and a star in the tiltyard. (Your elder cousin Richard is also a formidable jouster, which must be a source of grief to the young noblemen who have prepared for the dangerous sport all their lives, and feel born to win.) The important thing is, the King likes you.

You will marry the sister of Jane Seymour. (So the blacksmith's grandson is related to the King.) This family connection saves you when your father is executed. Richard Cromwell is a tougher character than you are, much more of a player, and his career is over, but though you do not inherit your father's title of Earl, you are granted a baron's title, and as Lord Cromwell you live and die a country gentleman, fathering many children and making a negligible impact on national life.

How could you possibly have lived up to expectations? In the third Cromwell novel, you will say to your father, 'You know everything. You do everything. You are everything. What's left for me?'

JANE BOLEYN, LADY ROCHFORD

We have to read you backwards, from your death on the scaffold eight years after the action of these plays. Possibly we are being unfair to you. But it's hard to avoid the conclusion that you were a strange and dangerous woman.

You are about thirty at the time of the death of Anne Boleyn, and have by then been at Court for fifteen years, so you know better than anyone the rewards and pleasures and dangers of Court life. You are the daughter of the scholarly Lord Morley, whose family seat is in Norfolk and who marries you into the Boleyn family, who have extensive property in the district. You are about twenty at the time of your marriage. You and George Boleyn live on a lavish scale in both Court and country, and after serving Katherine of Aragon, you become a lady-in-waiting to Anne. If George was as promiscuous as rumour suggested, you must have been embarrassed and miserable. You have no children.

When George was in court, accused of treason, he said that he was being convicted 'on the word of one woman'. (There are no trial records to help us, only sound bites.) It is difficult to see who he meant, if not you; ever since, it's been assumed that it was you who alleged that he and his sister Anne were lovers. This assumption receives support from near-contemporary sources, who refer to you as someone who hated your husband and wanted to be rid of him by any means. The incest accusation is so strange, and so *de trop*, that it seems unlikely that Thomas Cromwell dreamed it up; he had enough to convict George of treason, without any lurid additions.

After the executions, the whole Boleyn family were in disgrace. You left Court and, as the childless widow of a convicted traitor, your financial situation was shaky. Your former father-in-law turned his back on you, but Cromwell persuaded/bullied him into making you an allowance and you were soon back at Court as lady-in-waiting to Jane Seymour. It's this that has suggested to later generations that, at the time of the Boleyns' fall, you cut a deal with Cromwell: your testimony, in return for his protection.

You served Anne of Cleves and the fifth Queen, Katherine Howard, Anne's cousin, who was a feather-headed teenager. You were an experienced courtier and you knew what Henry would do to a wife he suspected of infidelity, and yet you helped Katherine meet her lover, and watched with every appearance of relish as she destroyed herself. It's hard not to believe you took a voyeur's pleasure in other people's disasters. But by this time your survival instincts had deserted you (or perhaps Thomas Cromwell had, as he was dead). After suffering some sort of breakdown, you were beheaded with Katherine.

MARY BOLEYN

You are the elder Boleyn daughter, the beauty of the family, a sweet-natured but brave and passionate woman, and in your later twenties when this story starts.

You are only about fifteen when the King's young sister Mary goes to France for a short-lived marriage to Louis XII; you are part of her entourage, and you stay in France after Mary is widowed and returns to England. You become the mistress of the new King, Francis I, and allegedly are involved with several other courtiers; Francis later refers to you as 'a great and infamous whore'.

Back in England, you are married to the young courtier William Carey, one of Henry's favourites. You become Henry's mistress and your husband profits from this by receiving grants and titles. You have two children, Henry and Katherine, who may or may not be the King's; propriety dictates that they are spoken of as your husband's. You are not calculating and you are not greedy. For which your family never forgive you.

You attend your sister through the period of her rise in the world, but she possibly finds your notorious past an embarrassment, as she has set herself up as a woman of unimpeachable chastity. William Carey dies during the sweating sickness epidemic of 1528, and you find you have no money. Anne assumes the wardship of your son, which means she will look after his education, but otherwise you're on your own.

In 1534, you turn up at Court visibly pregnant. You have made a secret marriage to William Stafford, a young soldier in the Calais garrison, who is well-connected but poor. Your uncle Norfolk, your father and your sister are outraged, and you are told to take yourself off to the country and not come back; your father cuts off the small financial support he has given you. You write a brave and heartfelt letter to Cromwell, telling him of your feelings for your young husband, complaining of the neglect you have felt in recent years, asking for his 'good help' and wishing him 'heart's ease'. You want to get back into the good graces of your family but you are unrepentant, saying of Stafford that 'I would rather beg my bread with him than be the greatest queen christened.' It sheds some light on your sister's marriage, which you have seen at close quarters; you'd rather be disgraced and forced into obscurity than endure her life as it is now.

You live quietly, your finances improve, you have several children with Stafford, and you survive your sister by seven years.

ELIZABETH, LADY WORCESTER

You're the woman who knows all the secrets. Unfortunately we don't know yours.

You are the wife of Henry Somerset, Earl of Worcester, and the sister of a prominent and well-informed courtier called Sir Anthony Browne. You are one of Anne Boleyn's circle, an attractive woman and much gossiped about. You have children with the Earl, but in the spring of 1536 you are pregnant with a baby the Earl suspects is not his. Your brother berates you, whereupon you say, 'Why are you pointing the finger at me? You should see what the Queen gets up to.' Or words to that effect.

Your brother tells Master Treasurer, William Fitzwilliam, and he tells Thomas Cromwell.

This happens in the fevered, poisoned days leading to the fall of Anne Boleyn. At the end of April, or early in May, you talk to Cromwell alone. By this time you are scared and so are the other women who are with Anne on a daily basis. You have debts your husband doesn't know about, which makes you feel vulnerable. And if Anne has a lover, or if the King thinks she has a lover, you are going to be in trouble for concealing her conduct.

But you are thirty-five, you are not a silly, defenceless girl. You want to distance yourself. You have been part of the tight little circle around Anne but you have to break out of it to save your reputation and possibly your life. Exactly what you tell Cromwell about the Queen is unknown, but it may be a great deal more than ever made its way on to the historical record. And the reward would be your immunity. Whatever bargain is struck, you come out of the process undamaged. You and the Earl are apparently reconciled and have several more children.

It seems to have been a historian, rather than a contemporary,

who started the rumour that your baby was Thomas Cromwell's.
It adds a nice complicated spin. In any event, the baby was a
girl, Anne, who later became Countess of Northumberland and
rode in a rebellion against Elizabeth I, actually taking the field
herself, though she was pregnant at the time. So whoever's
daughter she was, she was one of the more memorable products
of this miserable year.

MARY SHELTON

You are a younger cousin of Anne Boleyn and one of her ladies-
in-waiting. You are an editor and contributor to the book of
court poetry known as the 'Devonshire MS'. You are pretty and
sweet-natured, and several men, including the King, are a little
bit in love with you. You may have been Henry's temporary
mistress during one of Anne's pregnancies. For a few weeks in
1536, what you say and what you do is of crucial importance.
But verifiable facts about you are scant and you remain as
elusive as a smile in the dark.

In 1536, you are engaged to be married to Harry Norris, a
widower and head of the Privy Chamber staff, who is jealous
that Francis Weston is paying attention to you. It is when Anne
asks Norris why he doesn't go ahead with your marriage that a
quarrel between Anne and Norris explodes in the face of
startled courtiers. It is public and can't be hushed up, and after
it, Anne is panic-stricken. If she's not guilty, she looks and
sounds guilty. Like Lady Worcester, you have to extricate
yourself from a situation where you might be accused of
complicity with an adulterous queen.

You talk to Cromwell, but whatever you say does not survive
in a written form. If you and Elizabeth Worcester have offered
evidence against Anne, Anne never knows it.

Your feelings about the death of Norris and Weston are
unknown, but you will survive, marry a cousin and have
seven children.

SIR JOHN SEYMOUR

You are a member of an ancient family who came over with the
Conqueror and have held their lands in Wiltshire ever since.
You are also, if rumours are true, a disreputable old rogue. You
fought for Henry VII against Cornish rebels at the Battle of

Blackheath (not much of a battle) and for Henry VIII in his French campaign of 1513 (not much of a war). You married Marjorie Wentworth, a famous beauty from a good family. But your chief distinction is that, in your fifties, you had a long-running affair with the wife of your son, Edward.

This was great fun for gossips but grim for your daughter-in-law, who was packed off to a convent and kept there until she died. Grim for Edward, who was obliged to disinherit his two eldest sons, on the grounds that they might be yours.

It seems you were still in royal favour, because you were host to Henry VIII's hunting party at Wolf Hall in September 1535. You were probably incredulous when he showed an interest in your daughter Jane, the girl you had not managed to marry off. You made no objection to her new situation, but died before you could really capitalise on her position as Queen. She did not come to your funeral.

JANE SEYMOUR

Historians always seem to suggest that you were the stupid wife. You may have been the smartest of all. Certainly you are the most mysterious.

You were brought up in the country and given only a rudimentary, feminine education: no Latin, no French, just sewing and music. You were allowed to ride and hunt, which you did very well. You were well-connected in several family lines, and became one of Queen Katherine's ladies when you were about twenty. The King didn't even seem to notice you. Nor did anyone else. You were pale and small and presumably very observant.

You were with Katherine through the protracted process of her rejection by Henry, and transferred to Anne Boleyn's service when Katherine was sent away from the Court. Despite the superheated atmosphere that built up around Anne, you were never touched by a breath of scandal. When the King finally noticed you and begged you to be his mistress, you were supremely oblivious. You never thought of giving in to him. It is impossible to know whether, with Anne's example before you, you were playing your hand very cleverly, or whether you really just wished he would go away. A faction formed around you: the supporters of the dead Katherine, the supporters of her daughter Mary, all the anti-Boleyn courtiers,

the 'old families'. At some point, after talks with your brother
Edward, Thomas Cromwell decided to facilitate your rise in
the world.

You were formally betrothed to Henry on the day of Anne's
execution, and married a few days later. As Queen, you took as
your motto, 'Bound to obey and serve.' Your game plan was to
look at what Anne had done, and do the opposite. Ambassador
Chapuys thought you were very plain and said that, after so
many years at Henry's Court, it would be a miracle if you were
a virgin. But others described the newly married King as
'having come out of Hell into Heaven'. Given that you cannot
be shown to have played any direct part in Anne Boleyn's
downfall, you do seem to have been a good woman. You
admired Katherine and later did your best to act as a mother to
her daughter Mary, to reconcile Mary with the King and
persuade him to bring her to Court. You also worked hard to
reconcile him to the existence of the small Elizabeth, a child
whom he almost rejected after the execution of her mother. You
bore no grudges, and acted with charity. Conservative in
religion, you bravely asked Henry to restore some of the
suppressed abbeys. His response was so terrifying that you
never again questioned his policies or whims.

In your day, the Court was decorous. French fashions were
no longer seen. There was a return to the correctness of
Katherine's day. However, times had changed; in a match that
would have been unthinkable a few years before, your sister
married Gregory Cromwell.

By early 1537 you were pregnant, and ferociously hungry for
quail, which had to be sent by the dozen from Calais. In
October, you endured a three-day labour, gave Henry his heir,
and died several days later. Cromwell blamed your attendants.
He was upset to the point of being irrational. Perhaps he was
afraid of what your loss would do to Henry, or perhaps he
thought the importance of his family connection would
diminish; or perhaps he just liked you. After your death no
music was heard at Court for months. Henry's next marriage
was a disaster.

EDWARD SEYMOUR

You are a clever, serious and prudent man in your mid-thirties when the King becomes interested in your sister, Jane. You take every advantage of the turn of events, and, at least initially, manage your rise in the world smoothly, without causing the offence that the Boleyn family caused in a similar situation.

You grow up in Wolsey's household and at Court, and go to France as a page when Henry's young sister marries Louis XII. In 1523, you are part of the military expedition to France led by Charles Brandon. You are a good commander and will later lead major military actions in France and Scotland. Early in your career, you are favoured by Wolsey and seen as a loyal and useful servant of the State. You give an impression of being calculating and self-controlled. Unlike your sister, you are a religious reformer. You get on well with Cromwell, personally and politically.

You will become Viscount Beauchamp and Earl of Hertford. Henry remains close to your family after Jane's death. At Henry's own death in 1547, you emerge as Head of Government and Regent or 'Lord Protector' to Prince Edward. You are displaced in a coup in 1549, and executed, but not before you have executed your own brother, Thomas Seymour, for treason.

SIR WILLIAM KINGSTON, CONSTABLE OF THE TOWER

You are a courteous elderly man of military bearing. You began your career as a yeoman of the guard, see much campaigning, are knighted after the Battle of Flodden, and serve as an administrator in peacetime. You have been Constable of the Tower for ten years. Always correct towards your prisoners, you exemplify the Tudor bureaucrat's attitude to death; you need to get the paperwork right. When Anne Boleyn arrives at the Tower, you are told by Cromwell to report everything she says. You do this with meticulous care but remarkable obtuseness. When you hear her hysterical laughter you conclude 'this lady has much joy and pleasure in death'.

THE CALAIS EXECUTIONER

For a believing Christian of the sixteenth century, the most important moment of life is the moment when we leave it. We leave with our sins absolved, from a prolonged deathbed with family and a confessor at hand: or suddenly from the battlefield, in the midst of our anger and pride. We are struck down by disease, like one of the victims of the era's epidemics, 'merry at breakfast, dead by dinner'. Or perhaps we fall foul of the law. The procedures for judicial killing are rule-bound and fixed, like the rites of the church. As on a deathbed, the sufferer must show contrition. In any speech to the crowd, he or she must accept the sentence, and praise the king. When the priest has done his part he steps aside and you, the headsman, are the focus of all eyes.

For the client of the Calais headsman, severance occurs within the blink of an eye, between two pulse-beats. You depend on your victim's cooperation; to receive the killing stroke, he or she must kneel upright, in a posture of attentive prayer: remaining, with the courage instilled by a lifetime of self-discipline, rigid on the brink of eternity. Apprehensive about the pain, the Queen of England asks the Constable of the Tower how it will be. He tells her, 'There should be no pain, it is so subtle.' She puts her hand to her throat: 'I have only a little neck.'

She must not be frightened, she must not be alarmed. She must not know that you are her fate. As part of your contract, an allowance is made to purchase the clothes suitable for a gentleman, so that to the Queen you will appear just another witness in the crowd. (She has seen you before, perhaps, but does not quite recall; you, or some man like you, staring; she is used to that.) Only at the last second will she recognise you, as you kneel to ask her pardon before her blindfold cuts out the light. She must not know the angle of her death, its path through thin air: you will call out, 'Bring me the sword!' and her head will whip around, and you will not be where she thinks you are, and she will be dead.

A sword, a good sword, is a precious and beautiful possession, and a sword dedicated to a single purpose is a sacred object. You are proud of the weapon and proud of your craft, and proud to know that the King of England has heard of both. When the summons comes, and you embark to cross the

Narrow Sea, you mean to burnish your reputation. On the day, your performance is immaculate. Your fee is £23.6.8d. The blade of your sword is incised with the words of a prayer.

Characters

THOMAS CROMWELL
ELIZABETH (LIZ) CROMWELL, *his wife*
GREGORY CROMWELL, *their son*
RAFE SADLER, *a young gentleman – Cromwell's ward and secretary – later one of the King's gentlemen*
CHRISTOPHE, *a French boy and thief – Cromwell's manservant*
KING HENRY VIII
KATHERINE OF ARAGON, *the Queen*
PRINCESS MARY, *their daughter*
ANNE BOLEYN, *lady-in-waiting to Queen Katherine – later Queen*
HARRY PERCY, *a young lord – later Earl of Northumberland*
THOMAS WYATT, *a young poet, friend to King Henry*
CARDINAL ARCHBISHOP THOMAS WOLSEY, *Lord Chancellor*
MARK SMEATON, *his lutenist*
WILLIAM WARHAM, *Archbishop of Canterbury*
STEPHEN GARDINER, *later Bishop of Winchester*
EUSTACHE CHAPUYS, *Imperial Ambassador*
THOMAS CRANMER, *Anne's Chaplain – later Archbishop of Canterbury*
THOMAS MORE, *later Lord Chancellor*
SIR THOMAS BOLEYN, *later Earl of Wiltshire*
GEORGE BOLEYN, *later Lord Rochford*
MARY BOLEYN, *King Henry's mistress*
THE DUKE OF NORFOLK, *Thomas Howard*
THE DUKE OF SUFFOLK, *Charles Brandon, the King's friend and brother-in-law*
SIR HENRY NORRIS, *the King's Groom of the Stool*
SIR WILLIAM BRERETON, *gentleman of the King's Chamber*
FRANCIS WESTON, *one of the King's gentlemen*
OLD SIR JOHN SEYMOUR
MARJORIE SEYMOUR
EDWARD SEYMOUR

JANE SEYMOUR, *lady-in-waiting to Anne Boleyn*
JANE BOLEYN, LADY ROCHFORD, *wife to George*
MARY SHELTON, *lady-in-waiting to Anne Boleyn*
ELIZABETH, LADY WORCESTER, *lady-in-waiting to
  Anne Boleyn*
SIR WILLIAM KINGSTON, *Constable of the Tower*
CALAIS EXECUTIONER

And SERVANTS, MONKS, DANCERS, LORDS, LADIES,
BISHOPS, GUARDS, *etc*.

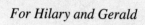

For Hilary and Gerald

WOLF HALL

ACT ONE

Scene One

Fanfares. A military dance for young men led by KING HENRY VIII, *watched by* KATHERINE OF ARAGON *and* PRINCESS MARY (*twelve*), *who absent-mindedly says her rosary.* MEN *joined by* LADIES. *Music softens.* KING HENRY *dances with* MARY BOLEYN. KATHERINE *displeased. All eyes on* ANNE BOLEYN (*yellow dress*) *who dances with* THOMAS WYATT. *Then she rejects him and dances with* HARRY PERCY – *very lovingly* – *which makes* WYATT *angry.* WYATT *leaves.* THOMAS WOLSEY *enters with his train, followed by* STEPHEN GARDINER, *upstaging* KING HENRY, *in every way possible. Thunder and lightning.* KING HENRY *and* KATHERINE *go off with* PRINCESS MARY. HARRY PERCY *and* ANNE BOLEYN *exit together. It rains. Night falls. Scene becomes* WOLSEY's *office.*

THOMAS CROMWELL *hurrying, wet, in riding gear.* STEPHEN *scowls as he leaves.*

STEPHEN. Cromwell. Late.

THOMAS. Yes – isn't it?

STEPHEN. No – I mean… (*Exasperated, he gives up and goes.*)

> THOMAS *goes into* WOLSEY's *splendid golden room. Big fire. Shadows.* MARK SMEATON *plays the lute.* WOLSEY *sits with his back to us.*

WOLSEY. Where were you when I needed you, Thomas?

THOMAS. In Yorkshire, Your Grace.

WOLSEY. Yorkshire?

THOMAS. Turbulent monks. You sent me there.

WOLSEY. You'll be hungry then. Fetch him something to eat. Cherries – he likes cherries.

SERVANT. There are no cherries, Your Grace.

WOLSEY. What? Why not?

SERVANT. It's April, Your Grace.

WOLSEY. Nonsense! It can't *still* be April! Why am I so ill-
served? Sorry, Tom – no cherries. Well, bring him something
– I don't know – a lettuce? Is there a lettuce? If you don't
give this one his feed he'll tear the place down.

> SERVANTS *appear to make* THOMAS *comfortable – take
his wet coat, build up the fire, bring wine and food – giving
the lie to* WOLSEY's *joke about being ill-served.*

What else would you like?

THOMAS. I'd like the sun to come out.

WOLSEY. You ask a great deal. It's almost midnight.

THOMAS. Dawn would do.

WOLSEY. We shall try the power of prayer.

> WOLSEY *looks at the* SERVANTS *– the signal to withdraw.*
MARK *stays.*

The King called me this morning – early. (*Yawns.*)
Exceptionally early.

THOMAS. What did he want?

WOLSEY. A son.

THOMAS. He's got one – young Richmond. And they say
Mary Boleyn's boy is his.

WOLSEY. Might be. It squalls, and it's ginger. Look, forget
Mary Boleyn – he needs a son born in wedlock. An heir to sit
on his throne when he's gone.

THOMAS. His daughter won't do?

WOLSEY. What – Mary? A girl ruling England? Don't be
absurd! Now you have a son – Gregory's a fine boy – I, God
forgive me, have a boy of my own – every lord, every landed
gentleman – every lackey can get boys… Only the King
can't seem to manage it. Whose fault is that?

THOMAS. God's.

WOLSEY. Nearer the King than God?

THOMAS. Queen Katherine?

WOLSEY. Nearer?

THOMAS. Yourself, Your Grace?

WOLSEY. Myself, My Grace. If the King lies awake at night, asking himself why his children die, the fault must be mine. Enough now, Mark.

Exit MARK.

Henry believes God won't give him sons because he and Katherine were never truly married.

THOMAS. He's just noticed? After eighteen years?

WOLSEY. He's reading his Bible. And though the Pope declared their marriage lawful – gave a dispensation – swept aside all impediment – in the Book of Leviticus the King has found the verse which forbids marriage with a brother's wife. Katherine was his brother's widow.

THOMAS. Then show him the contradictory verse. Deuteronomy says marrying your brother's widow is compulsory.

WOLSEY. The King doesn't like Deuteronomy. He prefers Leviticus. He says, 'If this is God's word, plainly written, no Pope has power to set it aside.'

THOMAS. Well, he's right there, isn't he?

WOLSEY. Is he?

THOMAS. You tell me – you're the Cardinal.

WOLSEY. I am a divided man: the Pope's voice in England – but first the King's loyal servant. Still… If we go to work in the usual way – offer Pope Clement a – a –

THOMAS. A bribe?

WOLSEY. God forgive you, Tom! A loan.

THOMAS. He may grant the King an annulment.

WOLSEY. There are precedents. Gold finds its way into the Vatican and the King gets a new wife. One who can breed.

THOMAS. What does Queen Katherine get?

WOLSEY. Jesu! She doesn't even suspect. It will be me who has to tell her. The King won't deliver bad news – he delegates it.

THOMAS. You'll have to pick the right moment.

WOLSEY. There is no right moment. She'll say, 'I am the daughter of two reigning monarchs and they send a butcher's boy to tip me off my throne!'

THOMAS. Then she'll threaten you with her nephew – the Emperor –

WOLSEY. But Charles won't go to war over his old aunt? Surely not!

THOMAS. He doesn't need to go to war. He can blockade us – starve us out – cut off our trade. When winter comes he can hold back the grain ships – and we'll be at his mercy. If I were you –

WOLSEY. Cardinal Cromwell – in charge! What a world that would be!

THOMAS. If I were you, I'd deal with the King's case here in London. You have the Pope's authority – get him his divorce before Europe wakes up to what's happening.

WOLSEY. When Europe wakes up it may break this country apart.

THOMAS. Then tell that to the King. He listens to you. He always has.

WOLSEY. He's listening to his conscience now. Which is an active one – a tender one.

THOMAS. Then… (*Taking this in.*) He's sincere in this matter?

WOLSEY. The King always believes what he says – at the time he's saying it. You know, Katherine and Arthur, they were children when they were married. Fifteen. Katherine always swore they lay beside each other chaste. Like brother and sister saying their prayers. She swears Arthur never touched her. Henry believed she came to him a virgin.

THOMAS. Couldn't he tell?

WOLSEY. He was a boy – seventeen! He was in love with her – how could he tell? Could you tell – the first time you… I know I couldn't! Anyway it suited him to believe her.

THOMAS. And now it doesn't.

WOLSEY. Still… if I do part him from Katherine, I could marry him smartly to a French princess.

THOMAS. You'd have to. We'd need the French as allies.

WOLSEY. Never a good position to be in!

THOMAS. If you *do* separate them, where will Katherine go?

WOLSEY. She's very pious. Convents can be comfortable.

THOMAS. What if she won't budge?

WOLSEY (*yawns*). Go home now, Tom. (*Calling to* SERVANTS.) Send Rafe Sadler in here! Your ward's been waiting for hours. Ah, Rafe –

Enter RAFE SADLER.

RAFE. Your Grace. I wish you'd talk to God about the weather. It's been raining for three years.

WOLSEY. I'll see what I can do. Take this man home to his family.

Starts to usher them out.

RAFE. We've missed him, sir. How was Yorkshire?

WOLSEY. Yes – how was Yorkshire? Did we get the money?

THOMAS. Your project's disliked there.

WOLSEY. I have the Pope's authority for it.

THOMAS. The Pope's no help when it comes to converting monks into cash.

WOLSEY. Thirty ill-run, over-wealthy monasteries must – and *shall* – amalgamate with larger well-run ones – like it or not. They are ill-run, aren't they?

THOMAS. Yes – treasure flows in at the front door, whores sneak out at the back –

WOLSEY. What became of poverty, chastity and obedience? Thomas, I *need* those funds – for my Oxford College and the school at Ipswich – my monument – my legacy when I'm gone.

RAFE. Ipswich, Your Grace?

WOLSEY. The town of my birth. Inglorious in every other respect. Go home now.

THOMAS. The laws relating to land –

WOLSEY. The law is an instrument for saying 'no'. I want to hear you say 'yes'. Find a way.

THOMAS. The Yorkshire gentry threatened to kill me.

WOLSEY. You don't look particularly killed. I may have to go to Yorkshire myself. I've often wondered what it's like. What do they eat up there?

THOMAS. Londoners when they have a chance.

WOLSEY. …but do they have any lemons.

RAFE. But surely… Your Grace is Archbishop of York? Were you never enthroned?

WOLSEY. When have I ever had time for my own spiritual affairs? Home! Come early tomorrow.

THOMAS (*struck by a thought*). You say the King is reading the Scriptures? Is he reading them in English?

WOLSEY. That… is forbidden.

THOMAS. Not to the King.

WOLSEY. Careful, Tom. Walls have ears. God bless you both.

They kneel, kiss WOLSEY's *ring, and leave.* WOLSEY *is robed, goes into his chapel and prays hard. A downpour.* THOMAS *and* RAFE *are escorted home to Austin Friars by* WOLSEY's LINKBOYS *and* GUARDS.

Scene Two

Home. THOMAS *greets* ELIZABETH *(LIZ)* CROMWELL, *his wife. A good fire.*

LIZ. Forget where you live?

> CHRISTOPHE *takes the wet clothes.*

THOMAS (*relieved to be home with her*). Oh, Lizzie...

LIZ. How was Yorkshire?

THOMAS. Oh, Lizzie...

LIZ. You went straight to the Cardinal?

> CHRISTOPHE *brings drink – exits.* LIZ *gives* THOMAS *the cup, they both drink from it, embrace. They've been apart a long time.*

THOMAS. The children?

LIZ. Blossoming. Anne wants to learn Greek. Grace wants to be an angel, and here's a letter from Gregory. It's in Latin.

THOMAS. Of sorts. (*Reads.*) 'Dear Father, I hope you are well. I hope my mother and my lovely sisters, Anne and Grace, are well. I hope your dogs are well. And now no more for lack of time. Your dutiful son, Gregory Cromwell.' Our son is no Cicero. Well, thank God he's not like I was at his age –

LIZ. What were you like?

THOMAS. I used to stick knives in people... What's new in London?

LIZ. The word on Cheapside is, the King's bought a huge emerald –

THOMAS (*opening his letters*). Has he? I wonder how much he paid for it –

LIZ. It's the size of a sparrow's egg. (*Shows him.*) It's *that* big.

THOMAS. Well, he's a big king, isn't he?

LIZ. It's not for him. It's for a woman – a woman's ring. So... who's the lady?

THOMAS. Queen Katherine. Surely?

LIZZIE (*scrutinising him*). You weasel! You've heard, haven't you?

THOMAS (*innocent*). You don't hear anything in Yorkshire.

LIZ. They're saying the King wants to do something very strange. And wrong. They say he wants to divorce the Queen? Is it true? – Because if it is, he'll set half the world against him.

THOMAS. Yes – Spain – the Emperor –

LIZ. No. I mean the women. All the women who have lost their children – all women who have daughters but no sons – all women who are forty…

THOMAS. It's just London gossip. Wolsey says the King is reading his Bible. If he's reading it in English that would be a great thing for us. All of us – men and women?

LIZ. Tom… I've something to tell you.

THOMAS*'s hackles rise.*

Thomas More has been here –

THOMAS. Jesus! (*Incensed.*) Did he threaten you? I'll kill him –

LIZ. He was very civil – courteous – you know his manner –

THOMAS. With the Bishop's men at his back?

LIZ (*nods*). He said, 'Your husband won't mind if I look through his library.'

THOMAS. Oh! (*Takes this in.*) He didn't find Martin Luther?

LIZ. No – you've Rafe to thank for that. But I wish you wouldn't keep those books in the house.

CHRISTOPHE *brings* THOMAS*'s night clothes, a candle, etc.*

THOMAS. I'll find a safer place for them… I might just… open a few more letters –

LIZ. You'll do no such thing! (*Going.*) It's three o'clock. You'll come to bed. Tell him, Christophe.

CHRISTOPHE. Go to bed now, master, or the mistress will
    beat me.

THOMAS (*half to himself*). If the King's in the market for large
    emeralds, he's in the market for a new mistress. 'So who's
    the lady?' Poor Mary Boleyn! He must be tiring of her –

CHRISTOPHE. And I myself wish to sleep. But until my
    master sleeps –

LIZ (*off*). Thomas – come to bed.

    House in darkness – silence.

Scene Three

MONKS *chanting. The Charterhouse. Dawn.* THOMAS
MORE, *strips to the waist, kneels before a crucifix. He begins
to flog himself.*

MORE.
    Mea culpa, mea culpa, mea culpa!

    Hide not Thy face from me, O Lord, on a day when I am
        sore troubled.
    I am like an owl of the desert – mine enemies reproach
        me –
    I mingle my drink with weeping – my bread turns to ashes
        in my mouth –
    Because of Thine indignation against me and Thy wrath.

    Mea culpa, mea culpa, mea maxima culpa!

Scene Four

Austin Friars. Next morning. Household bustle. CHRISTOPHE
*sharpening a razor. The house still dark, coming to life.
Candles.* LIZ, *doing six things at once.*

THOMAS. Morning, Rafe. Sun shining?

RAFE. Bucketing down, sir. (*Slaps down a satchel of books.*)

THOMAS. Wolsey's losing his touch.

CHRISTOPHE (*yawns*). I shave you?

THOMAS. No, you stay away from me – I lost enough blood in
    Yorkshire. (*Unwraps the books.*)

RAFE. Brother Martin Luther – and William Tyndale.

THOMAS. His Testament in English. Where did you hide
    them? (*Starts to read.*)

    CHRISTOPHE *opens the shutters.*

RAFE. In little Grace's bed with little Grace on top of them.
    When the Bishop's men looked in I was bathing her head.
    'Not too close,' I said, 'she has a fever.' And they ran.

LIZ. Those books – Out of my house – This morning.

RAFE. I'll take them to Gray's Inn.

LIZ. It's true about the fever, though – two deaths last week in
    Southwark –

THOMAS. Well… south of the river… It's only April – too
    early for the sweating sickness.

    He slaps his book shut. RAFE *puts it in the satchel.*

    They go towards York Place. CHRISTOPHE, *half-asleep,
    grabs a loaf, carries* THOMAS's *papers.*

RAFE. Thomas More took us by surprise.

THOMAS. I put you at risk.

RAFE. Isn't it wrong? That the word of God can breed such
    hatred?

THOMAS. Think about it – we're all intelligent men here –

CHRISTOPHE (*with half a loaf in his mouth*). Hun… mung… un… ungligent –

RAFE (*to* CHRISTOPHE). What!

THOMAS. Well, you and I are intelligent men. Christ said, 'I come not to bring peace but a sword.'

RAFE. Give me some of that. You're a pig, Christophe –

CHRISTOPHE. Oink! Oink!

MORE *shambles on, unnoticed, with a couple of* HEAVIES – *untidy, unkempt – buttons undone. He carries books and papers.*

THOMAS. Thomas More's living in a world long gone. He believes you stop men thinking by burning their books.

RAFE. But God invented the printing press.

THOMAS. The word is turning and More's left standing –

RAFE. Let's hope he's never raised to high office. Or we'll all –

MORE. Cromwell! Just the man I need!

THOMAS. Sir Thomas More. I hear you came looking for me. (*Takes the satchel from* RAFE.)

MORE. You were not at home. (*Good-naturedly.*) Neither were the heretic books you bring in from Germany. Where've you hidden them? At Gray's Inn?

THOMAS. You'll find nothing heretical on my shelves.

MORE. Well… your conscience is your own concern. You could be very useful to me, you know? You've lived in Antwerp? You know the heretic Tyndale.

THOMAS. I know *of* him. They say he's translating the Gospels into English –

MORE. False translations. Wicked, misleading deceptions.

RAFE. Why don't you translate the Gospels yourself, sir?

THOMAS. He distrusts the English language. If his native tongue had a neck, Master More would wring it.

MORE. It would help me greatly if you'd cross over and speak to Tyndale –

THOMAS. I serve the Cardinal –

MORE. I ask myself why? It's well known you're no friend to priests, yet you make yourself a willing drudge for the most corrupt priest in Christendom. Work with me. Persuade Tyndale to come home. For… an exchange of views – to end any misunderstanding between us.

THOMAS. In your torture chamber?

MORE. Oh, come! That's a slander. What need have I of a torture chamber?

THOMAS. Men go into your house hale and hearty – they come out half-dead.

MORE (*thinks – looks as if he's going to say something profound. But:*). Must be my wife's cooking. (*Nasty laugh.*) Come to Chelsea. Bring young Sadler with you. The food may not be of the quality, and I may say quantity, you're used to at the Cardinal's table, but the talk is excellent.

THOMAS. I'll think it over.

MORE. If Wolsey comes down, his dog will need a new master. Come to my whistle, boy – we should be friends. And let Tyndale know that if he won't come home I'll fetch him.

THOMAS. None of my business.

MORE. So you say – so you have asserted…

Before MORE *turns away,* CHRISTOPHE *moves in on him, thrusting his gnawed chunk of bread in his face.*

CHRISTOPHE. You want breakfast?

MORE *flinches*.

You call this the body of Christ, eh? Ting-a-ling-a-ling! (*Priestly drone.*) *Hoc est corpus meum* – Hocus Pocus Meum. (*Elevates the crust with both hands.*) Want some?

MORE (*controlling his rage*). In your place, Cromwell, I'd not keep blasphemers in my house. You're sailing close to the wind as it is.

MORE *ambles away, shedding papers. His* HEAVIES *pick them up and follow.*

CHRISTOPHE. Does he really have a torture chamber? I should very much like to see it.

RAFE. Yes – I think you've said enough to get you in.

THOMAS. What's wrong with that man, Rafe? Everything he was brought up to believe, he believes it still. What I grew up believing is chipped away – every month a little bit lost, and then a little bit more. I search my Bible – I can't find where it says monks. Or nuns – or purgatory, or fasting – or relics, or priests who can change bread into the body of Christ –

RAFE. It doesn't say pope either, does it?

THOMAS. No – I've never found where it says pope. And nor has Thomas More – that's why he wants to stop us looking.

CHRISTOPHE. *Hoc est corpus* – Hocus Pocus –

THOMAS. Christophe!

Scene Five

York Place.

STEPHEN. Late again. Why do you keep us waiting?

THOMAS. We stopped to watch a fight at the Abbey – a couple of whores and a young monk. Must have lost track of the time.

STEPHEN. Nothing you do would surprise me, Cromwell. The Cardinal tells me your father kept a low alehouse. In Putney.

THOMAS. He was a blacksmith too. Thirsty work.

STEPHEN (*looking him over*). You hide your origins well. Most of the time.

THOMAS. At least I know who my father was.

STEPHEN (*rising above the insult*). Can you shoe a horse?

THOMAS. I can make a knife.

Grabbing STEPHEN, *he suddenly pulls an imaginary knife and pretends to stab* STEPHEN, *who freezes in horror.*

THOMAS *goes in to* WOLSEY.

WOLSEY. What do you know of this Boleyn girl – not the King's mistress – the flat-chested one?

THOMAS. Anne Boleyn? Not much. Father married up – old Norfolk's sister – he's as cunning as a fox.

WOLSEY. I know he is – I open all his letters. The girl Anne was brought up in France – now she's in London – setting her cap at the Earl of Northumberland's son – Harry Percy –

THOMAS. She's wasting her time. Young Percy's marrying Old Talbot's daughter. It's all fixed.

WOLSEY. Which is why the King's ordered me to put a stop to their nonsense. 'Oh, 'Arry Percy, 'Arry Percy – 'ow I lurv you!' ''An I shall marry you, my pet, and you shall 'ave 'Arry's 'art, an' 'is 'awks an' 'is 'ounds, an' 'is 'ole hearldom.' It's no laughing matter. Over there – take notes. I want this on the record. (*Suddenly bellowing.*) Thomas Boleyn! Come in here.

Enter SIR THOMAS BOLEYN, *suave, middle-aged diplomat.*

BOLEYN. Your Grace.

WOLSEY (*grim as Hell*). Sit.

BOLEYN. I –

WOLSEY. Did you put her up to it – wagging her tail at that young fool Harry Percy? The King won't have it. I'll not have it!

BOLEYN. Surely Your Grace cannot think –

WOLSEY. You'd be surprised what I can think –

BOLEYN. Oh, come! Young people today –

WOLSEY. You Boleyns can't manage your women, can you?

Enter STEPHEN.

STEPHEN. Forgive me, Your Grace. Sir Thomas, your son George is here – (*Horrified*.) he's brought a woman.

WOLSEY. A woman? They'll be leading in bears next!

BOLEYN. My daughter-in-law, in fact –

Enter GEORGE BOLEYN *and* JANE BOLEYN, LADY ROCHFORD.

GEORGE. Your Grace.

WOLSEY. George, why have you brought your wife here? (*Baleful but polite*.) Sit, madam – pray sit.

GEORGE. She knows my sister Anne's secrets –

WOLSEY. Anne confides in her?

GEORGE. No, Your Grace. My wife listens at doors.

WOLSEY. Well, Jane… I knew your father – in gentler times than these. Are you happy with this popinjay he's married you to?

JANE ROCHFORD *keeps her eyes down*.

Thought not. So… what have you to tell me? What do Anne Boleyn and Harry Percy get up to behind closed doors?

Nothing.

Come on – squawk up!

BOLEYN. Well, the fact is… we may find…

WOLSEY (*bellows*). Shut your foolish mouth!

JANE ROCHFORD. Anne says they're married.

WOLSEY *gasps*.

They have taken their vows –

WOLSEY. Witnesses? Answer! Before witnesses? That's everything – tell me!

JANE ROCHFORD. I don't know.

WOLSEY. Has he had her?

JANE ROCHFORD. Oh, Your Grace…

WOLSEY. 'Oh Your Grace', what? (*Explodes – ugly.*) Come on, you gawking wet girl – what? What! I need to know how far this has gone –

BOLEYN. Your Grace – please moderate –

WOLSEY (*to* BOLEYN). What's the stupid lad been doing with his cock? Though I doubt a dunce like Harry Percy knew he had a cock until your slut of a daughter started helping him look for it –

GEORGE. Oh!

WOLSEY. Has he had her!

JANE ROCHFORD. I don't know.

WOLSEY. Good! Good. You *don't know*. Or you won't say. And we're going to keep it like that.

JANE ROCHFORD. I –

WOLSEY. Do you understand me?

BOLEYN. The facts remain. If a promise of marriage was made before witnesses, it holds good in law – especially –

WOLSEY. Especially if he's shoved it up her. Listen to me, Boleyn. You'll take your girl Anne down to Kent and keep her there. You pimped her sister Mary to the King in the hopes of rich rewards – now you think you'll pimp the other one to Harry Percy and get your hands on his earldom. If Anne's a whore you'll need to keep it quiet – or you'll have her on your hands costing you bed and board till she's an old crone.

GEORGE. But if there were witnesses –

WOLSEY. Let them show their faces – I'll deal with them. Are there letters?

BOLEYN. I have a few –

WOLSEY. Burn them.

GEORGE. Harry Percy may not accept –

WOLSEY. You leave that foolish boy to me.

GEORGE. You don't know my sister Anne.

WOLSEY. No, but I'm sure I could if I paid cash down.

GEORGE. Anne always gets what she wants.

WOLSEY. George – I always get what I want. Get out – the whole pack of you.

BOLEYN (*under his breath*). Butcher's boy! (*As he passes* THOMAS.) Butcher's dog!

BOLEYNS *leave:* BOLEYN *trying to keep his composure and his smile,* GEORGE *furious.* JANE ROCHFORD *trails behind and takes a long look at* THOMAS. *He rises to bow her out. A backward glance.*

WOLSEY (*making a big thing of introducing a series of dog images, whistles, laughs*). Here, boy! Here! Come out, dog! Good boy!

THOMAS. I never knew Your Grace could be so terrifying.

WOLSEY. Oh, it was an act! I'm an excellent actor – you should see me play Herod of Jewry. Boo!

WOLSEY *laughs and roars, throwing up his hand. Strange moment. A shadow of the arm falls on the wall.* THOMAS *leaps away – reaching for an imaginary dagger – on guard. Shock.*

Tom? What did you think I was going to do?

THOMAS. When you've lived in Italy as I… have…

WOLSEY. I suppose the Vatican must be very like Putney. Did you kill him? (*Studies* THOMAS*'s face. Concerned.*) Have you made a good confession?

MARK *comes in, unnoticed.*

THOMAS. It was a long time ago. I was a soldier, Your Grace.

WOLSEY. Even soldiers have hopes of Heaven. I could hear your confession here and now – absolve you.

Silence.

THOMAS. There's a little knife – an estoc. If someone comes at you – out of the shadows… He's just a body – he doesn't have a name.

WOLSEY. Do you no longer believe in the sacrament? I've never asked you what you believe.

MARK. Lord Percy is here, Your Grace.

WOLSEY *and* THOMAS *adjust their faces*.

WOLSEY. Very well, Mark.

MARK. Do you wish me to stay and play for him?

WOLSEY *and* THOMAS *burst out laughing*.

WOLSEY. No – thank you, Mark.

MARK – *not seeing the joke – is hurt. Exits*. STEPHEN *brings in* HARRY PERCY, *nervous*.

STEPHEN. Henry Percy, My Lord.

HARRY PERCY. Your Grace.

WOLSEY. God's life, Harry, I'm told you're as good as married to a common trull!

HARRY PERCY. I am betrothed to Anne Boleyn, sir. And I resent the –

WOLSEY. Hold your tongue!

HARRY PERCY. I will not! Why shouldn't I have her? I know she's only a simple maid –

WOLSEY. Simple? That's you, Harry – you're the simpleton. As for a maid? That's surely not her.

HARRY PERCY. I love her.

WOLSEY. Courts are no place for love, Harry. So it's time to move on. You'll forget this Anne Boleyn, and you'll marry Mary Talbot as the King commands.

HARRY PERCY. I won't though. I'd be miserable.

WOLSEY. You can wake up miserable as dawn on Ash Wednesday every day of your life, but you'll do your duty to your noble house, and to your country.

HARRY PERCY (*with a mighty effort at clarity*). If you take Anne from me, I'll die.

WOLSEY (*bursts out laughing*). Nobody ever died of love, Harry. You'll die in battle, defending England from the Scots, and leave behind you many sons and a marble tomb. That's your destiny. That's what your family is for – it's what it does best. It's *all* it does. And if you're not man enough, I'll take away your earldom and give Northumberland to one of your horrible young brothers.

HARRY PERCY. You can't do that, Wolsey.

THOMAS. You'll find he can.

HARRY PERCY. I don't know you, do I? You speak to a lord only when you are spoken to.

WOLSEY. Oh, I've done with you, sir – take him away, Stephen. It must be dinner time.

STEPHEN. I often ask myself if I'm Your Grace's secretary or doorkeeper at the madhouse. Come, Sir Henry.

HARRY PERCY. Your Grace! I am married! Words were spoken! Vows were made.

WOLSEY (*gently*). Consider them broken.

STEPHEN *ushers* HARRY PERCY *out*.

And that's the last we'll hear of Anne Boleyn.

Scene Six

The dance takes shape around ANNE. *Bright lights. Arthurian masque at Court – mounted* KNIGHTS (*Vices*) *attack the Castle of Perseverance, defended by* LADIES (*Virtues*). WOLSEY *arrives in his Chancellor's chain looking magnificent – takes centre stage –* THOMAS *and* RAFE *stand apart.* KING HENRY, *as Love's Champion, dances with* MARY BOLEYN. GEORGE *dances with* ANNE. GEORGE *and* KING HENRY *change partners. Exit* KATHERINE, *angry with* MARY BOLEYN.

RAFE. Is that Anne Boleyn?

THOMAS. See the emerald on her finger?

RAFE. It's the size of a sparrow's egg.

THOMAS. Worked it out?

RAFE. So that's why the King wouldn't let Harry Percy have her! (*Looks at* WOLSEY *enjoying himself.*) Wolsey doesn't know, does he?

THOMAS. Not yet. You're going to tell him.

RAFE. What?… Me?… Now?

THOMAS. In you go.

> RAFE *whispers in* WOLSEY's *ear. Shock.* WOLSEY *stares at* RAFE *– rises to leave. A point is reached in the dance where* ANNE *blocks his exit. Hand in hand with* KING HENRY, *she speaks.*

ANNE. I am Perseverance.

> WOLSEY *bows to* KING HENRY.

WOLSEY. Lady, forgive me… I fear I have been…

> WOLSEY *blunders off.* RAFE *follows.* ANNE *stands in* THOMAS's *path, looks him up and down.*

ANNE (*flat – stating the fact*). Thomas Cremuel.

> THOMAS *bows – hurries after* WOLSEY.

ACT TWO

Scene Seven

York Place, KATHERINE *with* EUSTACHE CHAPUYS. *Carts loaded down with papers, their wheels very squeaky, dragged into the court by* LAWYERS.

KING HENRY. We must submit ourselves to God's will. It's the good of my soul I'm thinking of, Katherine. (*He believes this.*)

KATHERINE (*passionate but cool and self-assured*). My soul is in the hands of God and my confessor. I shall submit myself to God's will. But not to the will of the Cardinal – who calls me concubine and your sister – not your wife.

KING HENRY. This is not Wolsey's doing. I have consulted my own conscience – and the sacred texts. Were there no impediment – I'd choose you for my wife above all ladies. I need a son –

KATHERINE. I have given you sons.

KING HENRY. They died! \

KATHERINE. For shame! Every day I pray for their little souls. Do you pray, Henry?

KING HENRY. I'd live with you as my wife still if I could be easy in my conscience. But God's will be done! Katherine, don't you see – it's why He has not blessed us with male children? My crown cannot pass to one born of a sinful union.

KATHERINE. 'Sinful union'? What then is your union with the Boleyns? A pure one? Ambassador Chapuys, you are new to London. You hear everywhere the name of Boleyn. Do you not wonder, who are these people? The King knows them very well. First the mother – well, you were only a boy then – unmarried –

KING HENRY. Katherine –

KATHERINE. And then Mary – he got a bastard boy on her –

CHAPUYS. Did he?

KATHERINE. And now it's to be the other sister – Anne –

KING HENRY. That is not the truth… I believe we should separate until the Cardinal's court delivers its ruling on our marriage. Ambassador Chapuys, will you –

KATHERINE. God made you King of England, and He made me England's Queen. I know my duty. I shall remain at your side. (*Tears.*)

CHAPUYS. Madame – come –

KING HENRY. I cannot bear to see you cry. Oh, Katherine… (*Bows.*) My Lady.

KATHERINE. I am your Lady… Never forget it. You do this out of hatred, Wolsey – you tear apart our marriage. You fear my country Spain – you favour France – you take the French King's gold –

KING HENRY. Oh, everybody takes money from King Francis, Katherine –

WOLSEY. I've never favoured France – nor the Emperor neither. (*Slight bow to* CHAPUYS.) I favour peace.

KING HENRY. We have sinned together – we suffer for it. Accept it.

KATHERINE. Is that what you do with Anne Boleyn? Suffer?

KING HENRY. She is an honourable lady. And chaste.

KATHERINE. Ha! She consorts with wicked men – reads their heretic books. She is entwined in heresy and will snare you too. Sin if you must – if you cannot keep your marriage vows… But do not sin with *her*.

KING HENRY. I forbid you to slander the lady! Your duty is to obey me, as a good subject should.

KATHERINE. I obey you as your wife –

KING HENRY. You are not my wife.

CHAPUYS. With great respect, Majesty, that is for the courts to decide.

CHAPUYS *gives* WOLSEY *a hard look – bows to* KING HENRY. *Exeunt* KATHERINE *and* CHAPUYS. BISHOPS, *the* DUKE OF NORFOLK, *the* DUKE OF SUFFOLK, *others assemble. More cartloads of documents are dragged squeaking in.* WOLSEY *takes his seat, towering over them.*

WOLSEY. Majesty – I have convened this court to inquire into the lawfulness of your marriage –

KING HENRY. Marriage so-called –

WOLSEY. To Katherine of Aragon –

KING HENRY. My late brother's wife – now his widow.

WOLSEY. You must bring before us the Pope's dispensation that permitted you to marry.

KING HENRY. Here it is. Examine it. (*Sincere.*) I am confident this court will find the document in some way defective.

CHAPUYS. My Lord Cardinal, as Ambassador to the Emperor Charles V, I'm instructed by his Imperial Majesty, on behalf of his aunt, Queen Katherine, to hand to you the Pope's dispensation. (*Does.*)

WOLSEY. Which is the original?

CHAPUYS. Ours.

KING HENRY. Mine.

CHAPUYS. Ours is the fuller version. With helpful notes.

KING HENRY. Ambassador Chapuys, I've no quarrel with your document – and no interest in it. Six times Katherine and I have lived in hope of an heir – six times our hopes have been dashed. What can this be but the judgement of Heaven? Why, after twenty years, am I left with one child – my daughter Mary – so frail any vagrant wind may destroy her? What have I done – what has the good woman I supposed my wife done – that God should take my children? I look to this court for an answer. I look to you, My Lord Cardinal, for remedy.

WOLSEY *bows slightly.* KING HENRY *joins the* BOLEYNS. WOLSEY, RAFE *and* THOMAS *go to* WOLSEY'*s room –* WOLSEY *in a vile temper, shedding vestments.* MARK *is playing his lute.*

THOMAS. Could have been worse.

WOLSEY. Could it? Could it! How!

The handcarts trundle in, squeaking.

Oh, dear God in Heaven – this affair of His Majesty's will
follow me to my grave.

RAFE. You'll outlive us all, Your Grace!

WOLSEY. It's killing me, Rafe. Eighteen hours' toil every day
for twenty years – I'm Cardinal Archbishop of York and I
don't even get Sundays off. What, then, will be my reward
for a lifetime of loyal service to Our Sovereign Lord?
(*Playing with a ring on his finger.*) I wonder which it is?

THOMAS. Your Grace?

WOLSEY. Which ring? They say I have a magic ring. It enables
me to fly – it detects poisons, renders ferocious beasts
harmless, ensures the favour of princes. Look. Which one do
you think it is? If I knew, I'd have a copy made and give it to
you. God! If only Anne Boleyn would grant Henry his
pleasure he might take an easier view of life and talk less
about his conscience! He does have a conscience, you know.
Time was, I could bend it to my purposes and always for the
good of the State. Why does Flat Chest hold him off, Tom?
Why the delay?

MARK. She hopes to be the new wife perhaps?

WOLSEY. Mark? What did you say!

MARK. His wife. When Your Grace lends me to play at Court, I
hear what the ladies are whispering. Ladies know more than
men about such things – men are the last to know. Anne
Boleyn won't let the King touch her until she's his wife. She
means to be Queen.

WOLSEY. Take it from me, boy, you yourself stand more
chance of being England's Queen… When I get the King his
divorce, he'll marry a Princess of France.

MARK. No, he'll marry Anne. She made him swear it.

THOMAS. Men will swear anything to get a woman into bed –

MARK. He's not got her into bed – that's the point, you see –

THOMAS. Now you go to bed, Mark, before I kick you. And take your fucking lute with you.

Exit MARK.

WOLSEY. I am weary – weary of it all. When the work's going well we don't notice life draining out of us… But this case – (*Picks up documents from one of the carts*.) I'm in the mire and I doubt I'll pull myself out. The wolves are circling – licking their chops. Go home, Tom. I hope you've sent your family out of the city? The sickness is back – you can't stir out without seeing funerals…

THOMAS. I think Wolsey might come down. He makes so many enemies. 'Man is a wolf to man.'

RAFE. What will become of us?

THOMAS (*shakes his head, he has no answer*). We should go. But not a word of this at home… I don't want them frightened.

RAFE (*miserable*). No – not a word.

THOMAS. Take heart, Rafe. (*Sincere but not quite convincing himself*.) I'll pick a way through for us. I will.

Scene Eight

Later. Austin Friars. Boxes, chests and bundles being piled up.
CHRISTOPHE supervising. LIZ and the girls are leaving
London at last to avoid the sweating sickness. THOMAS and
RAFE working at his table. LIZ in a corner sewing.
GREGORY CROMWELL brings more candles.

GREGORY. I've brought more candles, Father.

THOMAS. Thank you, Gregory.

GREGORY. They said you were working. I thought you might
    need... more light. (*Shuffles* THOMAS's *papers.*)

THOMAS. Gregory – what are you doing?

GREGORY. Trying to be helpful.

THOMAS. I was making copies of those letters.

GREGORY. Oh, sorry. (*Picking up a small, brightly coloured*
    map.) What's this map? I like maps... (*Reads, enjoying*
    saying the names.) Loo–goo–vaa–lee–um. Ponzeeleeus...
    Are they towns in Italy?

THOMAS. No. One's Carlisle, the other's Newcastle. It's the
    Scots border.

GREGORY. Oh. (*Slight pause.*) Father?

THOMAS (*not looking up*). What?

GREGORY. Do you think you could stop writing?

THOMAS. Give me a minute. (*Signs letters, finishes.*) Yes?

GREGORY. Are we rich?

THOMAS. I always thought we would be. One day.

GREGORY. We are rich. I know we are. Why are we rich?

THOMAS. Well... Because... Rafe – why are we rich?

RAFE. Well, Gregory... Suppose you want a low-interest loan
    from a German bank –

GREGORY. Why would I... want a loan from a German bank?

RAFE. Your father will get you the best terms. Or say you're a
    London merchant – your ship's been holed as she comes into
    port –

GREGORY. I'm a sailor now?

RAFE. No – the ship's owner. It's loaded with gunpowder and sugar, Bay of Biscay salt and powdered pearls. But the whole cargo sinks beneath the waves. Who makes good the loss? The harbourmaster's Flemish, the ship's captain's French, so they're shouting in three languages. Send for Master Cromwell – everyone goes home happy. Or suppose you're a landlord –

GREGORY. Wait. Am I still this same London merchant?

THOMAS. You could be.

RAFE. You want to put up your rents by ten shillings, so your tenants are rioting. Send for Master Cromwell. He'll show those tenants why their rents should be *twenty* shillings. He'll arrange a marriage for you, or break off a betrothal – he's read more books than anybody – or if you want some Venetian glassware – or a Turkey carpet –

GREGORY. Why would I? I don't have a house.

RAFE. You could buy one –

GREGORY. How would I get the money?

RAFE. With a loan from the German bank.

THOMAS. Does that answer your question, Gregory?

GREGORY (*brightly*). Yes it does… (*Thinks about it.*) I don't understand it though.

THOMAS (*laughing*). Oh, my son!

GREGORY. What I mean is… if the Cardinal comes down, shall we be poor?

THOMAS. He won't come down.

GREGORY. He will if he can't get the King his divorce. That's what they're saying in the kitchen.

THOMAS. Ah, in the kitchen!

GREGORY. If Wolsey's no longer here to protect us… What's to stop Thomas More coming and smashing up our house?

Nobody wants to answer this.

RAFE. We should go to bed now –

THOMAS. Yes – go – you're off to the country tomorrow.

GREGORY. I'd rather stay here with you.

THOMAS. I need you to look after your mother and sisters for me.

GREGORY. Yes, I'm very tired, though I don't know why I should be.

THOMAS (*worried*). Tired? What sort of tired? Aches and pains?

GREGORY. No – just tired-tired. Goodnight, Father. (*Kisses* THOMAS.)

THOMAS. Goodnight, my son.

GREGORY. It's not the fever – it's just bedtime. (*Yawns.*) D'you remember when I was a devil in the Christmas play?

THOMAS. I do. I remember.

GREGORY. Wrapped in a black calfskin with my face dyed black?

Exits with RAFE.

LIZ. Sometimes I think he's still three. (*Sewing.*) Is it true that Katherine still makes her husband's shirts?

THOMAS. Lizzie! How could I possibly know a thing like that?

LIZ. If I were her, I'd leave the needle in them.

THOMAS. I'm sure you would.

LIZ. They say she's not stopped crying since he left her.

THOMAS. He hasn't left her. That's the thing. Katherine still has her household. And now Anne Boleyn has a household too. The King runs back and forth between them and they both shout at him. They're leading him a dog's life. Last time I saw Katherine she wasn't crying. She was briefing her lawyers.

LIZ. Men say, 'I can't endure it when women cry' – as if it were nothing to do with the men at all… The crying.

THOMAS. I've never made you cry, have I?

LIZ (*a long look*). Yes you have. But only with laughter.

THOMAS. Come to bed.

LIZ (*absorbed*). Just finish this bit. (*Struck by a thought.*) Who does the King sleep with?

THOMAS. Nobody. He won't have Katherine in his bed – Anne won't have him in hers. I imagine he wanders the cold passages of his palaces in his nightshirt looking for somebody who *will* have him.

LIZ. Nobody should be all alone.

THOMAS. The Cardinal says he pities him. I know it's not permitted to touch a king. But I'd like to shake him. If he were our neighbour I'd go round and say, 'Sort it out, Harry! You're the scandal of the parish.' (*Silence.*) I ought to make a will.

LIZ (*reaching for his hand*). Tom, don't die.

THOMAS. I don't intend to. Good God, no!

LIZ. Don't die. Don't leave me alone.

THOMAS. I'll never leave you, Liz.

> LIZ *has disappeared.* THOMAS *stares at the place where she has been. He looks up. A bell tolling before coffins. Sung Requiem. He's in the street with* RAFE *and* CHRISTOPHE – *a funeral procession coming towards him. Then* GREGORY *joins him – the relief is overwhelming.* THOMAS *is left in the street with* RAFE *and* CHRISTOPHE. *It snows.*

Scene Nine

THOMAS, *grim, hurrying along with* RAFE. CHRISTOPHE *carrying document cases.* MORE *falls in.*

MORE. Heard the news from Rome, Cromwell?

THOMAS. I've heard the Emperor's troops are in the city.

MORE. *In* the city! They're sacking it, man! Plundering churches – looting and burning – raping holy nuns – wives and virgins.

THOMAS. So the French would have us believe –

MORE. The Pope's in the Emperor's prison. In the circumstances His Holiness is hardly likely to annul the marriage of the Emperor's aunt, is he? The Queen will see the hand of God in it – saving her husband from himself.

RAFE (*cold*). How will it save His Majesty?

MORE. By keeping him married – preventing his fall into error. That's how Katherine will see it – her people will rejoice. Not the Cardinal, of course. The King has little patience with those who fail him.

THOMAS. Rafe, we must turn around and go to York Place.

MORE. Naturally he'll lose his place as Chancellor.

THOMAS. Do you hope to step into it?

MORE. Bless you, no! If it's offered I shall refuse. My books and my family are enough for me.

THOMAS *turns and meets his gaze.*

Though, of course, if one could do some good in that office...

They fix each other. MORE *looks away first. He ambles off. Noise in York Place starts.*

Scene Ten

Bursts of noise within. SUFFOLK *shoves* THOMAS WYATT, *agitated, bloody and dishevelled, out onto the stage.*

SUFFOLK. Stay out of this, Wyatt – the Cardinal's seeing nobody – take yourself off!

SUFFOLK *goes back in, bawling. Enter* THOMAS, RAFE *and* CHRISTOPHE.

RAFE. Master Wyatt? What's happening?

THOMAS. God Almighty, sir – Look at you!

WYATT. The Duke of Suffolk –

THOMAS (*appalled*). You've not been fighting with Suffolk again –

WYATT. No, no – Suffolk – the Duke of Norfolk – they've brought half of East Anglia with them and they're breaking up the house –

THOMAS. Dear God! (*Fierce.*) Wait here – stay out of it.

WYATT. No – I have to see the Cardinal – (*Waving his summons.*)

THOMAS. You'll make matters worse – you always do, sir. Wait here – leave this to me. Christophe.

The Dukes' SERVANTS *are taking the house apart – bundling up parchments, scrolls, missals, pictures, hangings, plate, chests – others remove* WOLSEY's *coat of arms.* STEPHEN *calmly makes an inventory.*

STEPHEN (*to the plunderers*). For God's sake, gentlemen – you must line those chests with a double thickness of cambric. Those vestments have taken nuns a lifetime to embroider.

NORFOLK (*covered in holy medals and reliquaries – he clanks as he moves*). Aha! Here's blacksmith's boy –

SUFFOLK. The butcher's dog –

NORFOLK. Come in – come to me!

SUFFOLK. Explain it to him – he's dismissed as Chancellor. Go on, tell him – I can't make him understand.

NORFOLK. He must hand over the Great Seal of England –

SUFFOLK. And his chain of office –

NORFOLK. I want that chain. Give me the chain, Wolsey –

THOMAS *steps protectively in front of his master – his Putney instincts and his need to treat the* DUKES *with impeccable courtesy at odds within himself.*

THOMAS. He can't. The Chancellor may surrender the chain and the Great Seal only to the King himself.

SUFFOLK (*threatening*). Harry's in Windsor.

THOMAS (*in* SUFFOLK*'s face, but remaining calm*). The Master of the Rolls would do.

SUFFOLK. Then fetch him!

THOMAS (*civil but with an infuriating smile*). The Master of the Rolls is in Windsor too. With the King.

NORFOLK. Oh, bugger his rolls! I want that chain!

He grabs it – pulls WOLSEY *about.*

WOLSEY (*frail, bewildered*). Handle me gently – I warn you! Norfolk, the King loves me – he can't rule without me. When he's had his frolic with your niece, I'll be recalled – then I may come to your houses and turn you out! Hands off me! Wait! (*Pause.*) If it is His Majesty's will… then I cannot see why the law should hinder it.

He drops the chain. NORFOLK *gets it.*

SUFFOLK. Where's the seal?

STEPHEN. Here it is. (*Hands it to* SUFFOLK.)

NORFOLK. The King wants rid of you by nightfall. Anne's moving in and needs the place scrubbed clean. Can't have the smell of butcher's boy hanging in the air – now, out you go!

A statue of the Blessed Virgin Mary is carried across the stage. The WORKMEN *take off their caps and do reverence.* NORFOLK *falls to his knees, jangles his relics and crosses himself. Then all resume the squabble where they left off.*

THOMAS. York Place belongs to the Archdiocese of York. When was Anne Boleyn made Archbishop?

NORFOLK. You'd do well, Cromwell, not to question the King's pleasure.

STEPHEN. Have you thought where you might take him?

NORFOLK. To the Tower if I had my way – and you with him, Cromwell.

WOLSEY (*overhearing*). Why would the King send me to the Tower?

STEPHEN. Your Grace, I'll take my leave. His Majesty has sent for me.

THOMAS. Why?

STEPHEN. He has taken me into his service. I'm to be Master Secretary. I shall have my own barge. And he's promised me the manor at Hanworth – the gardens are a delight. The house will need considerable renovation, of course –

WOLSEY (*sarcastic*). Then Cromwell here's your man. He'll get you antique statuary from his Italian friends – fountains – he'll plant you a knot garden if you pay him well enough.

STEPHEN. Your Grace, His Majesty cannot countenance failure – accept it. You've had many good years in his service. Perhaps the days remaining to you should be spent in the service of God? Prayer and contemplation, My Lord – prayer and contemplation.

WOLSEY (*bitter*). God keep you, Stephen.

NORFOLK. And you, Cromwell, get back to your smithy.

Exit STEPHEN *with the* DUKES. CHRISTOPHE *thumps a* PLUNDERER *trying to conceal a silver chalice. He hands it to* WOLSEY. *Enter* RAFE.

WOLSEY. Everything I own I have from the King. If it pleases him to take my house I am sure we have other roofs to shelter under. (*Throws the chalice to* THOMAS.)

THOMAS. We'll go to Bishop Waynflete's old manor in Esher.

MARK. Oh *no*! Surely we can do better than that! Nobody's been near the place for years. It's probably fallen down.

THOMAS. The roof is sound – it will do for the present.

RAFE. Your Grace's barge is ready.

THOMAS. We'll go up river – and the horses will meet us at… at Putney.

MARK. Oh God! Putney? Do we have to?

THOMAS. Come. We've done more difficult things these last years than get the household to Esher. I think we can find some bedlinen and soup kettles – and whatever else we can't do without.

Barge arrives. WOLSEY, THOMAS, MARK *and others get aboard. Noise of crowd jeering.*

Sit down, Mark, or you'll have us over.

MARK. I'm not sitting there – the seat's wet.

THOMAS. Sit on it, or I'll throw you in the river!

WOLSEY. Why do they hate me? I've persecuted none of them – every year when wheat was scarce I saw they were fed. When the apprentices rioted – while they stood garlanded with nooses that were to hang them – I went on my knees to the King for them… Why is the King angry with me? 'Put him to work,' they said. But I said no – he's a young man. Let him hunt, joust, fly his hawks – play his music. He was forever plucking… something or other. And singing.

MARK. You make him sound like Nero.

WOLSEY. God help me! I never said so – he is the gentlest, wisest prince in Christendom – I'll hear no word against him.

Waynflete's semi-derelict house. The bedraggled procession arrives and looks about. Lights are fetched. There's a hole in the roof – water pouring in – and the floor is muddy.

THOMAS. Well… This house looks pretty enough.

RAFE. A sound roof?

MARK (*to* CHRISTOPHE, *who is curious about* MARK*'s lute case*). Get your filthy hands off my instrument.

SERVANTS *work efficiently. They bring boxes, sacks and bundles. Light fires, etc.* WOLSEY *collapses on a stool.* MARK *tunes his lute and makes himself useless.*

THOMAS. We'll soon have everything in good order. Come on then – go and get the kitchen cleaned up. Mark, put down that lute and pick up a broom.

MARK. What?

THOMAS. A broom – sweep the floors.

MARK. The floor is mud. You can't sweep mud.

WYATT *slips in unnoticed*.

WOLSEY. The old King was a hard man – but his son... so sweet a nature... Never spared myself. Rising early, watching late... Tom Wyatt, where did you spring from? What sort of trouble is it this time?

THOMAS. It'll be money –

WOLSEY. Or drinking. Continued with a breaking of windows – ending in rioting and beating the watch –

WYATT. I followed you – I have a summons, Your Grace. I am to appear before the justices –

CHRISTOPHE (*passing by and snapping the neck of a rat on the word 'justices'*). Supper, huh? (*Exits*.)

WOLSEY. Give it here – give it here...

WYATT. Could you –

WOLSEY. Wait – let me read it. Does your father know of this? (*Reads*.)

WYATT. No, Your Grace – I thought –

WOLSEY. You thought you'd be used more mildly if you came to me.

WYATT. Yes, Your Grace, I did.

WOLSEY. I'll talk to the Sheriff of London – if he'll talk to me... Will anybody talk to me ever again?

THOMAS. Tomorrow His Majesty will begin to miss you.

WYATT. Sir, I am grateful. It won't –

WOLSEY. It won't happen again? What kind of simpleton do you take me for? Of course it will happen again. Look at you!

WYATT *shifts uncomfortably in his torn clothes.*

I do this for your father's sake. He's been a good friend to
the State, and to me. Friendship's proving a costly business.
(*To* THOMAS.) You see, Thomas – what it will be like
without me? All the young lords in jail. Who else is
summoned with you?

WYATT. William Brereton, Francis Weston –

WOLSEY. They can rot – I'll not lift a finger…

WYATT. I shall go to the King for you –

WOLSEY. And make things worse? Stay away from His Majesty.

WYATT. We must repair this. Someone has poisoned his mind
against you. Norfolk has always been your enemy –

THOMAS. No – Thomas More. It was Thomas More.

WYATT. The King needs you. I'll tell him so – he'll listen –

WOLSEY. I forbid it. Anything you say will be turned against
you – and me. And when they come for me, where is the
kind protector who will turn away the Sheriff's men from my
door? Not that I have a door any longer. Or a roof…
(*Looking up at the leak.*) While I am… in eclipse, Cromwell
here will look after you. He'll be like a father to you –
though not so kind a one as I have been.

WYATT. He won't beat me, will he?

THOMAS. He might.

WYATT. I am in your debt – and his.

WOLSEY. And that's another thing. You're always in debt –

WYATT. Your Grace, I cannot bear to see you in this place. If
you'll not let me plead to the King for you, what can I do?

WOLSEY. Go and sit quietly in a room by yourself. And think
upon the misery you've brought upon your unhappy father.
Can you manage that? (*As* WYATT *leaves, to himself.*) I
wonder if *I* can manage it. (*To* THOMAS.) And then there
are the women. That boy is much troubled by women.

THOMAS. That's all I have to cope with then? Debts, drinking,
fighting and women?

CHRISTOPHE. He's a real man! (*Jumps on* MARK.)

MARK. Get off me! What's…?

> CHRISTOPHE *shoves a rat down his britches.*

> Oh! Horrible!

CHRISTOPHE. You not like her? You like better her brother?

> *As* CHRISTOPHE *chases* MARK *out,* MARK *collides with* THOMAS.

WOLSEY. Why do you employ that boy?

THOMAS. No one else will.

WOLSEY. There's no braver young man in all England than Thomas Wyatt – nor a more honest one. Be patient with him, Tom – if you make him your friend you'll not lose by it. Now what about my supper?

> *Enter* RAFE.

RAFE. There's a rider coming.

THOMAS. Christophe!

> CHRISTOPHE *comes to heel, ready for a fight.*

WOLSEY. They're going to arrest me!

THOMAS. No – they'd send more than one man.

RAFE. It's Harry Norris, the King's Groom of the Stool.

> SIR HENRY NORRIS *and* PAGE *enter lathered from their gallop.* NORRIS *hands his riding cloak to* THOMAS, *as if he were a servant.* THOMAS *holds the cloak as if it were an offence to the human spirit.* NORRIS *makes a low bow to* WOLSEY – *smiling and courteous.*

WOLSEY. Now, Sir Henry – get your breath back. What can be so urgent?

NORRIS. His Majesty has commanded me to ride after you and resolve this misunderstanding. He loves you for your faithful service and –

WOLSEY (*at once on his feet – horribly eager*). Thank God! Oh, Thomas, we're going home!

THOMAS *walks away – he knows what's coming and can't bear it.*

NORRIS (*embarrassed*). Ah… No. If you could… (*A back-off gesture.*) Until the Lady Anne's temper cools…

RAFE. It was Anne Boleyn then?

All look at NORRIS.

NORRIS. Your Grace, all it needs is a little time. To heal the… The King will calm her – you may be sure of that. Ladies are…

WOLSEY. I know the King –

NORRIS. He is – and he will continue to be your good master. He sends you this ring.

WOLSEY *kneels reverently in the muddy patch – receives the ring – kisses it.*

WOLSEY. He is the kindest and most merciful of rulers. (*Tears.*) Sir Henry, how can I reward you?

NORRIS. Oh, really… there's no –

WOLSEY. This is a piece of the true cross. Cherish it. (*Hangs his jewelled reliquary around* NORRIS*'s neck.*)

NORRIS. It's… too much.

THOMAS (*to* RAFE). Five for a florin in any workshop in Italy. (*Gives cloak to* CHRISTOPHE.) Come, Your Grace – let me help you up.

WOLSEY (*putting on the ring*). I must return the King a gift. But I've nothing – what can I send him?

NORRIS. Something perhaps for the Lady Anne? His Majesty would like that.

WOLSEY. Yes – but what?

CHRISTOPHE *catches* THOMAS*'s eye and lifts his rat three inches.*

RAFE (*looking at* MARK). The Lady Anne likes music.

THOMAS. Mark, put down your broom, boy, and go with Sir Henry Norris.

MARK. Oh! Willingly! Gladly!

WOLSEY. He's a pretty thing, isn't he – and he plays very nicely. Would she like him? I'll be sorry to lose you, Mark – but you'll be happy with Lady Anne.

MARK. I shall be happy – at last, I shall be happy!

THOMAS. Christophe – Sir Henry's cloak.

PAGE *steps forward*. CHRISTOPHE *drops it in the mud*.

CHRISTOPHE. *Oh – pardonnez-moi! Je suis désolé!*

NORRIS. Your Grace.

PAGE *helps* NORRIS *with the cloak*. NORRIS *bows. We see a rat tied to his cloak.*

WOLSEY. All it needs is a little time. You'll see. But I'm hungry. What's for supper? The King cannot rule without me – I do everything for him. Who else can run the country? Norfolk would start a war with France and Thomas More would burn all the Bible scholars –

THOMAS. If Jesus Christ came down among us, Thomas More would burn him for a heretic.

WOLSEY. May God forgive you, Tom! (*Laughter becomes tears*.) I have two hundred servants at York Place – where will they go?

THOMAS. We'll find new places for them –

WOLSEY. But they're my people. When I am back in the King's favour… (*Sees* THOMAS*'s face, the truth hits him*.) I think I should… Oh, Mother of God… Mother of God. (*Overcome with misery and fear*.) It is All Souls' Eve. I feel the dead all around me. I'll go say my prayers.

All go out. THOMAS *remains, takes out* LIZ*'s prayer book, reads, turns upstage*. RAFE *returns. We may or may not see* LIZ'S GHOST *in the shadows. Is that her white cap?*

RAFE. He'll never recover from this, will he? (*Pause*.) Are you crying, sir?

THOMAS. I am… Sorry.

RAFE. That's her prayer book.

THOMAS. Look, Anne wrote her name in it.

RAFE. Anne Cromwell.

THOMAS. Grace couldn't read but she loved the pictures – I...
(*Weeps.*) I don't know where the dead go, Rafe. I don't know
if they come back... but I wish they would. I need to see Liz
just once more. That day... She was well at breakfast time
when I left her... I've lost my girls. And now I've lost my
master – everything I've worked for – all the years of my life
– just slipping away – it's going so fast. Rafe, you must leave
me – go back to your family –

RAFE. No, sir, I'm staying. You've brought me up since I was
seven. You taught me to look the world in the eye. I will not
leave you. I will not.

THOMAS. Without Wolsey here to protect us, Thomas More
will wipe his boots on us. You'll be on one of his lists.

RAFE. Go to the King.

THOMAS. He won't see me.

RAFE. Stand in his light till he does. What have you to lose?

THOMAS. Well... You're right. What have I to lose?

CHRISTOPHE *returns. His presence brings them back
to earth.*

CHRISTOPHE. He says his prayers. Now he shouts for his
food. He say, 'Who is cooking tonight?'

THOMAS. I'll cook.

RAFE. Cook what?

CHRISTOPHE, *ever hopeful, holds up a rat.*

THOMAS. There's always something. Think I can't do it? I was
once the best cook in the whole of Italy.

Enter WYATT.

WYATT. His Grace says he wants turbot. And he hopes you
remembered to bring plenty of lemons.

Scene Eleven

KING HENRY *and his men go into his chamber.* NORFOLK *comes out.* THOMAS *arrives.*

NORFOLK. Cromwell! You've got a face coming here. Wolsey sent you to grovel, did he?

THOMAS. No, My Lord, I thought I might offer some help to the King.

NORFOLK. Help? You?

THOMAS. Help him understand where the Cardinal's money is.

NORFOLK (*understanding this*). Crack open the treasure chests, eh? One obstacle in your path, Master Cromwell. (*Hugely enjoying this.*) The King has never forgotten that in his last Parliament you spoke against his French wars.

THOMAS. He's not still dreaming of invading France, is he?

NORFOLK. God damn you, man – we own France! We have to go and get it back. What's wrong with you people? How could a blacksmith's son understand – understand the – er – what do you call it?

THOMAS. *La gloire?*

NORFOLK. Precisely.

THOMAS. I was a soldier, My Lord.

NORFOLK *turns, surprised – even impressed?*

NORFOLK. Not in any English army, I'll be bound.

THOMAS. I fought at Garigliano.

NORFOLK (*contempt*). By God! Johnnie Freelance, eh. (*Interested despite himself.*) Which side? French or Spanish?

THOMAS. French.

NORFOLK. There – see! I knew there was something about you I didn't like… Picked the wrong side there, lad!

THOMAS. I noticed.

NORFOLK. Bloody massacre! Bet you ran like a Frenchman too?

THOMAS. I went north – got into the cloth trade. Silks mostly. Good market with the soldiers over there.

NORFOLK. By the mass, yes. Those Switzers, they dress up like play actors! Makes 'em easy targets. Can you handle a longbow?

Doors thrown open. KING HENRY, *boar-spear in hand, is some distance away with a group of* COURTIERS, *dressed for hunting.* NORRIS *comes forward.*

NORRIS. Master Cromwell.

THOMAS. Sir Henry.

NORRIS. I was sorry to hear of your wife's death.

NORFOLK. What? Lost your wife?

THOMAS. Yes, My Lord. To the sickness…

NORFOLK. Well, you can get another easily enough. You can have mine if you want her. I'd be glad to get her off my hands.

KING HENRY *notices* THOMAS, *who kneels.*

KING HENRY. Thomas Cromwell? Stand up, man – off your knees. So… How is… (*Leads* THOMAS *apart.*)

THOMAS. The Cardinal cannot be well until he regains Your Majesty's favour.

KING HENRY. Forty-four charges against him, master – forty-four.

THOMAS. Saving Your Majesty, there's an answer to be made to each one.

KING HENRY. Could you make those answers here and now?

THOMAS. Yes. Would Your Majesty care to sit?

KING HENRY. I heard you were a ready man.

THOMAS. Would I come unprepared?

KING HENRY (*smiles*). Another day I'd put you to the test. But I've business with the new Chancellor then I'm off hunting with Suffolk. St Hubert's, you know. Will the cloud lift, d'you think? D'you hunt yourself?

THOMAS. I favour any sport that keeps young men off the battlefield.

KING HENRY. The chase prepares us for war... (*A hard look*.) Which brings us to a sticky point, Cromwell.

THOMAS (*cheerfully*). It does indeed.

KING HENRY. Six years ago you said in the Parliament I could not afford a war.

THOMAS. Seven years ago, Majesty. No ruler in the history of the world has ever been able to afford a war. Wars are not affordable things. No prince ever says, 'This is my budget, so this is the kind of war I can have.' No. War uses up all the money you've got – then it breaks you and bankrupts you.

KING HENRY. When I led my soldiers into France in the year...

THOMAS. 1513.

KING HENRY. 1513, I took the town of Thérouanne – which in your speech you called –

THOMAS. A doghole.

KING HENRY. A doghole. How could you say so?

THOMAS (*shrugs*). I've been there.

KING HENRY (*anger*). And so have I – at the head of my army! Listen to me, master – you said I should not fight because the taxes would break my country. What's a country for but to support its prince in his enterprise? What use is a king that can't fight? Should I stay indoors and ply my needle like a girl?

THOMAS. Well, it would put a smile on the face of Your Majesty's Treasurer.

KING HENRY (*flash of fury, then laughs*). I'm King of England. If I choose to war in France, what shall constrain me?

THOMAS. The distances – the harbours – the terrain – the people – the winter rains and mud. When Your Majesty's ancestors fought in France, whole provinces were held by England. From there we could provision and supply armies. Today we have only Calais.

KING HENRY. I know. (*Sunny smile*.) We'll need to capture a
sea coast and take back Normandy. (*Laughs*.) Well reasoned,
Cromwell – I bear you no ill will. Only I fear you have no
experience in policy, or the direction of a campaign.

THOMAS. None.

KING HENRY. You know money though, don't you? Wolsey
says you understand Church finances.

THOMAS. I love a balance sheet as Your Majesty loves hunting.

KING HENRY. He said 'Every monastery in England – Thomas
Cromwell will tell you what it's worth.'

THOMAS. Monks are very cunning when it comes to hiding
their wealth. But the full amount could be brought to light.

KING HENRY. And the total would be? (*Waits*.) I would be
interested to know.

THOMAS. Yes you would, Majesty.

KING HENRY. I don't see how you would make the calculation.

THOMAS. I trained in the Florentine banks. And in Venice.

KING HENRY. Oh? (*Thrown*.) The Cardinal told me you were
a common soldier.

THOMAS. I was that too.

KING HENRY. Anything else?

THOMAS (*meets his gaze unflinchingly*). What would Your
Majesty like me to be?

KING HENRY. You have a bad reputation, Master Cromwell.

THOMAS *bows*.

You don't defend yourself?

THOMAS. Your Majesty is able to form your own opinion.

KING HENRY. I am. I will.

SUFFOLK (*clumping in*). Ready, Harry? Cromwell. (*Grins*.)
Shouldn't you be comforting your fat priest?

KING HENRY *angry,* SUFFOLK *doesn't notice*.

You know – they say Wolsey once rode out with his servant Robin. They came to the head of a valley where, looking down, he saw a very fair church with its lands about. He says to Robin, 'Who owns that? I wish it were mine.' –

THOMAS. And Robin says, 'It is, My Lord. It is.'

SUFFOLK. You've heard it?

THOMAS. They tell that story all over Italy. Of one Cardinal or another…

KING HENRY *meets* THOMAS*'s eye.*

Only there the servant isn't called Robin.

KING HENRY. Cromwell… One word more. (*Whispers.*) I miss the Cardinal. Every day I miss him. I'm going to give you a thousand pound – take it to him with our blessing. And I've told them to return some necessities for his house in Esher – tapestries, plate, bed-hangings – that sort of… you know. Don't tell the Duke of Norfolk. Tell no one. Ask Wolsey to pray for me. Tell him to go up to Yorkshire. He's never been enthroned as Archbishop. Tell him to busy himself with that.

THOMAS. Majesty.

KING HENRY *joins* SUFFOLK. THOMAS *leaves as* STEPHEN *arrives with* MORE.

MORE. Cromwell. What are you doing here?

STEPHEN. How was your interview with His Majesty? Unpleasant I should think.

THOMAS. Stephen, can't we drop this? This rancour between us?

STEPHEN. No – I don't see that we can.

MORE *and* STEPHEN *go in to* KING HENRY. MORE *kneels.* KING HENRY *puts the Chancellor's chain round* MORE*'s neck.* STEPHEN *hands* KING HENRY *the seal.* KING HENRY *hands it to* MORE.

MORE. I have your word, Majesty, that you will not press me? On that… matter?

KING HENRY. Oh, Thomas!

MORE. Your word – the word of a king?

KING HENRY. If your conscience tells you you cannot come with me in this matter of my new marriage, then… But I wish you'd tell me your objection.

MORE. I do not say I object.

KING HENRY. I must have a son! All Europe knows and accepts it.

MORE. Good men pray for it.

KING HENRY. My father fought his way to the English throne. It wasn't given to him – he took it. And he gave England peace. Good order – the rule of law. That was his legacy to me. If I have no son, the old families of England will fight over the Crown like dogs with a bone. They haven't gone away – those people. They stand in the shadows, watching me. I could die of the plague. I could fall in the joust. Do you know how many men died at Towton? In one battle? Thirty thousand. Thirty thousand Englishmen. Do you wish those times back?

MORE. No man has been more loyal to the House of Tudor than I have.

KING HENRY. But it won't count – will it? If there are no Tudors left? Forty years of peace, Thomas! I'll not throw that away because the Pope wants to keep me shackled to an old woman who was never my wife. Anne Boleyn will give me a son. She has promised me a son.

MORE. Sons are the gifts of God.

KING HENRY. It's Anne. You don't like her?

MORE, *kneeling, returns his gaze.*

Is it because she loves the Gospel?

MORE. I love the Gospel.

KING HENRY. In English?

MORE. I fear error – mistranslation may be the unwitting servant of heresy.

KING HENRY. Thomas, I need your help.

MORE. In that matter – in all matters – you shall have my
  prayers.

KING HENRY. Oh, you should have been a churchman. Why
  weren't you?

  KING HENRY *stumps off followed by* SUFFOLK *et al.*
  MORE *fingers his chain – gets slowly to his feet –
  looks bleak.*

Scene Twelve

York Place.

CHRISTOPHE. Anne Boleyn's a witch, master – she has
  witched the King. (*Believing this absolutely.*) Wear a holy
  medal to protect you. I give you mine – my mother gave me.

THOMAS. I'm touched, Christophe. But there are no such
  things as witches.

RAFE. Put it round your neck – just to be on the safe side.

  CHRISTOPHE *puts the medal on* THOMAS. *He and* RAFE
  go. MARY BOLEYN *comes out.*

MARY BOLEYN. Ah – the new man at Court! I'm Mary
  Boleyn – the Easy Armful – sister to Flat Chest. I believe
  that's what the Cardinal calls us?

THOMAS. No! Does he?

MARY BOLEYN. These days you're always with the King,
  Master Cromwell. How suddenly you've risen in his favour!
  And today my sister sends for you too.

THOMAS. Do you know why?

MARY BOLEYN. She's bored. It's the week of Christ's
  Passion so Henry's crept back to his wife… He hasn't the
  face to be seen with his concubine during Holy Week.

THOMAS. Well, she'll get him back after Easter.

MARY BOLEYN. Anne always gets what she wants. (*A touch
  of bitterness.*) My sister's everything now… We heard your
  wife died? And your little daughter?

THOMAS. I... I have a son.

MARY BOLEYN. We know. Anne has all the Cardinal's men in her little black book. She's forever writing, devising punishments. She pinches me, you know. Want to see my bruises? When she's Queen her enemies will feel it. You'd do well to keep in her good books. And out her bad ones.

Enter MARK *is his new kit.*

THOMAS. Mark? Is it you? How are you?

MARK (*sulky shrug*). As you see.

THOMAS. Must feel strange – being back at York Place – now the world's so altered?

MARK. No.

THOMAS. Don't you miss My Lord Cardinal?

MARK. No.

THOMAS. Happy?

MARK. Yes.

THOMAS. The Cardinal will be pleased. Shall I take him your good wishes?

MARK. I wouldn't bother. He's finished, isn't he?

MARY BOLEYN. Come in. Don't stare at her flat chest.

ANNE *plays with a tied bunch of rosemary, plucking it nervously. Suddenly she's all sweetness and light and playful French Court. In attendance are* JANE SEYMOUR *and* JANE ROCHFORD.

ANNE. Aha – Cremuel! I wanted to see for myself this paragon who so enchants His Majesty. Suddenly everything – everything is about *you*. The King does not cease to quote his Master Cremuel. 'Cremuel is so *right*. Cremuel is at all points correct...' Also, 'Maître Cremuel makes us laugh.'

THOMAS. I do make him laugh – sometimes.

ANNE. Can you make me laugh, do you think? I seldom... laugh – if I think about it. I should like to try. Come here, Milksop.

JANE SEYMOUR, *terrified, comes to her.*

Men frighten her because she does not know what they are.
See – this is a man. Have you seen such a man? Come here,
you. (*To* MARK.) Stand side by side. Observe, Milksop. This
is a boy, we think – one day we must find out – and this is a
man. (*To* MARK.) Oh, don't pout, sweetheart – you know
how I like to tease. I can never remember his name but he
sings sweetly. He was a gift. From the Cardinal.

THOMAS. My Lady – since the Cardinal came down, how
much progress has been made in your cause?

ANNE. None. (*Pulls a funny, sad face.*)

THOMAS. Consider how bound to you His Grace would be, if
by your means he was restored to the King's favour.

ANNE. Oh, but what would be the point of that? He cannot
help me. He promised he would free the King from
Katherine – but then he did not – he would not. I think he did
not want it.

THOMAS. Are you any better off now Thomas More is
Chancellor?

ANNE. No – no. Truly I am not. It is terrible. He will not work
for the annulment – he refuses – and still Henry appoints
him. I cannot explain it. Can you explain it to me, Cremuel?

THOMAS. His Majesty has known More since he was a boy.
Perhaps he needs old friends about him – with the Cardinal
gone – and his wife gone –

ANNE. Oh, Katherine is not gone! He is with her now. They are
praying together about their sin.

THOMAS. It's all they have left in common.

ANNE (*laughs*). See! You can make me laugh. (*Serious.*) I don't
believe in those kind of prayers. (*Studies him.*) And nor do
you. I know everything about you. I have you in my books.

THOMAS. The good ones I hope – not the bad ones.

ANNE (*serious*). You favour the Gospel. For you – very
dangerous. I favour the Gospel – for me not dangerous.
(*Softly.*) I can protect you…

GEORGE *enters suddenly*.

GEORGE. Sister? What... what in the name of Jesus! Surely you're not talking to Wolsey's people?

ANNE. We were discussing our faith. (*Suddenly angry*.) Oh, and of the time, the time, the time all this is taking!

MARY BOLEYN. She's not getting any younger.

ANNE. He says if Wolsey were returned to the King's Council he'd work tirelessly in our cause.

GEORGE. Face it, Cromwell, Wolsey's finished. I don't see why we should dance attendance on Rome anyway.

THOMAS. Is that a question? Do you want an answer?

GEORGE. Not from you, Putney boy! (*Laughs*.)

ANNE. Do you have better ideas, sweet brother? No you don't – he doesn't have any ideas at all. Everything is in here – (*Touches his codpiece*.) and nothing in here – pretty, pretty head – empty, empty, empty. One simple thing we ask of Wolsey, and he could not do it.

THOMAS. It was hardly simple.

ANNE. One simple thing –

THOMAS. You know very well it was not simple.

ANNE (*teasing*). Then perhaps I am simple?

THOMAS (*studies her*). You may be. I hardly know you.

A pause as if she can't believe it – then she laughs as if she's heard something outrageous.

GEORGE. What did he say! I'll knock him down!

ANNE. Wolsey can't help me... but this one might. (*Strokes* THOMAS*'s cheeks with the rosemary*.) When you think of something, come and tell me about it. (*Leads* GEORGE *off*.) Knock him down? You're a fool, brother. Look at him. Look at you...

MARY BOLEYN *follows* THOMAS *out. Doors slam.*

THOMAS. There have been rumours that your sister is –

MARY BOLEYN. She's not. She'd call on me to let out her
bodices. Besides she can't be – because they don't. He's not
got above the knee. Sometimes she lets him pull her shift
down and kiss her breasts.

THOMAS. I'm surprised he can find them.

MARY BOLEYN *laughs boisterously.* JANE SEYMOUR
appears at the door.

JANE SEYMOUR. Lady Anne wants you, Mary.

MARY BOLEYN. Oh, by all the saints!

She goes. JANE SEYMOUR, *very nervous, makes a huge
effort.*

JANE SEYMOUR. I wanted to say…

THOMAS. Lady?

JANE SEYMOUR. I have heard that your wife died… And
your little daughters… I am truly sorry. I shall pray for you.

THOMAS. May I know your name, My Lady?

JANE SEYMOUR. Oh, I'm nobody. I'm only Jane Seymour.

Interval.

ACT THREE

Scene Thirteen

Burst of music. In the Council meeting.

KING HENRY. Finally it stops raining, and here we are wasting the day in a Council meeting.

STEPHEN. Majesty, we are not halfway through the business of the morning.

KING HENRY. Get on with it then!

STEPHEN. Preparations for Wolsey's enthronement in York Minster are in hand –

NORFOLK. It's about time – he's been months getting there –

SUFFOLK. He's marching up through Yorkshire like a conqueror – an army at his back –

THOMAS (*entering*). Not true, Your Grace.

SUFFOLK. He means to rule us all from York as he once did from York Place.

THOMAS. He wishes only to serve God, and his King. And he needs me at his side. I ask Your Majesty's permission to ride north.

KING HENRY. I need you at *my* side. There are difficult matters I must… Difficulties. I'll say this for you, Cromwell – you stick by your man.

THOMAS. Why would I not? I've had nothing but kindness from him. Majesty.

He starts to go.

KING HENRY. Where are you going?

THOMAS. Lady Anne has sent for me, Majesty.

KING HENRY. She spends more time with you than she does with me. You and her Gospel men… If I did not know her chaste I should suspect your honesty, sir. (*Gets up, signals the others to stay where they are*.) A word. Stephen Gardiner tells me Wolsey has been writing to the King of France –

THOMAS. I don't believe it.

KING HENRY. Letters have been intercepted. Cromwell, this is breaking my heart – the Cardinal was like a father to me. These letters. It smacks of treason.

THOMAS. You can't believe it, Majesty. Treason? The Cardinal?

KING HENRY. Never tell a king what he can or cannot believe.

THOMAS. Majesty.

KING HENRY (*lowers his voice*). Look at Archbishop Warham. (*He is fast asleep*.) That is how my affairs are. Yet many authorities advise me that I should consider my marriage to Katherine dissolved in the eyes of Christian Europe, so I may remarry when and where I please. But others say –

THOMAS. I am one of the others.

KING HENRY. Dear Jesus! I will be unmanned by it!

THOMAS. You have to take Parliament and the English people with you on this matter or the rights of your heirs will be challenged.

KING HENRY. My will is not enough then?

THOMAS. No, Majesty. For the sake of your son – I mean the son of any future marriage – I think it's not enough.

KING HENRY. Nan's threatening to leave me. There are other men, she says, and she's wasting her youth. Other men! What am I to do? I put all my trust in Wolsey –

THOMAS. And we would not have failed you, he would not. But certain men hindered him, turned against him.

KING HENRY. Still you speak for him! Tell me this, Cromwell. Who'll get me my divorce? Do you know Anne's chaplain – Dr Cranmer? She puts great faith in him.

THOMAS. The Cardinal thinks very highly of him.

KING HENRY (*quizzical look – could go either way*). I've a mind to make you one of my Council? They're all against it

– the Dukes, Archbishop Warham, Gardiner – Thomas More especially. That's why I might just… do it. I can't let you go to York. No. This… difficulty… I want you to speak to Katherine for me – I shall speak to her no more. (*Aloud.*) You've all failed me! (*Storms out.*)

SUFFOLK. Harry? Harry – where are you going? (*Runs after him.*)

STEPHEN *helps the almost defunct* WARHAM *out of the chamber.*

MORE. It falls to you, Cromwell, to help His Majesty unravel Wolsey's affairs. He was an exceedingly rich man and his… empire must be dismantled. You know where all the money came from and where it is now.

THOMAS. Oxford and Ipswich are to be the Cardinal's monuments –

MORE. Monuments? It would go better for the Cardinal if the world could forget him – and all his works –

THOMAS. What money's left, is for them.

MORE. Ipswich is a lost cause. Wolsey's birthplace. It rankles. The King might take over the establishment in Oxford.

THOMAS. As… Cardinal College?

MORE. He will rename it of course… I see you take it hard. Well, here's more bad news for you. (*Relishing the moment.*) The King is minded to appoint Stephen Gardiner to the Bishopric of Winchester.

THOMAS (*to himself*). God save us.

MORE. Wolsey's richest diocese. Stephen will be in a position to do much good.

THOMAS. Yes – for himself. You once called yourself Wolsey's friend – can't you see how much we need him back at the King's side? Speak for him to the King –

MORE. I am his friend. Only I could never stomach the greed he has for ruling over men – I warned him against it. (*Smiles.*) That's true friendship – to speak hard truths.

THOMAS. A true friend wouldn't slander him to the King –

MORE. I slander no man – I do no man harm –

THOMAS. Then how did you come by this chain of his? Eh? (*Flicking it*.)

MORE. I never wanted it.

THOMAS. Fell from Heaven around your neck, did it?

MORE (*losing it*). God has thrown Wolsey down from all his pomp and power and I give thanks for it! I rejoice that I had a hand in his destruction. (*Exits*.)

RAFE. Is it good policy to bait a Lord Chancellor?

THOMAS. He enjoys it. If he wakes up in the morning and finds himself cheerful, he goes along to the Charterhouse to beg a flogging from the monks.

RAFE. Sir… Don't you think it's time… you let the Cardinal go?

THOMAS. No. I want him back at the King's side.

Scene Fourteen

York Place. ANNE *beating up* JANE SEYMOUR. THOMAS CRANMER *looks upset*, GEORGE *angry*, MARY BOLEYN *disgusted*, MARK *amused*.

ANNE. I needed you, Cremuel – where have you been?

THOMAS. I had business with the King.

GEORGE. You! What business?

THOMAS. Matters concerning the Cardinal –

ANNE. One day there'll be a great reckoning for him – but don't blame me for it – let him blame his own pride –

CRANMER (*gently*). A little charity, madam? The Cardinal needs our prayers.

ANNE. You know Dr Cranmer, my chaplain? He's just returned from Rome.

THOMAS (*they embrace*). The Cardinal was very sorry you would not come join in his college in Oxford. He'd have made you very comfortable.

CRANMER. Oh well, you know… I was very comfortable in Cambridge.

GEORGE. Wolsey is going about York like a rebellious prince with eight hundred men at his back –

THOMAS. Not true.

ANNE. He is exchanging letters with Katherine – they're plotting with the Pope – they mean to force the King to banish me from Court –

THOMAS. Slanders.

CRANMER. Can we be sure? It would be a mistake on the Pope's part to interfere –

ANNE. The King will not be forced! Is Henry a mere parish clerk? A child? This could never happen in France. There, churchmen bow to their king's commands – 'One king, one law, is God's ordinance in every realm!'

CRANMER. That is Master Tyndale's view, Lady – unfortunately Tyndale is a heretic. Discretion, madam –

ANNE. 'The subject must obey his king *as he would his God*!' I have read this – the King has read it!

THOMAS. Heavens! Does Sir Thomas More know?

ANNE. The Pope shall learn his place – I am the woman to show him what his place is! Wait! I've something to show you –

MARY BOLEYN. Oh, sister – do not give it currency.

ANNE *throws a book at* MARY BOLEYN.

ANNE. Fetch it! – to me. Give it!

JANE SEYMOUR, *in tears, brings the drawing.* ANNE *smacks her.*

This milk-faced creeper found it in my bed when she turned down the sheet. Look! That is Katherine – this is Henry in the middle –

THOMAS. I supposed so from the crown –

ANNE. And this is me – with no head! Read. '*Anne sans tête.*'

CRANMER. Give it to me – I'll destroy it.

ANNE. But never mind who grudges me – I mean to have him.

GEORGE. My sister always –

ANNE. I shall be Queen! And I shall punish who has done this thing.

CRANMER. Madam, I beg you – be calm. A piece of paper cannot harm you.

ANNE (*suddenly afraid*). How can they come in my own chamber, Cremuel – with all my servants here watching? It was Katherine's people – that much I know. I am not safe – not even here.

She whirls away – all but CRANMER, THOMAS *and* JANE SEYMOUR *following.*

JANE SEYMOUR. Oh dear. I fear this may be a long winter.

THOMAS *hands* JANE SEYMOUR *a small gift wrapped in a scrap of silk.*

THOMAS. For you, Jane.

JANE SEYMOUR. Gold thread! Thank you –

THOMAS. From Venice –

JANE SEYMOUR. I expect Lady Anne will take it from me. We're embroidering initials on everything she owns. 'H' and 'A' intertwined.

CRANMER. Isn't that a little premature?

JANE SEYMOUR. 'H' and 'A' – so it says 'Ha ha!' – all over her undergarments. Unfortunate, don't you think?

CRANMER. You're old John Seymour's daughter – from Wolf Hall?

JANE SEYMOUR. One of them, sir.

CRANMER. I thought the Seymour girls were with Queen Katherine.

JANE SEYMOUR. I was happy to serve her. But I must go where my family tell me. Thank you, Master Cromwell. (*Exits.*)

CRANMER. Gifts to Court ladies, Thomas?

THOMAS. I feel sorry for Jane, that's all. Would you ask Lady Anne to stop slapping her about?

CRANMER. You must make some allowance for My Lady – she's very fragile. I believe she's a little afraid of what she's begun – but her faith in the Gospel is firm. She will bring Henry to it, and that would bring grace to England, would it not? But the old families are against her – and most of Henry's friends – pulling him and pulling him away from her, when she is so near. I look at the men about the King – his advisers – all able men no doubt – but it seems to me they are utterly lacking in any sympathy for his situation. Nor is there any kindness in them – no charity – no love.

THOMAS. I know. That's what the Cardinal is for.

Scene Fifteen

Impressive procession. 'WOLSEY' (MARK), in full regalia, is rehearsing. He ascends the throne. HARRY PERCY, terrified, enters at the head of a band of SOLDIERS.

WOLSEY. Harry Percy! Welcome to Cawood, Harry. Have you come for my investiture? It's tomorrow, you know, in the Minster – this is a rehearsal. I fear you've missed dinner. Had I known you were coming...

HARRY PERCY (*trembling*). My Lord – I arrest you for high treason.

WOLSEY. Do you now?

Scene transforms into a nightmare masque at Court. The masque is brightly lit, the 'audience' in semi-darkness. The effect is hellish. WOLSEY is tormented by DEVILS.

DEMON FOUR (FRANCIS WESTON). Come, Wolsey – we must fetch you to Hell! Beelzebub, our master, is waiting supper for you.

DEMONS prod WOLSEY with forks.

WOLSEY. Supper? What wine does he serve?

DEMON TWO (NORRIS). Beelzebub has wines of the very best. Had you not heard? The Devil is a Frenchman!

Catcalls, boos, anti-French jeering.

DEMON THREE (GEORGE). Now hang him up! Hang him and bowel him for a traitor! Bowel him! Is there a butcher in the Court?

ALL DEMONS. Not any more!

WOLSEY *hung and drawn – lengths of red cloth and sausages pulled out.*

NORFOLK. There! Do you see! I always said my niece would have his guts!

WYATT. Shame! Shame on you, Norfolk! Shame on you all!

Music stops. The masque falters – a moment's silence – actors thrown.

NORFOLK (*afraid, clutching his relics*). Who said that?

Worried whispers. Then the DEMONS *recover and press on with a chant.*

DEMONS. Down, down, down to Hell! (*Repeated five times.*)

WOLSEY *is dragged into Hell. Cheers. Musical climax. Fireworks. The* DEMONS *take their bow.* ANNE *goes straight to* NORRIS. LADIES *flirt with* DEMONS. THOMAS, RAFE *and* GREGORY *watch.*

NORFOLK (*approaching* THOMAS). When I find who cried 'shame' I'll have his balls boiled in broth. You didn't see who it was, did you, Cromwell? (*Glares suspiciously at* COURTIERS *talking with* LADIES.) Look at that lot – talk, talk, talk – it's unmanly, that's what it is. Look at Harry Norris simpering over my niece.

THOMAS *looks, and notes* NORRIS's *devotion.*

I mean, you don't *talk* to women. It's not what they're for, is it?

Exits in a huff.

ANNE *sees* THOMAS – *her smile fades. She leaves.*

BRERETON. Ah, here's the fat butcher! How did you like our play, Cromwell?

WESTON. Keep up, Brereton. Wolsey was the fat butcher. Cromwell's the grim blacksmith.

THOMAS. Quite right, Francis Weston.

WESTON. Your father was an Irishman, they say.

THOMAS. First I've heard of it.

BRERETON. No – he was a moneylending Jew.

WESTON. The Irish are violent little people, aren't they? Lady Anne says you had to flee England at the age of fourteen after escaping from prison.

THOMAS. Now that *is* true.

WESTON. How did you escape?

THOMAS. An angel struck off my chains.

WESTON (*believing this absolutely*). Really?

Other DEMONS *laugh at* WESTON's *gullibility – led by* NORRIS.

NORRIS. Foolish boy!

WESTON. Don't call me boy!

WESTON *almost hits* NORRIS. *The incident is ended by* GEORGE's *arrival.*

GEORGE (*unmasking*). It's like the shirt of Nessus. I was roasted alive.

THOMAS. So you should be, George Boleyn. You make a fine devil.

BRERETON. We should have dragged you to Hell along with your master, Cromwell. But don't worry – some dark night the Devil will come for you. And if he doesn't, I will.

THOMAS. You too, Norris? I'd imagined you were old enough to know better.

GEORGE. How did you creep in among your betters, Cromwell – go away! There must be horses in need of shoeing somewhere.

THOMAS. Oh, very witty, George! But who was our Lord Cardinal.

In a single rapid movement he whips off the WOLSEY *mask and reveals* MARK – *exposed and frightened.*

MARK. It was like being on the rack. You've sprained my wrist – how am I going to play my instrument?

BRERETON. You don't need both hands to wank yourself off with, do you?

WESTON. Not that I've heard.

MARK (*to* THOMAS). You see how they pick on me? It's not my fault – Lady Anne made us do it.

THOMAS *takes a step towards* MARK. *He flinches.*

It was only a play!

Exeunt MASQUERS, *subdued, angry that the fun has been spoilt, muttering low threats against* THOMAS. *Quietly.*

THOMAS (*suddenly on guard*). Who's there? Come out of the shadows – stand where I can see you… Tom?

WYATT. Master Cromwell.

THOMAS. Tom Wyatt. What are you doing here? It was you, wasn't it? Who called out 'shame'?

WYATT. Yes. I'm sorry. It is – a shame.

THOMAS. Then there are two of us who think so, Tom.

WYATT. All this cruelty – why the cruelty? The one they chose to arrest him was Harry Percy.

THOMAS. There was certainly malice in that – but not Harry Percy's malice.

WYATT. Who then? Who would…?

THOMAS *gives him a hard look.*

Of course – of course it was.

THOMAS. Anne hated him.

WYATT. He gave his whole life for the King.

THOMAS. When he was arrested, the people knelt in the road and wept. Crowds stood in the dark with lighted candles – praying for him. His friends kept on telling him, he'd come before the King and clear his name.

WYATT. He could have done so – I'm certain of it.

THOMAS. Do you think they'd have ever let him? No, he knew –

WOLSEY'S GHOST. You are leading me in a fool's paradise. I know what they have provided for me – what death they have prepared for me.

THOMAS. They'd got as far as Leicester Abbey – at dusk they were setting the wax candles on the cupboard, and my master asked –

WOLSEY'S GHOST. Whose shadow is that that leaps along the wall? Where is Tom Cromwell – why isn't he here?

THOMAS. God forgive them – they told him I'd be with him by nightfall. He'd taken no food for days – he felt a pain around his heart, a sharp pain, a crushing pain...

WOLSEY'S GHOST. A pain as cold as a whetstone. Believe me, death is at the end of this.

WOLSEY'S GHOST *fades away*.

THOMAS. The monks knocked together a box of unplaned boards... And they buried him with no ceremony. Look... (*Hushed.*) He sent me his ring.

WYATT. Anne, Anne, Anne!

THOMAS. Stay away from her.

WYATT. I have stayed away. I stayed away for a year. How much staying away can a man do? I'm a hopeless case.

THOMAS. Tom, I promised the Cardinal I'd keep you out of trouble. I can pay your debts, but I can't keep you sober, and it seems I can't keep you away from Anne Boleyn. Listen to me. Your enemies are whispering to the King that you've slipped in before him –

WYATT. Ha! Suffolk told him she was soiled goods and was banished from Court for saying so. Look… you know I'm no liar. If Anne is no virgin it's none of my doing. For two years I was sick to my soul at the thought of another man touching her. But I was not the duke or the prince she was fishing for. Yes – she liked me – she liked to keep me in thrall. Some days she'd even let me kiss her – others not. That's Anne's tactic, you see? She says, 'Yes, yes, yes…' And then she says 'no'. And the hardest thing to bear… is her hinting that she says 'no' to me – but 'yes' to other men. So I'm forever asking myself how I've fallen short – why I can never please her. Why she's never given me the chance.

THOMAS. Well, you write better poems than the King. Your verses please her. Harry Percy can barely write his own name.

WYATT. Half the Court swears it was Harry Percy who took her maidenhead – the other half swears it was me. But only I can swear it was not.

THOMAS. How many lovers has she had?

WYATT. Ten – twenty – a hundred? None? Who knows the truth? You're the cleverest man in England now the Cardinal's dead. What's your opinion?

THOMAS. I think she's made a fool of you, Tom. But you should go down on your knees and thank God she's never let you touch her. The King's jealousy will make him a dangerous man once he marries her.

WYATT. Will they be married?

THOMAS. I think I can get him his annulment. Cranmer and I have been busy.

WYATT. What if you get him excommunicated?

THOMAS. It's a risk. Thomas More says in the old days, when King John and all England was excommunicated, the cattle didn't breed, the corn wouldn't ripen, the grass stopped growing, and birds fell out of the air… If that starts to happen we can always rethink our policy.

Scene Sixteen

Windsor.

KATHERINE *and* MARY *on.* SERVANTS *show* THOMAS *in.*

THOMAS. Madam. Madam, your daughter is ill. She should sit.

KATHERINE. This is Cromwell, Mary. He used to be a
   moneylender. Then one day he found he had a talent for
   legislation – and the laws he writes are written against the
   Church. He will induce the King your father to call himself
   Head of the Church in England.

MARY. Whereas the Pope is Head of the Church everywhere.
   From the throne of St Peter flows the lawfulness of all
   government. And from no other source.

THOMAS. Yes, but won't you sit, Lady Mary?

   MARY *looks at her mother but gets no response.*

KATHERINE. Master Cromwell would sever England from
   Rome. I fear he will sever us from the grace of God.

   MARY *looks at the stool.*

   You are a princess. So stand up.

THOMAS. I mean only to clarify, or define, for the King a
   position previously held – one that ancient precedents –

KATHERINE. Ancient precedents? You and Cranmer are still
   drafting them – the ink's not yet dry.

   Hunting horns, off.

MARY. Is my lord father leaving?

KATHERINE. No – he would have come to say goodbye to us.

THOMAS. His Majesty is going to Chertsey – to hunt for a
   few days.

MARY. Is the person with him? The concubine?

THOMAS. He'll ride by way of Guildford to visit Lord Sandys
   – he wants to see his handsome new gallery at The Vyne.

KATHERINE. I am to follow? When?

THOMAS. He'll return in a fortnight.

MARY. A fortnight? Alone with the person?

> MARY *sways.* THOMAS, *who has been expecting her to faint and watching her out of the corner of his eye, moves like lightning, catches her, positions her on the stool, holds her briefly and steps away from her, all in the course of his next short speech. There is no break in the dialogue. From this point,* MARY *fixes her eyes in wonder on him.*

THOMAS. Before His Majesty returns, you are to go to another place – The Moor in Hertfordshire.

KATHERINE. Do you think me a box – or a package – to be bundled up and sent to Hertfordshire? I am England's Queen. (*Falters.*) I knew that one day he would go and not come back. I never imagined he would send a man like you to tell me… (*Breaks down.*)

THOMAS. Madam –

KATHERINE. Do you make your own wife cry, Cromwell?

THOMAS. Accept the King's will, madam – take it gently. Or he may separate you.

KATHERINE. From my daughter?

THOMAS. Advise your daughter. Conciliate him.

KATHERINE. You mean conciliate his woman.

THOMAS. Madam… one honourable course is open to you. Withdraw from the world – enter a house of religion. If God calls you your marriage can be dissolved. England – all Europe would applaud your sacrifice. And the King would be good to you.

KATHERINE. And the Princess? Mary, could you make such a sacrifice?

MARY. Gladly! I should like it above all things.

KATHERINE. Then… you may tell the King I will become a nun. Princess Mary and I shall tidy ourselves away. My one condition is that Henry must become a monk.

THOMAS. Madam. (*Bows, smiling.*)

KATHERINE. Mark my words – my husband is changeable. Let the concubine remember that. One day you may have cause to remember it yourself.

THOMAS *bows. As he leaves the sun comes out. He takes a deep breath of fresh air, throws off his coat, and loosens the neck of his shirt.*

Enter CHAPUYS *in a hurry – rushing to comfort and confer with* KATHERINE.

THOMAS. Ambassador Chapuys –

CHAPUYS. Is it true? Has he left her?

THOMAS. News travels fast – (*Bowing and turning away.*)

CHAPUYS. Ill tidings fly on raven wings.

They bow and part. Then CHAPUYS *turns.*

Cromwell… listen to me. Your King, all Europe knows, is set on a devilish and destructive course – he will reduce his country to a tangle of wreckage.

THOMAS. Ambassador Chapuys, I think you misunderstand –

CHAPUYS. No – you stop – you listen! The Emperor will not see his aunt insulted, nor the Princess Mary's rights taken from her and given to whatever bastard Henry gets next –

THOMAS. His Majesty has no intention –

CHAPUYS (THOMAS *tries to interrupt but* CHAPUYS *overrides him*). Let me tell you what will happen. The Pope will excommunicate him – all Christian princes will prepare for war – England will stand alone – my master will invade – your Tudor King will go down – then what will become of Thomas Cromwell?

He sweeps on, leaving THOMAS *standing. For once* THOMAS *is shaken. The scene goes dark – resolves itself into a violent knocking. In the darkness shouts of 'Cromwell! Cromwell!' that begin Scene Seventeen.*

ACT FOUR

Scene Seventeen

Christmas. Darkness. Violent knocking. Confusion at Austin Friars. CHRISTOPHE, *half-dressed, opens the door.* BRERETON *bursts in – an armed guard. Enter* RAFE *and* GREGORY, *bleary-eyed – half-dressed.*

BRERETON (*bellowing*). Cromwell! Cromwell!

GREGORY. Is my father arrested?

BRERETON. He'll be hung up next to the grand thief his master if I get my way – Cromwell!

CHRISTOPHE *picks up an axe.* THOMAS *arrives.*

THOMAS. Christophe, put that down. Merry Christmas, William.

BRERETON. I warned you I'd come for you. King's at Greenwich. He wants you. Now.

GREGORY. Are you arrested?

THOMAS. Back to bed, Gregory.

GREGORY. No – I'm coming with you.

RAFE. So am I –

CHRISTOPHE. We are all coming, master.

THOMAS. What does he want me for?

BRERETON. How should I know? But I hope it'll be something nasty.

CHRISTOPHE (*aside*). Shall I smack him on the mouth?

THOMAS. Another time perhaps. William, go ahead with the gentlemen of the guard – we'll follow when my boys are dressed.

BRERETON. Forget it. I was ordered to fetch you and fetched you'll be.

Scene Eighteen

A chill, pale light. There is no fire – or a very feeble one – which gives neither heat or comfort. An eerie silence. KING HENRY is wearing only his nightshirt – he is almost in shock – shivering, cold, and full of fear. It's as if he's seen a ghost.

CRANMER. We meet under the strangest of circumstance. I've been with him these last three hours but it's you he's calling for.

KING HENRY. Between Christmas Day and Epiphany, God permits the dead to walk. This is well known.

In his mind, he relives his encounter with the ghost – which he devoutly believes was a real one. THOMAS says nothing. CRANMER waits for THOMAS to speak.

I have seen my dead brother. He was here in this room.

THOMAS (*bows his head as if to acknowledge the ghost. Gently and reverently*). How did he show himself to Your Majesty?

KING HENRY. There was a white fire around him… a strange light… in his hand he held a book… he was dressed in his robes of estate… Arthur died at Ludlow. In winter the roads are impassable. They had to take his coffin in an ox-cart. I cannot think it was well done. They buried him at Worcester… It troubles me I never saw him dead –

CRANMER. The dead do not come back to complain of their burial –

KING HENRY. Never saw his face in death till this night… His body shining white. Why does he come back – why?

CRANMER. It was not his body. It was an image formed in your mind. You've read St Augustine on these matters.

KING HENRY. He looked sad… so sad. He seemed to say, 'You have taken my kingdom – you have taken my wife.'

CRANMER (*hint of impatience*). Your brother died before he could reign. It was God's will. As for your marriage – we know it is contrary to Scripture. It is a sin – *that* we acknowledge. But God will grant you mercy.

KING HENRY. Can there be mercy for me? When I come before God's judgement throne, Arthur will plead against me – and I must stand there and bear it. I – I alone! I'm afraid.

CRANMER. Majesty, you must –

THOMAS*'s look stops him.*

THOMAS. Did your brother speak to you, Majesty?

CRANMER. No.

THOMAS. Did he make any sign?

KING HENRY. No.

THOMAS. Listen to me. (*Grips* KING HENRY*'s arm.*) Lawyers say '*Le mort saisit le vif*' – the dead grip the living. If your brother visited you it's not to accuse you – only to remind you that you are vested with the power of both the living and the dead. You've inherited his rights – and the rights of all England's kings who came before you. Your brother Arthur brings you this sign: Examine your kingship. Exert it.

KING HENRY. Cranmer?

NORRIS *brings* KING HENRY *a huge dressing gown of russet lined with sable, and swiftly exits.* KING HENRY *wraps himself comfortably in its warmth. There is no break in the dialogue.*

CRANMER. My opinion remains –

THOMAS (*signalling* CRANMER *to be quiet*). What is written on King Arthur's tomb?

KING HENRY. '*Rex quondam, rexque futurus.*'

THOMAS. The former king is the future king. Your father made living proof of it. He came out of exile and claimed his *right.* That right is now your own and it must be held and made secure in every generation. God took your brother from us – God set you in his place. It is God who sends your brother's spirit to you – urging you to be the king he would have been. Your brother cannot fulfil King Arthur's prophecy – so he wills that task to you.

KING HENRY (*considers – then is gripped by a different panic*). But the book – he held out a book.

THOMAS. What could it be but the Word of God – set down in our own English tongue? Your brother receives the Gospel from God's own hand. He offers it to you. Take it, Majesty. Accept God's gift.

KING HENRY *looks at* CRANMER, *who is staring at* THOMAS *in nervous awe.*

CRANMER. Perhaps… I cannot see anything against it. Though I would still counsel you against heeding dreams.

THOMAS. The dreams of kings are not the dreams of lesser men.

CRANMER. Well…

KING HENRY. But why now? Why does he come back now? I've been King twenty years.

THOMAS. Because the time has come for you to be the ruler you should be – sole and supreme head of your kingdom.

KING HENRY. Very well. Anne tells me I should no longer bow to Rome. (*Stands.*) I understand. I knew who to send for. I always know. Thank you, Thomas. Where's Norris? Norris! What time is it?

Re-enter NORRIS.

NORRIS. Four o'clock, Majesty. Four more hours until dawn.

KING HENRY. Make up the fire. Have my chaplain robe for mass. Go and get the…

NORRIS. Majesty.

KING HENRY. Gentlemen. Goodnight.

THOMAS *and* CRANMER *leave.*

CRANMER. You're a man of ready wit and vigorous invention, Thomas. But I doubt I could find authority in the Gospel for it.

THOMAS. Still, it could be a good night's work, for the Gospel.

CRANMER. Do you imagine it to be a book of blank sheets on which Thomas Cromwell may print his desires? When you touched the King – took his arm in your grasp – I winced. To touch the King! Are these your sons?

THOMAS. Gregory's my son. This is Master Rafe Sadler who's like a son to me. And Christophe – he could be my son – the Cardinal used to tell people I'd fathered a whole tribe of children. This one was caught robbing my master in France. I took him into my service.

CRANMER. A thief?

THOMAS. Thieves may come to paradise, I suppose? Didn't Christ himself say so?

GREGORY. Father? Are you in any danger?

THOMAS. No. The King had a dream, that's all.

GREGORY. A dream! He got you out of bed for a dream?

NORRIS (*passing with a 'stool'*). Believe me – he gets one out of bed for much less… (*Exits.*)

GREGORY. Was it a bad dream?

THOMAS. He thought so. It isn't now. Dr Cranmer, tell Lady Anne we did a good night's work for her.

Scene Nineteen

THOMAS *and the boys get in a boat.*

THOMAS. It's as if England's other affairs no longer exist.

GREGORY. All because he wants Anne Boleyn?

CHRISTOPHE. I go trit-trot about London – I listen. They say first Henri goes to it with old mother Boleyn – good luck to him! Then he goes to it with sister Mary – well, it is what kings do. But now he lusts after sister Anne – which is a witch with twelve fingers and seven teats. '*Ma foi!*' they say 'Where will it end?' But all the while Nan the Witch say '*non*' to the King, she's doing it with brother Georges – her own brother!

RAFE. George Boleyn?

CHRISTOPHE. Like dog on bitch – like man on boy – 'filthy French tricks'! When English say something filthy they call it 'French' –

GREGORY. Can't you keep your voice down, Christophe?

CHRISTOPHE. Why? We're in the middle of the fucking River Thames! Ha! Anne won't let Henry do her because if she say '*oui*' he say: '*Ah, thank you, madame, merci bien!* Now *au revoir, putain* – trit-trot, trit-trot!' So she say: 'Oh, Majesty! *Pardonnez-moi*, I never could permit…' But Georges shoves it up her every night – bonk, bonk: 'Oh, my lady sister – hurry, hurry! Let me unload my big wagon!' 'Quick! Quick!' she say, 'shove it up the back way – where it will do no harm!'

RAFE. And this is what London is saying of a future Queen of England!

THOMAS. Thank you, Christophe, for the information. (*Gives money.*)

GREGORY. Ought he to speak like that? And be paid for it?

THOMAS. Certainly – let him go trit-trotting around the city and bring me word what people say of the King's great affairs. Government should always listen to the voice of the people.

Scene Twenty

Council – STEPHEN (*now Bishop of Winchester*) *smirks,* WARHAM *asleep. Enter* THOMAS, CRANMER *and* RAFE. *Enter* KING HENRY.

KING HENRY. Cranmer?

CRANMER. Majesty, have you ever found a passage in Scripture where it says England is subject to Rome?

KING HENRY. There's no such a passage.

CRANMER. Nor can I find where it says a king – appointed under God to rule his people – is subject to any jurisdiction out of his own realm.

KING HENRY. Go on.

CRANMER. Where in Scripture does it say that England's gold must be sent each year to Rome –

THOMAS. So the Pope can clothe and feed his whores?

KING HENRY. Well… I've never understood by what authority
His Holiness takes my money. He speaks to me as if I were
his subject. But it's always been so. Hasn't it?

THOMAS. Fetch the books, Rafe.

Exit RAFE.

STEPHEN. Majesty, is this the time and the place –

THOMAS. His Majesty asked Dr Cranmer to consult the
universities of Europe on questions concerning his marriage
to Queen Katherine – and to enquire into the nature of those
authorities deemed competent to pronounce the marriage
lawful or otherwise.

STEPHEN. The authority of Rome –

THOMAS. The authority of Rome is what's in question.

KING HENRY. Is it? In question?

RAFE, GREGORY *and* CHRISTOPHE *bring in huge piles
of books and papers on carts. This time, in contrast with the
earlier scene, the carts glide smoothly as* THOMAS *has
oiled the wheels.*

CRANMER. The Pope holds you his subject, Majesty. He
demands tribute. You ask if it's always been so? In these
books, we have found matter to show that in times past the
King of England was the Head of his Church in England.

THOMAS. He always was, always ought to have been, and
ought to be so now.

STEPHEN (*picking up a book*). Geoffrey of Monmouth? *A
History of the Kings of Britain*? But –

CRANMER. Geoffrey of Monmouth was a fine churchman and
a great scholar – though an Oxford man. We have traced for
Your Majesty the devious means and doubtful ways by
which the natural order of things was subtly twisted and
perverted for the benefit of Rome. A corrupt Church made
the English King Rome's subject and leached away his
wealth – to his shame, and the shame of all England.

THOMAS. We can show legal proofs that England should be an Empire entire of herself –

KING HENRY. Will it take long?

CRANMER. It will get you your annulment –

KING HENRY. Truly? But can it be legal? These powers you say I ought to have… if I take them back… Could I just… 'take them back'? How would that be lawful?

THOMAS. Parliament will make it lawful.

CRANMER. Once accepted by the bishops, it will be lawful in any court.

KING HENRY. The Pope named me Defender of the Faith… would that not be taken from me?

CRANMER. When you are rightfully Head of your Church, you can order religion in your realm and defend it as your own conscience, subject to God, dictates.

KING HENRY. I'd preside in the Church courts?

THOMAS. Who else?

KING HENRY. Could I bring in my own case and sit in judgement on it?

CRANMER. Subject to your own conscience.

KING HENRY. Ah, but could I grant my own divorce?

THOMAS. Your Archbishop could.

KING HENRY. Warham? I doubt that. But when God gathers Warham to his bosom…

THOMAS. A third of the wealth of England is in Church hands. Would it not be more useful to the Crown? Christ did not bestow on his followers grants or offices of state. When the gold we send to Rome is diverted into your treasury –

KING HENRY. No… I'm not sure. But… could it be… that this may at last…? I must go to Anne. No word of this to Thomas More – go no further until we have discussed it with the Lady Anne. Cranmer – come and argue your case.

Exeunt with CRANMER.

RAFE *and* GREGORY *cart out the books.* STEPHEN *collects his papers.*

THOMAS. You were very quiet, Stephen. Where do you stand?

STEPHEN. Mmmm? Behind the King.

THOMAS. Whatever your private opinion?

STEPHEN. Always behind the King.

THOMAS. I knew you were bishop material. How's your new house at Hanworth coming along?

STEPHEN. It is my joy – my consolation. Though the glaziers, gardeners, and other craftsmen you sent me are robbing me blind.

THOMAS. No – they are the best. The best is expensive. By the way, I am hearing strange rumours about you.

STEPHEN. What rumours?

THOMAS. It's whispered that you keep two women in your household dressed as boys.

STEPHEN. Do I? Better than two boys dressed as women. Now that would be opprobrious. (*A dry laugh.*)

HARRY PERCY *is heading towards* THOMAS, *drunk and in tears. He sees him.*

HARRY PERCY. It's time somebody in this place spoke the truth! The Cardinal can't stop me now, Cromwell, and nor can you.

MARY BOLEYN (*off*). Harry!

MARY BOLEYN *runs on laughing – she's been chasing* HARRY PERCY.

HARRY PERCY. Words were spoken. Vows were made. (*Exits.*)

THOMAS. Harry Percy! What's the matter?

MARY BOLEYN. The marriage is off! The King came to tell her you'd finally cleared a way through to an annulment and then –

THOMAS. What?

MARY BOLEYN. Harry Percy's wife is demanding a divorce. He's not been to her bed for two years – says his conscience won't let him because *they're not legally married*. (*Laughs*.) They never have been! How could they be since he's married to Anne Boleyn!

THOMAS. What!

MARY BOLEYN. The King's a bachelor again but Anne's a married woman! Don't laugh though – arrange your face –

ANNE*'s room*. BOLEYN *at the table*. GEORGE, *head in hands* – NORFOLK *staring into an unlit fire*. MARK, *overlooked, plays a sad song*. THOMAS *and* MARY BOLEYN *arrive*.

JANE ROCHFORD. Better send Anne away until the King's rage cools. Pack her bags.

GEORGE. Say another word, wife, and I may strike you!

JANE ROCHFORD. The King can have nothing to do with her – if she's concealing a secret marriage –

GEORGE. I wish you were concealing a secret marriage – I wish I could divorce you – but Jesus, no chance of that! The fields were black with men running in the other direction.

JANE ROCHFORD. She could still be his concubine. It's all she's fit for –

BOLEYN. Please!

ANNE. Harry Percy spoke of love – he wrote me verses – I was a girl – I thought there was no harm.

NORFOLK. Do something, Cromwell!

THOMAS. One moment. (*Slaps* MARK *across the head*.)

ANNE. What did you just do?

THOMAS. Hit Mark.

ANNE. Mark? Is that his name?

THOMAS. Cheer it up, can't you – or get out.

NORFOLK. How did he get in here!

MARY BOLEYN. He's always in here –

NORFOLK. Get out! – Out! Or I'll spit-roast you like a sucking pig!

MARK *runs*.

THOMAS. Well, Lady – you have astonished me. (*Pause*.) Harry Percy writes verses! (*Straight face*.) Do you still have them?

ANNE. Of course not!

THOMAS. That's as far as it went? Verses? There was no promise, no contract – nor any talk of them?

GEORGE. And no consummation of any kind?

MARY BOLEYN. Hardly. Our sister is a notorious virgin.

THOMAS. What has the King said?

JANE ROCHFORD. He stormed off –

MARY BOLEYN. Left her standing –

BOLEYN. In this exigency there are a –

NORFOLK (*exploding*). Oh, by the thrice-beshitten shroud of Lazarus! While you talk of exigencies and approaches, Boleyn, your daughter's slandered and whored up and down, the King's mind poisoned, and this family's fortune is unmaking before your eyes!

GEORGE. What I say –

NORFOLK. Hold your tongue, fool of a boy!

GEORGE. Harry Percy was once persuaded to forget his claims. If he was fixed once –

ANNE. The Cardinal fixed him! Fool! And most unfortunately the Cardinal is dead.

Abashed silence – they absorb what she's said.

THOMAS (*disguising his triumph*). The Cardinal would have known how to save you, Lady. Though, were it not for Wolsey, you would indeed be married to Harry Percy.

ANNE (*snaps*). At least I would occupy the estate of wife, which is an honourable estate!

MARY BOLEYN. Not in Harry's case – he's drinking himself to death –

NORFOLK. I'll go beat his skull to a pulp! No – why keep a dog and bark yourself? You do it, Cromwell –

THOMAS. Harry's Earl of Northumberland now. God forbid I lay hands upon an English peer!

NORFOLK. Wolsey's dead – but he taught you his trade. So go find Harry Percy – and fix him.

THOMAS. If Harry swears you betrothed yourself to him – if he can produce witnesses – you are a married woman in the sight of God, and in the courts of law. And you'll never be Queen of England. I'll speak to Harry but I'm afraid…

BOLEYN. Perhaps if we faced him with the possibility of –

NORFOLK. Face him with my arse! You're a great fool and getter of greater fools, Boleyn. Leave everything to the Cardinal's man!

THOMAS *leaves*. RAFE, GREGORY *and* CHRISTOPHE *fall in*.

RAFE. We've found him.

CHRISTOPHE. At the sign of Mark and the Lion – drunk – we take you there.

Scene Twenty-One

A room in Mark and the Lion – the lowest tavern in London.
HARRY PERCY sits drinking on his own. A BODYGUARD
protects him. WHORES hang around on stage. When RAFE,
GREGORY and CHRISTOPHE enter they accost the boys. A
CLEANING WOMAN is mopping the floor of sick. Her tub of
dirty water is placed centre-stage left. CHRISTOPHE is the
only one pleased to see the WHORES.

GREGORY. Jesu! More Boleyn ladies!

WHORE. How about it, sunshine? Only a penny – and I've not
got the French pox.

CHRISTOPHE. Ha!

> THOMAS *enters. He gives the* BOYDGUARD *a look – he*
> *runs. The* WOMEN *melt away.*

THOMAS. Now, My Lord – what's to be done here? I've heard
your wife is petitioning for a divorce – surely not? Tell me,
how can I help you?

HARRY PERCY. Get away from me, Cromwell –

THOMAS. Mary Talbot is as lovely a lady as any in the
kingdom –

HARRY PERCY. But she's not my wife. I am married to Anne
Boleyn. I spoke the truth before and Wolsey bullied me out
of it. But Wolsey's dead, and I'm not a boy any more. I stand
by my promise to Anne and she must stand by hers to me.
The King talks about his conscience – he bellows about it to
all Europe – and then he sets out to steal another man's wife.
Go ask him how will he stand on the Day of Judgement
when he comes before God naked – stripped of his retinue.

THOMAS. And how will you stand when you come before
the King's Council, stripped of your earldom, bankrupt
and broken?

HARRY PERCY. What? What are those papers?

THOMAS (*a file of papers*). I have here a list of your creditors.
Goes back ten years. Among many others, you owe money to
the King. And to me.

HARRY PERCY. I've never borrowed money from you.

THOMAS. When your creditors got tired of waiting, they sold your debt on. To me. I could call in these debts tomorrow, I could ruin you, My Lord.

HARRY PERCY. You can't take away my earldom.

THOMAS. You hold your earldom from the King. Your task is to secure the north. But your coffers are empty. Men will not fight for a kind word –

HARRY PERCY. They are my tenants – it is their duty to fight.

THOMAS. With rusty swords? From behind crumbling walls? If you can't hold the line against the Scots, the King will take your titles, your land and your castles and give them to someone who can.

HARRY PERCY *slumps over the table and shakes with sobs.*

Come – you may have made some childish promises –

HARRY PERCY. No! We swore our oaths in front of witnesses. You don't grasp it. And once we were contracted she showed me such freedom –

THOMAS. Stop there! Any word or hint that you have been in any way *free* with Lady Anne – you'll answer to me and to the Boleyns –

HARRY PERCY. Who are you? Who are the Boleyns? I'm the Earl of Northumberland!

THOMAS. And the Duke of Norfolk will come and bite off your bollocks. He asked me to mention it.

HARRY PERCY. I love Anne! And she loves me –

THOMAS (*angry, threatening*). She despises you! Who wouldn't? A drunk and a pauper. The only way you'll please Anne Boleyn is by freeing her… So she can become Queen of England.

HARRY PERCY. How can I? What happened, has happened. I can't change the past!

THOMAS. Oh, the past changes all the time. I'll show you how easily it can be altered. You must swear on the Gospel that you made no agreement with her.

HARRY PERCY. I can't lie to God! I'd put my soul in danger –
and when you stand before God –

THOMAS (*grabs him by the throat – glares in his face*). You
don't have a soul, Harry. You've mortgaged it. Come on – if
you're going before the Council we'd better get you sobered
up. Christophe?

CHRISTOPHE *shoves* HARRY PERCY'*s head in a bucket
of water.* RAFE *and* GREGORY *watch, horrified.*

HARRY PERCY. Aghh! Take your hands off me.

CHRISTOPHE *ducks him again.*

Don't you know who I am?

CHRISTOPHE *ducks him.*

I'm the Earl of – (*'Northumberland' bubbles under water.*)

THOMAS. Oh Christ – Enough!

Scene Twenty-Two

Council assembles. NORFOLK *in the chair.*

NORFOLK. We have to wait for Archbishop Warham.

Door creaks open. Nothing happens. Then very slowly,
WARHAM *shuffles in. He's almost extinct.*

THOMAS. I hope I see you well, My Lord of Canterbury.

WARHAM. Cromwell. You – a Councillor! What's the world
coming to? I'll not be sorry to go out of it.

MORE. Now you're of this Council, Cromwell, I trust you will
tell the King what he ought to do – not merely what he can do.
'If the lion knew his strength it would be hard to rule him.'

THOMAS. Conceal his powers from him? Would that not be
treason, Lord Chancellor?

HARRY PERCY *brought in by* MINDERS.

NORFOLK. Harry Percy – you are here to deny before this
Council…

KING HENRY *arrives, louring*. NORFOLK *jumps up –*
KING HENRY *takes his place*.

Harry Percy, answer to the Council – were you ever
contracted to the Lady Anne Boleyn?

HARRY PERCY. No.

NORFOLK. Were promises of marriage made between you –
promises of any kind?

HARRY PERCY. No.

NORFOLK. Did you ever fu… ff… ff… er –

THOMAS. Has there been carnal knowledge between you?
Answer. Answer upon your honour.

HARRY PERCY. Upon my honour, no. No! No! No!

KING HENRY. It'll take more than your word.

HARRY PERCY (*panic-stricken*). What…

THOMAS. Approach His Grace of Canterbury, My Lord.

WARHAM *has difficulty lifting a large Bible*. BOLEYN
tries to help. WARHAM *bats him away*.

WARHAM. Harry Percy, you have chopped and changed in this
matter. You have asserted it, denied it, asserted it – now you
are brought here to deny it again – but this time not only in the
sight of men. Now… you will put your hand on this Bible, and
swear before me and in the presence of the King, and his
Council that you are free from unlawful knowledge of the
Lady Anne, and free from any contract of marriage with her.

HARRY PERCY (*hand on Bible, shaking*). I swear.

NORFOLK. You'd wonder how the whole thing got about in
the first place.

He advances on HARRY PERCY. HARRY PERCY *places
his hands over his balls*. NORFOLK *thrusts his face into*
HARRY PERCY'*s*.

We shall hear no more of this, boy.

WARHAM (*shuffles up to* KING HENRY, *who kisses his ring*).
Henry, I have seen you promote within your Court and
Council persons whose principles and morals will hardly
bear scrutiny. (*Hard look at* THOMAS.) I have seen you
deify your own will and appetite, to the sorrow and scandal
of Christian people. I have been loyal to you to the point of
violation of my own conscience. I have done much for
you... But now I have done the last thing I will ever do.

Scene Twenty-Three

Burst of music 'A Te Deum'. Few witnesses – the BOLEYNS.
STEPHEN *marries* KING HENRY *and* ANNE. *Then* MARK
plays the lute and sings 'What Shall I Do For Love?'

MARK (*sings*).
        Alas what shall I do for love
        For love alas what shall I do?
        Sith now so kind I do you find,
        To keep you me unto.

STEPHEN. Please God put a male heir in her belly before
    Christmas.

THOMAS. Shall I tell you a secret, Stephen?

STEPHEN. What?

KING HENRY. Cromwell. Now that Warham is dead I shall
    make Cranmer Archbishop. And you... Well, what will I
    make of you? I don't know... yet.

STEPHEN. An Ambassador, Majesty? Poland? Hungary?

KING HENRY. Before there is any issue from my new
    marriage – which God grant will be soon – Cranmer must
    make a dissolution of my so-called marriage. Convene a
    special court. Katherine may send lawyers – or attend
    herself. You, Cromwell, shall go and tell her. But what is to
    become of my sweet daughter Mary?

THOMAS. Be kind to her, sir.

KING HENRY. I must make her a bastard. Anne insists upon it.
    We must settle England on our son.

Exits with ANNE *and* BOLEYNS.

THOMAS. Hungary, Stephen? Really!

STEPHEN. I thought you might enjoy it. The secret – tell me the secret.

THOMAS. She's already with child.

STEPHEN. If you tell it in that tone, people will think you mean to take the credit.

THOMAS. So now she needs rest and quiet. She's talking about a house for herself – a retreat. Shady trees – fountains – walks – rose arbours… Close to the King at Whitehall –

STEPHEN (*getting the drift*). Cromwell –

THOMAS. I mentioned your new place at Hanworth –

STEPHEN. Cromwell, I have just paid a fortune to that crew of French glaziers you recommended –

THOMAS. Perfect! Light and airy – just the place for a growing child –

STEPHEN. And the antique statue of the Three Graces dancing you had sent from Rome –

THOMAS. No. Well, I have to admit that came cheap from a man in Shoreditch –

STEPHEN. She's not having it! I refuse! I'm not budging – Anne Boleyn can't take my house.

THOMAS. I think you'll find she can. She took York Place from the Cardinal, did she not? You were there. You made the inventory. You are witness to what she can do.

STEPHEN. What kind of monster have you brought among us?

THOMAS. You played your part. You've just married her. Bishop. (*Leaves.*)

STEPHEN *follows him – angry. As they go:*

STEPHEN. God damn you, Cromwell! Who are you? What office do you hold? You're nothing! Nothing! I suppose in a world where Anne Boleyn can be Queen, Thomas Cromwell of Putney can be Prince of Thieves –

THOMAS. I suppose you're right.

STEPHEN. What else have you faked?

THOMAS. Oh, drop it, Stephen – I'll get you your money
back…

Scene Twenty-Four

Ampthill Manor.

KATHERINE. Married? The rites may have been performed but
Anne Boleyn is not his wife. If he places a crown upon her
head it won't make her Queen – if she gives him a son her
bastard can never reign. Tell Henry I'll not come to
Cranmer's court. My case is in Rome, awaiting the attention
of the Holy Father.

THOMAS. Slow, isn't he?

KATHERINE. Only the Pope can settle the King's affairs.
Certainly not Dr Cranmer.

THOMAS. Archbishop Cranmer.

KATHERINE. A heretic?

THOMAS. Whatever you call him, madam, he will annul your
marriage.

KATHERINE. Then the Pope will excommunicate him.
Bishops and even kings must come to judgement. (*Pause*.)
So she is with child. It means nothing. A child in the womb
is not an heir in the cradle. As I know.

THOMAS. My Lady –

KATHERINE. What will happen to the Princess Mary?

THOMAS. I will do all I can for her.

KATHERINE. Tell the King I will pray for him. He needs to be
on the side of the light. He is not a man like you, who packs
up his sins in his saddlebags until they grow too heavy – then
dumps them on the highway or drops them overboard into

the sea. Henry errs, but he craves forgiveness. I believe – I will always believe – he'll turn from his path of error in order to be at peace with himself. Peace is what every good Christian prays for.

THOMAS. What a placid end you make, madam. Like an abbess. You're sure you won't think it over? I mean about becoming an abbess?

KATHERINE. I'll stay here. The King's true subject... and his wife.

THOMAS (*bowing out*). Madam.

KATHERINE. Cromwell... I believe you are my friend.

THOMAS. I am the King's servant.

KATHERINE. If the day comes when I can no longer protect her, do not let them harm the Princess Mary. I commend her to your care.

THOMAS. Madam.

RAFE *enters*.

Not over yet.

RAFE. You have to feel sorry for Katherine.

THOMAS. Do you? I'll tell you a little story... Henry went to France to have a little war – as Englishmen do – and left her as Regent. Down came the Scots. They were well beaten at Flodden and their King had his head cut off. Katherine – angelic Katherine – was going to send the head to her husband in his camp. But they advised her such a gesture was 'un-English'. She sent instead the surcoat in which the Scottish King had died – stiff, black and crackling with his pumped-out royal blood.

RAFE. Jesus.

THOMAS. If Katherine had been a man she'd have been a greater general than all the heroes of antiquity. In a fair fight between her and Henry, I know who I'd put my money on.

Scene Twenty-Five

A garden. Mid-May. Birdsong. THOMAS *and* ANNE *are at their most intimate and triumphant – it's the high point in their cooperation, best-friendliness, and joint purpose – they are in a state of exhilarated tension – almost flirting. She has her hand on his arm. She teases him – strokes him with a bunch of flowers.* MORE *is waiting for* KING HENRY. *He scrubs very nervously at his inky fingers and cuffs.*

ANNE. One by one my enemies are swept aside. (*Stares at* MORE.) What *is* Sir Thomas doing?

THOMAS. He's lost his contest with the inkpot again.

ANNE (*hand on mouth – tries to stop herself laughing*). Stop! I mustn't laugh!

THOMAS. Go on – laugh.

ANNE. Don't – they'll see us. (*Satirical – gently mocking.*) More's his friend. It's breaking Henry's heart…

THOMAS. Laugh – you can't resist it.

ANNE. No more than you – they're coming.

Enter KING HENRY, NORFOLK, STEPHEN *and others.* MORE *kneels. He continues to nervously play with his fingers. He won't look* KING HENRY *in the eye. He takes off the chain and puts it in* KING HENRY'*s hands.* KING HENRY *lays it on a cushion held by a* SERVANT.

He's reluctant to let go that chain, is he not? He was a fool to accept it. He thought Henry was a child who could be led. But now I have humbled him. (*Looks at* THOMAS.) As I humbled Wolsey before him. All subjects must learn humility.

THOMAS. You set us a daily example, Lady.

ANNE *looks affronted – then laughs and squeezes his arm.*

NORFOLK. He has misplaced the Great Seal.

THOMAS (*to* ANNE, *aside*). He's misplaced his whole career.

ANNE *stops herself laughing.*

NORFOLK. He thinks he may have left it in the privy. Go look, Gardiner.

STEPHEN (*sotto voce*). You go look, My Lord!

NORFOLK. I am the realm's foremost peer.

STEPHEN. And I am Bishop of Winchester.

NORFOLK (*hissing*). Then go and look. Bishop!

Face-off. STEPHEN *goes.*

ANNE. I wonder what he's thinking. He never says.

THOMAS. He dare not.

ANNE. He will never accept me – not as Henry's wife, nor as his Queen. That's the truth of him.

THOMAS. Perhaps. We'll never know.

ANNE. If I were King I'd find out.

THOMAS. He's no longer a threat to you. Be charitable. Let him go.

A flash of anger from ANNE, *because* THOMAS *has abandoned the battle of wits.* JANE ROCHFORD *arrives and watches them. She is furious to see them so intimate. As if she hates to see others relaxed and happy.* STEPHEN *arrives with the Great Seal. Thrusts it at* NORFOLK *and storms out.* NORFOLK *gives it to* MORE *who gives it to* KING HENRY *who gives it to a* SERVANT.

ANNE. At last! We're rid of him. (*Laughs.*)

JANE ROCHFORD (*at* ANNE). Oh, look at you with your blacksmith's boy! It's a pity you didn't meet earlier in life.

THOMAS. Lady Rochford!

JANE ROCHFORD. Enjoy it while you can. You'll never be rid of Thomas More. They may put a crown on your head but Katherine will always be his Queen – he may claim to be your husband's loyal subject but he's the Pope's man first. And when he speaks, or writes, all Europe listens. That's why Europe's princes despise you.

ANNE. When this Prince is out of me, the people of England will love me!

JANE ROCHFORD. No they won't. They'll never love you – no more will they love Cromwell here. They love Queen Katherine because she's a fit wife for England's King. While you are… Well, what are you?

KING HENRY *and* MORE *turn and look at the confrontation.*

KING HENRY. Anne?

ANNE *exits in the other direction.* KING HENRY *exeunts with* NORFOLK *and others.* JANE ROCHFORD *smiles at* THOMAS *and follows* ANNE. MORE *kneels as* KING HENRY *leaves. He is battered and bewildered and deeply wounded. Almost in a state of collapse from the strain of what he has just done. He keeps feeling for his missing chain.* THOMAS *marches up to him and bounces him to his feet.*

MORE. Thank you.

THOMAS (*brushes him down*). What will you do?

MORE. Write. Pray.

THOMAS. Write just a little, perhaps, and pray a lot.

MORE (*gently*). Is that a threat?

THOMAS. Are you coming to the Lady Anne's coronation?

MORE. No I'm not.

THOMAS. Yes you are. I have arranged everything. The last detail is for you to show your support. In public.

MORE. As things are, I can't afford a new coat.

THOMAS (*produces a purse*). Your friends had a collection.

MORE (*turns it over suspiciously*). This is from you?

THOMAS. You think you have no friends?

MORE. I don't know, Thomas. I have to walk my own path.

THOMAS. Turn up, bow, smile and the thing is done. They're married. She will be Queen. She's carrying his heir. Accept it.

MORE. Now that *is* a threat.

THOMAS. It's a warning – friend to friend.

MORE (*rattled*). Who are you, Cromwell?

THOMAS (*expressionless*). Blacksmith's boy.

MORE. You would sell yourself to the Turk if the price were right.

CHAPUYS (*entering*). Sir Thomas, may we speak?

MORE (*polite but weary*). No, Ambassador Chapuys – I've nothing to say.

CHAPUYS. The Emperor, my master, admires the stand you are taking.

MORE. I assure you, I have taken no stand.

CHAPUYS. You have resigned.

MORE. For reasons of health.

CHAPUYS. But surely… You've resigned in protest against the shameful treatment of Queen Katherine – and against your King living openly and adulterously with a concubine – I have written to the Emperor.

MORE. No – no! (*Rubbing his chest.*) Chest pains – here – around the heart.

CHAPUYS. But Anne will never be crowned? England will never accept one so low? Royal blood must have royal blood –

THOMAS. You'll get nothing out of him, Ambassador.

CHAPUYS (*civil*). Then may I enquire, Master Cromwell, are you to succeed him as Lord Chancellor.

MORE. God!

THOMAS. Not I, sir.

CHAPUYS. Then shall it be Bishop Stephen?

THOMAS. No. (*Smiles.*)

MORE. Let me explain. Gardiner is the King's right hand – Cromwell his left – but they hate each other. So we'll have some fool Jack-in-Office as Chancellor while the two of them scrap like terriers, and England's affairs are shredded between them. (*Exits.*)

CHAPUYS. Do you not covet this office?

THOMAS. I don't need a gold chain, Eustache – I watched it strangle Wolsey. The secret, you see, is to be close to the King – always with him – every day. Come home with me to supper – I'll explain it all to you. We are neighbours in the city, you know?

CHAPUYS. Of course we are! My master the Emperor is a most generous prince. If I could reassure him that your King will never crown his concubine...

Music. As ANNE's *coronation – the most magnificent, climactic scene – begins,* MORE *hurries away from the sound and sight of it. Blend into next scene.*

Scene Twenty-Six

June 1533. Huge music – Court in coronation robes. ANNE *enters through clouds of incense with* LADIES – *two* BISHOPS *lift up the hem of her robe – she prostrates herself before the altar, helped by* LADIES – *not easy as she's so pregnant.* ANNE *is anointed,* CRANMER *presses the ivory sceptre into her hand and crowns her.*

NORFOLK. Didn't I tell you? Say what you will about my niece, she always gets what she wants. Even the heavens lend their blessings – look how the sun shines on her.

A dance celebrating childbirth. Gifts for a male child displayed in the dance. Armour, weapons, ships, boys' toys. Everybody possible joins in. ANNE *and* KING HENRY, *triumphant, watch.*

An elaborate cradle crosses the stage. Everybody adores it as if it were the Blessed Virgin Mary's statue in the sack of York Place. ANNE's LADIES *draw* ANNE *away. A clap of thunder. Darkness. All run for cover. A joyful peal of bells which falters and peters out into silence.*

Jesu! After all this – a girl! A useless, mewling, ginger puke-pot of a girl!

KING HENRY *arrives*. CRANMER *takes him aside*. KING HENRY *takes the blow perfectly*.

KING HENRY. Healthy? Then I thank God for his favour to us. (*Going.*) Call her Elizabeth. Cancel the jousts.

NORFOLK. One thing was required of her – one simple thing and she fails us. A girl!

KING HENRY (*almost off*). Archbishop Cranmer. Cromwell – nobody else.

They go apart with KING HENRY.

(*Perplexed – baffled.*) A girl – another girl? After all Anne's promises… She promised me – she *promised*!

THOMAS. One day we'll make a great marriage for her. Your Majesty is young enough. The Queen is strong – her family fertile. You'll get another child soon.

CRANMER. Perhaps God intends some peculiar blessing by this Princess.

KING HENRY (*considers*). Dear friend, I am sure you are right.

CRANMER. Next time it will be a boy.

KING HENRY *goes off, with* SUFFOLK *and others*.

KING HENRY. Next time – next time I shall have a son. God knows we are both young enough. Assure yourselves – believe me – God intends some peculiar blessing by this Princess.

Scene Twenty-Seven

The Court assembles. Foreign AMBASSADORS *if possible.*
ANNE'*s* LADIES *bring on Princess Elizabeth, strip her naked,
and lay her in a crib.*

JANE ROCHFORD. The Queen wishes to show Princess
Elizabeth to the world. Rumours are running all over Europe
she was born with teeth – that she has six fingers on each hand
– and that she is furred all over and has a tail – like a monkey.

GREGORY. That's horrible! But she wasn't, was she? Born
with teeth?

MARY BOLEYN. No, Gregory. She hasn't got fur either.

JANE ROCHFORD. She has ginger bristles. You could exhibit
her at the fair as a pig baby.

MARY BOLEYN (*cooing over the crib*). Don't you think she
looks like the King, Gregory?

GREGORY. She could be anybody's.

THOMAS (*raising his hand to hide a smile*). My son means
that all babies look alike.

WYATT. For God's sake, Gregory! People have gone to the
Tower for saying less.

GEORGE. She is all Boleyn.

JANE ROCHFORD. *All* Boleyn? How could that be possible?
Think before you speak, husband.

Enter ANNE *and* KING HENRY *with* AMBASSADORS – *a
group of French, Venetian, German – and* COURTIERS, *as
many as possible.* ANNE'*s women and* THOMAS'*s group
drop back. The foreigners file past the baby, bowing to* ANNE
and KING HENRY. ANNE *is menacing in the scene but
never angry, nor raises her voice. She has a delicious secret.*

FRENCH AMBASSADOR (*presents a tacky gift*). Good baby,
good baby... She is very...

GREGORY (*to* RAFE). She has no tail. He looks disappointed.

ANNE (*sweetly*). My dearest wish is that one day she shall marry
a Prince of France. You will say so to King Francois.

FRENCH AMBASSADOR. Majesty. (*Bows to her. As he turns we see his grimace.*)

ANNE. Wait, monsieur! Cremuel – tell the Ambassador of the bill you are bringing into Parliament.

THOMAS *looks at* KING HENRY.

KING HENRY. Yes – explain the succession to him.

Elizabeth cries. LADIES *whisk the crying child away.*

ANNE. Tell him, Cremuel.

THOMAS. I –

ANNE. I wish it made clear to your master, and to all Europe, that a bill is going through Parliament which settles the succession of England on my children. Mine. Not Katherine's. When a son is born to me he shall succeed to the thone of England. And my daughters are and shall be royal princesses. Cremuel's bill declares that Katherine's child Mary is a bastard –

KING HENRY. No it doesn't.

ANNE. What?

KING HENRY. Well… not exactly.

ANNE. What? She is not? How is she not? Katherine was never your wife –

KING HENRY. That is true –

ANNE. She was never your wife so the child you got on her is a bastard – is that not so, Cremuel?

THOMAS. My bill puts Mary out of the line of succession. It's enough –

ANNE. It is not enough –

THOMAS. It's just as good as –

ANNE. It is no good to me. I want her made a bastard. Your bill will make her a bastard.

KING HENRY. Madam, we don't want to provoke…

THOMAS. We don't want to provoke, without good cause, her cousin the Emperor.

ANNE. You don't want to provoke him? No? Then I shall provoke him for you. I shall tell you, Ambassador, what will happen to Mary. The Princess Elizabeth is to have her own household and the bastard Mary will join it as her servant. She will go on her knees to my daughter. And if she won't bend her knee then she shall be beaten and buffeted until she does bend. She will call my daughter Princess, or I shall make her suffer.

KING HENRY. Sweetheart, there's no need for this. Of course everybody will call her Princess. Cromwell means to seal the act with an oath. All my subjects will swear to uphold the rights of Elizabeth – and any other children we are blessed with.

STEPHEN. All your subjects? *All* of them?

THOMAS. The people of England will stand behind their King. They'll declare their loyalty to him and to his heirs.

STEPHEN (*amused*). What – you'll trudge up and down the muddy lanes of England swearing shepherd lads and ploughboys?

THOMAS. A ploughboy's oath is as sacred as any bishop's.

STEPHEN. Or any blacksmith's boy's, or Putney drab's?

KING HENRY. The intention is, Gardiner, that every person of consequence shall be sworn.

STEPHEN. And if they refuse?

ANNE. Will it be… treason?

THOMAS (*cautious*). It could be.

STEPHEN. I wonder what Thomas More will say to your oath.

KING HENRY. Thomas More is my most loyal subject and my dear friend. He will be sworn.

STEPHEN. I doubt it.

KING HENRY. I say he will be sworn. (*Quietly.*) Gardiner, why do you do this? (*Explodes.*) You obstruct me and exasperate me at every turn! (*Roaring*.) All I ask is a country godly and quietly governed, and some peace and quiet for myself!

ANNE. Perhaps, Bishop, in serving His Majesty as Master Secretary, you have neglected your diocese. As a good shepherd you should mind your sheep.

STEPHEN. My flock is safe in fold.

ANNE. Perhaps you should go count them.

STEPHEN. I assure you, madam –

ANNE. Go! Count!

STEPHEN. Who will do Master Secretary's job?

KING HENRY. Cromwell will. You have leave to go.

STEPHEN. But if –

KING HENRY. You have leave!

STEPHEN. Majesty. (*Bows out – black look for* THOMAS.)

ANNE. Cremuel. Thomas More? I too wonder what he will say to your oath. You will make him swear. And anyone who resists me. Do it for my peace of mind. At such a time as this my peace of mind is very precious to me. Very. Precious.

KING HENRY (*amused but puzzled*). Indeed, sweetheart?

ANNE. Because I have a great desire to eat apples.

KING HENRY. What are you saying?

ANNE. What can it mean? My craving for apples?

KING HENRY. Oh, Nan! Already?

ANNE (*goes to* WYATT *and takes his hand*). Fetch me some apples, Tom – apples from Kent. Yes, you can tell them. Tell everybody – shout it to the world. (*In a world of her own – ignores* KING HENRY.) Write proclamations – the King shall have his son and heir. And any man who'll not accept his titles shall die a traitor's death.

ANNE *exits with* WYATT, *followed by the Court.*

THOMAS. I am happy for you, Majesty.

KING HENRY. Why did she go first to Wyatt?

THOMAS. Sir?

KING HENRY. What is it to him if she craves apples?

THOMAS. Sir, I've no wish to disappoint the Queen –

KING HENRY. No – you'd better not!

THOMAS. Gardiner may be right. I believe Thomas More may refuse the oath.

KING HENRY. Then you'll make him sign it.

THOMAS. All Europe will wait to see what he –

KING HENRY. Find a way. Thomas More must swear to the act.

THOMAS. It won't be easy –

KING HENRY (*explodes*). Do I retain you for what is easy? Jesus pity my simplicity! – I have just promoted you to a place in this kingdom no one of your breeding has ever held in the whole history of the realm! Cromwell, you are as cunning as a bag of serpents, but do not be a viper in my bosom. You know my decision. Execute it. Find a way. Just do it. Do you understand me?

Scene Twenty-Eight

Lambeth Palace. CRANMER *pacing, agitated.* THOMAS *comes in with papers and scrolls.*

SUFFOLK. If he won't take the oath, Harry will throw him to the lions… Like that fellow in the Bible… Jonah.

CRANMER. Daniel.

NORFOLK. We'd better have him in then.

CRANMER. Perhaps he'd agree to swear if we promised to keep his compliance secret? Then he wouldn't lose face.

THOMAS. He wouldn't, but *we* might.

MORE *is brought in by* GUARDS – *dishevelled as usual, suffering from hay fever.*

MORE. Spring is here. Soon we shall be dancing round the maypole. (*Nods to* CRANMER.) Thomas. (*To* NORFOLK.) Thomas. (*To* THOMAS.) Thomas. (*To* SUFFOLK.) Charles.

THOMAS. Have a seat, Thomas.

MORE *sits – takes out spectacles, a book, papers, as if he's settling down for the day.*

NORFOLK. Here is the oath. (*Unscrolling a large document.*) And here's a list of those who have sworn to it – bishops, priests, Members of Parliament – all accept Henry as Head of the Church in England, and his daughter Elizabeth as his only heir.

MORE (*mild – polite*). Thank you. I've already seen it.

NORFOLK. And will you here and now swear to it?

No response.

THOMAS. He's already said he won't.

SUFFOLK. He may have changed his mind. Just sign it, man – then we can all go to dinner.

MORE *smiles at his simple idiocy.*

CRANMER. Why will you not take the oath? Is it because your conscience will not let you?

MORE. Yes.

NORFOLK. Yes, and...? And?

MORE. Yes and nothing.

NORFOLK. You object to it but you won't say why?

MORE. Yes.

CRANMER. Are there parts of the oath you could accept? (*Silence.*) Or do you object to each and every clause of it?

MORE. I've nothing to add. So I'd rather say... nothing.

CRANMER. And you feel no doubts about the stand you are taking?

MORE. I have taken no stand.

CRANMER. Surely you have doubts? Because a majority has studied and sworn this oath of loyalty to the King, and found no difficulty with it –

MORE (*reasonable*). 'A majority'? You claim the majority. You say you have Parliament behind you. I have the whole of Christendom behind me – together with the angels and the saints, and all the company of the Christian dead, for as many generations as there have been since the Church was founded, one Church, undivided –

THOMAS. Oh, for the love of God! A lie is no less a lie because it's the old lie – the thousand-year-old deception! Your undivided Church is hacking at its own limbs – in the low countries burying women alive – in Paris slowly roasting them so their suffering is increased –

MORE (*patient*). The body is burnt but the soul is saved. Better to burn with earthly fire than in the flames of eternity.

CRANMER. If you will not take the oath what conclusions must we draw?

NORFOLK. Where does your loyalty lie?

SUFFOLK. What is the King to think?

MORE. I know nothing of what's in the King's mind. And certainly he can draw no inference from my silence.

NORFOLK. Oh, but he can though! So what are we to say to him? You must give us your reasons.

MORE. How will you compel me?

CRANMER. In the name of Christ, don't destroy yourself! Help the King. Help your country.

MORE. That is my intention – with prayers, certainly. With oaths? No.

NORFOLK. We've a war coming, sir – can't you grasp that? We'll have the Emperor's soldiers running up and down The Strand – stabling their horses in the Abbey – they're planning an invasion! Then where do you stand? Do you want Henry – who loves you – on the throne, or some Papal puppet? How will that be lawful? What will your conscience tell you then?

MORE. May I go home now?

CRANMER. No.

MORE. The Tower, then? I'm prepared for that. I've brought a
bag with everything I need –

SUFFOLK. You know what the end of this will be? They'll
drag you to Tyburn, strip you naked, slit you open, haul out
your guts and burn them in front of your eyes. Is that what
you want – a traitor's death? Every heretic in London
jeering at you while you gasp for your last breath in a pile
of your own shit?

This gets to MORE. *He is trembling. He tries to pack his bag
but he is shaking too much and fails.*

MORE. God will strengthen me.

SUFFOLK. You think so?

THOMAS *picks up documents and books from the table and
packs them for* MORE.

MORE (*whispering*). God bless you, gentlemen.

THOMAS (*to the guards*). Show Sir Thomas every mark of
respect.

MORE *is taken away.*

CRANMER. What will you do?

THOMAS. Trick him into it. When he questioned heretics –
people he called heretics – he'd say 'You can lie to them – you
can make a promise and break it – it's all God's work. You can
trick them,' he'd say, 'trickery is allowed.'

CRANMER. But you'll see he comes to no harm?

THOMAS. Don't worry – I'll keep him alive. I'm trickier than
he is.

CRANMER. If we give him a few days to think things
through… Perhaps the King won't force the point.

THOMAS. The King would leave him comfortably in the
Tower until he comes to his senses –

NORFOLK. Not my niece though. She'll hound Henry until he gives her his head on a platter.

SUFFOLK. Like that scarlet whore in the Bible. Jezebel.

CRANMER. Herodias.

> *Pause.* THOMAS *roars with laughter and* CRANMER *joins in.* NORFOLK *and* SUFFOLK *look blank. The laughter is cut by a hideous scream.*

Scene Twenty-Nine

A scream like an animal in pain followed by wailing, then rhythmic keening – ominous music. A macabre procession. JANE ROCHFORD, JANE SEYMOUR *and other* LADIES *come out of* ANNE*'s chamber with bloody bedlinen. Then we are in* KING HENRY*'s bedchamber – as for his 'dream'.*

KING HENRY. A boy – I know it was a boy. Women keep these things secret but she has miscarried my son. They lit fires in the Queen's apartments to burn what has bled away. If there was anything to bury… Why will God not give me a son, Cromwell?

Whose fault is it? –

Anne blames Katherine – says she ill-wishes me. She comes in the night with her cold heart and her cold hands that smell of the grave – and lies between me and the woman I love… the woman I…

What's become of your ready answers? Help me… just… do something, Cromwell. When I ride out now the people shout at me. They rise up out of ditches to tell me I should take Katherine back. And this one uses me worse than if I were a cur. Yes – I am King of England and I am treated worse than a dog. I begin to suspect…

THOMAS. What? What do you suspect?

KING HENRY. Don't you fail me too, Cromwell – don't you fail me.

Scene Thirty

A year has passed. Four a.m. Dawn breaking. Cold light. A wet July day. MORE *is kneeling saying the rosary.* THOMAS *in the murk.*

MORE (*calling*). Has my confessor come? Thomas? Come in, come in.

THOMAS. Your last meal?

MORE. Milk pudding.

THOMAS. It will never sustain you on the scaffold.

MORE (*taking the dish and stirring it*). It's what I asked for. Nourishing. There's enough here for dinner as well – but I won't need it. (*To himself.*) Wasteful, really. (*To* THOMAS.) What time must I be ready?

THOMAS. The King grants you mercy.

MORE. Mercy? (*Gapes at* THOMAS. *Shakes and turns away to hide his face and puts down the dish.*)

THOMAS (*appalled at the confusion – because he didn't mean to ignite false hope*). It's to be the headsman, not the hangman. You should thank me, Thomas. I went on my knees – I begged for you. (*Studies* MORE.) You're afraid of pain. I thought at the last you might despair of God's grace.

MORE. I'm still afraid. The axe is a terrible thing. I am human.

THOMAS. I would have left you, you know. To live out your life – in prayer and repentance. If I were King.

WOLSEY'S GHOST. *Homo homini lupus.*

THOMAS. Man is wolf to man.

MORE (*recovering, his anger builds*). Well, the wolves are unleashed now – Henry begins to feel his power. He didn't know the half of it until you showed it to him. You have lifted him up into God's place. Now you shall suffer the terrible strength of it. His kingdom – his people – his Church –

THOMAS. The King didn't want your death –

MORE. And nor did you. What use is my death to you? You wanted my compliance. I've beaten you both – this is a terrible defeat for you.

THOMAS. I feel it as a defeat.

MORE. Don't let it make you bitter.

THOMAS. Write to him.

MORE. I'm done with writing.

THOMAS. I'll write it. You just sign it.

A smile between them.

You don't want to live, do you? You want martyrdom.

MORE. I am my own worst enemy. I've been told that all my life.

THOMAS. Then I'll leave you.

MORE. Say a prayer for me. I'll say one for you. (*Exits*.)

WOLSEY'S GHOST. Say one for me too... If ever a man picked up an axe and cut off his own head...

THOMAS. What sort of a day will it be?

WOLSEY'S GHOST. It will be raining. Hard.

THOMAS. That's the trouble with England. The weather – rotting the grain in the fields – another bad harvest – then hoarding – then hunger – then riots – then hangings...

WOLSEY'S GHOST. Well, you can't do anything about the weather, Tom.

THOMAS. No, but I can change everything else. I don't want this country to be like my father's house in Putney – shouting and fighting all the time. I don't want children growing up on the street. I want it to be a place where everybody knows what he has to do – and feels safe doing it. You used to say the English were a frivolous, wretched people –

WOLSEY'S GHOST. Set down on a foggy island at the edge of the world – abandoned by God for century upon century – no grace, no light, no learning – nothing but rain – mud – blood...

WOLSEY'S GHOST *joins two others –* MORE *and* LIZ – *backs to the audience.*

THOMAS. But now, I think, we have reached a new age. Still rain, mud, and blood, but we are listening to God now – we are turning his way. Slowly, slowly, we are working out our salvation.

KING HENRY *enters.*

KING HENRY. I miss the Cardinal. Every day I miss the Cardinal of York. What am I to do, Thomas? I cannot sleep – if I shut my eyes I'm afraid I will be murdered. I have such doubts... Save me. Tell me what to do...

He sees JANE SEYMOUR. *The* GHOSTS *turn.*

End.

BRING UP THE BODIES

The full cast enters. THOMAS WYATT *addresses the opening lines from his sonnet to* ANNE BOLEYN, *observed by* KING HENRY, *all three of them observed by* THOMAS CROMWELL.

WYATT.
>Whoso list to hunt, I know where is an hind...
>But for me, alas!, I may no more:
>The vain travail hath wearied me so sore
>I am of them that furthest come behind –
>Yet may I by no means my wearied mind
>Draw from the deer... But as she flee-eth afore
>Fainting I follow... I leave off, therefore –
>Sithens in a net I seek to hold the wind...

Prologue

WOLSEY'S GHOST. *A forest – the first three scenes (design and light) must tell us we are in a forest, and that the realm of nature, the unseen and the unforeseen is encroaching on Wolf Hall. We must feel we are out of London. Distant hunting horns.* WOLSEY'S GHOST *scents the air and disappears.* DEMONS *reprise elements of the Wolsey masque. The masque changes to a hunt. A hart crosses the stage and exits.* ANNE, *looking hunted, crosses the stage. Horns draw nearer and nearer. Hounds baying louder and louder.* HUNTSMEN *blow a kill.* HUNTSMEN *bring on the deer stuck with crossbow bolts. Laughter. Enter* KING HENRY VIII (*who has fleshed out*), FRANCIS WESTON, SIR WILLIAM BRERETON, SIR HENRY NORRIS, *with crossbows.* KING HENRY *cuts the heart out of the deer.* HUNTSMEN *blow.*

KING HENRY. My hounds must have their fee! Norris. Brereton. Weston.

> *Playfully he smears bloody hands on the faces of* BRERETON, WESTON *and* NORRIS. *A* SERVANT *pours a bowl of water for* KING HENRY, NORRIS *hands* KING HENRY *a towel.* HUNTSMEN *begin to butcher the deer.*

BRERETON. Let Cromwell do that – our 'fat butcher'.

WESTON. How many more times! Wolsey was the fat butcher
  – Cromwell's –

THOMAS. I'm the grim blacksmith.

> *Rain – a downpour.*

KING HENRY. God granted me the stewardship of this kingdom… I wish He'd given me lands with less rain and more sunshine in them.

ACT ONE

Scene One

Enter OLD SIR JOHN SEYMOUR, EDWARD SEYMOUR *and* MARJORIE SEYMOUR.

SIR JOHN. Welcome, Majesty! Welcome to Wolf Hall.

KING HENRY. Sir John Seymour! Very glad to see you.

SIR JOHN. Majesty.

KING HENRY. We've hunted our way through Somerset and Wiltshire – to bring you venison.

SIR JOHN. Majesty.

KING HENRY. I am your guest. We'll stay –

THOMAS. Five days.

KING HENRY. Five days. Then on to Farnham and so to London…

SIR JOHN. My… er… wife.

MARJORIE. Your Majesty does us great honour…

SIR JOHN. My son Edward you know –

KING HENRY. Yes – we remember Edward from the late Cardinal's household –

EDWARD (*kneeling*). Majesty.

KING HENRY. Get up, Edward.

EDWARD. And my sister Jane, sir.

KING HENRY. Ah, Jane we know! Jane… Now we visit you at home, will you be less shy? At Court we get hardly a word from her. Oho, did you ever see such a blush! Never – unless upon a little maid of twelve.

JANE SEYMOUR. I cannot claim to be twelve.

KING HENRY (*smiles upon* JANE SEYMOUR *two seconds too long. Recalls himself*). That small sheep – over there, Cromwell – what would you say it weighs?

THOMAS. No more than thirty pounds, sir.

WESTON. He should know. He used to be a shearsman, didn't he?

KING HENRY. We'd be a poor country without our wool trade, young Weston. Jane?

KING HENRY *offers* JANE SEYMOUR *his arm. They go into Wolf Hall.*

SIR JOHN. Tell me, Master Cromwell – when will you marry again? Don't you live miserably – with no women in your life?

THOMAS. I'm never miserable, Sir John. The world is too good to me.

SIR JOHN. We've many fresh girls in our Forest of Savernake. Don't be alone in the world – marry again, man!

THOMAS. I have my son Gregory with me.

GREGORY (*bows*). Your servant, Sir John.

Dinner served.

SIR JOHN. Boys are very well, but a household's no home without women. There's my daughter Jane – such a good girl –

KING HENRY. She is, she is! Tomorrow you'll hunt with me, Jane.

SIR JOHN. Put her in the saddle and Jane's the Goddess Diana – good strong thighs on her – she'll make some man a fine wife – though I never troubled her much with schooling. What do girls want with foreign languages? They're not going anywhere. Am I right, Cromwell?

THOMAS. Well… I had my daughters taught equal with my son.

WESTON. What? In the tiltyard?

THOMAS *smiles, patiently.*

EDWARD. It's not uncommon for city daughters to be taught their letters –

WESTON. Cromwell's daughters! Can you imagine them? You'd not want to bump into one of them on a dark night in Putney!

GREGORY. My sisters died, sir. You insult their memory –

JANE SEYMOUR (*steers* GREGORY *away, hand on his arm*). You men think we do nothing but sew and gossip. But I've lately got some skill of the French tongue –

SIR JOHN (*spluttering*). Have you, Jane?

JANE SEYMOUR. Mary Shelton is teaching me.

KING HENRY. Mary Shelton is a kindly young woman.

WESTON. Very skilful in the French tongue!

JANE SEYMOUR (*to* GREGORY). When we leave our studies, we speak of love.

KING HENRY (*laughing, intrigued*). Do you, Jane?

JANE SEYMOUR. Which gentlemen are fittest to be lovers, who burns with secret love for the Queen – who among you writes the best verses –

KING HENRY. No harm in verses.

WESTON. Even to married ladies.

General laughter.

KING HENRY. Now tell us – who writes you verses, Jane? Who are *your* suitors?

JANE SEYMOUR. You must put on a woman's gown, Majesty, and ply your needle if you want to know that.

KING HENRY. I shall! I'll come and search out all your lewd secrets – unless we can find someone more maidenly for the task? Gregory, you're a pretty fellow – or that boy Mark – the musician? Now there is a smooth and girlish countenance.

JANE SEYMOUR. Oh, we barely count Mark a man – he's always among the ladies. If you want to know our secrets, ask Mark.

THOMAS. I'll remember that.

KING HENRY. What sort of a day shall we have tomorrow? The Cardinal reckoned he could change the weather. 'A good enough morning,' he'd say, 'but by ten it will be brighter.'

EDWARD. Some men have a weather eye – that's all it is, sir. It's not special to cardinals.

KING HENRY. I should never have stood in awe of him.

WESTON. He was too proud – for a subject.

KING HENRY *falls asleep*.

So you'll hunt with us tomorrow, Lady Jane?

JANE SEYMOUR. If His Majesty wants me. I do as I'm told.

WESTON. The Queen would be angry if she knew.

THOMAS. Make sure she doesn't find out, then – there's a good boy.

SIR JOHN. He's fallen asleep.

EDWARD. Whose office is it to wake him?

WESTON. Harry Norris – but His Majesty's sent him across country with love letters for Queen Anne.

THOMAS. Francis Weston, your gentlemanly touch is required.

WESTON. I wouldn't dare.

KING HENRY *sinks toward the table, snorts*.

SIR JOHN (*whispering*). Make a noise – wake him naturally. Tell a joke, Edward – and we'll laugh. Suddenly.

EDWARD. A *joke*? (*Affronted*.) I think not.

BRERETON. You wake him, Cromwell. No man so great with him as you.

THOMAS. Not I.

JANE SEYMOUR *taps the back of* KING HENRY*'s hand. His eyes flick open*.

KING HENRY (*rises*). Well… Early start tomorrow. Oh… Where's Harry Norris?

THOMAS. Ridden to the Queen, sir – with your letters.

KING HENRY. Then… Weston – follow me. Jane – goodnight.

Smiles at her – is about to say something else – but then goes abruptly. All follow except EDWARD.

SIR JOHN (*to* THOMAS *as he goes*). Good girl my daughter… er… Jane. Supple. Good breeder for some man.

EDWARD. Stay, Master Cromwell… (*Smiles.*) My sister's not spoken for, you know? You'll have gathered my father has hopes –

THOMAS. I like Jane, Edward – always have. I admire her loyalty. But I'm too old for her now.

EDWARD. Queen Katherine was always good to her.

THOMAS. And Jane misses her. As many do. Our present Queen knows it, so…

EDWARD (*encouraged to press on and get the gossip*). I hear she can be a shrew?

THOMAS. She is a very gracious lady – when everything's going her way. But when she is crossed… (*A 'take cover' gesture.*) I disappoint her, you know. She wants me to arrange a French marriage for her daughter Elizabeth.

EDWARD. And you won't?

THOMAS. The French say Elizabeth is a bastard, and Princess Mary Henry's only heir. But I daren't tell Anne that. My head would wobble on my shoulders.

EDWARD. You surprise me, Master Cromwell. I imagined you were in great favour. You still work together? For the Gospel?

THOMAS. We work together, yes. I owe her a lot. But truth is, I'm grown too great for the Queen's liking. She wants the Boleyns to be the only people the King listens to.

EDWARD. They say her father gets the rough side of her tongue.

THOMAS. He does indeed –

EDWARD. While brother George gets…

THOMAS. What? What does he get?

EDWARD. Many things are said of Queen Anne I dare not repeat. Forgive me – we're hunting tomorrow – I'm ready for my bed.

THOMAS. Edward, when we leave Wolf Hall, we should go next to Farnham – but I'm told the plague's in the town. I may bring His Majesty to stay at your house at Elvetham.

EDWARD. Oh no – please… I'm not provided. Could you not take him to the Westons at Sutton Place?

THOMAS. The Westons can go to the Devil. No – I have my reasons. Make sure your sister Jane is there to welcome us.

EDWARD. Well…

THOMAS. If you love me, Edward – do me this favour. You'll not lose by it.

Scene Two

GREGORY *is already in bed, half-asleep.*

GREGORY. Father… King Solomon had seven hundred wives and three hundred concubines.

THOMAS. He did.

Pause.

GREGORY. Didn't the Pope have something to say about it?

THOMAS. God was angry with King Solomon and took the kingdom from his heirs.

GREGORY. Father… I've been thinking about purgatory.

THOMAS (*interested*). Have you?

GREGORY. Yes – I know we used to have it. But do we have it still?

THOMAS (*wishes he knew*). When we get back to London you can ask Archbishop Cranmer. He'll tell you the latest thinking.

GREGORY. Because if there's no purgatory, where do the dead live now? When I say my prayers for my mother and my sisters… Well, I'd be sorry to think they can't hear me.

THOMAS. Say your prayers anyway… And go to sleep now.

GREGORY. Am I to marry Jane Seymour? Is that what you've been discussing with her brother Edward this past hour?

THOMAS. Go to sleep.

He's already asleep.

You're a good boy. (*Prays.*)

WOLSEY'S GHOST (*appearing*). He *is* a good boy –

THOMAS. Wolsey? –

WOLSEY'S GHOST. Fine archer, fine horseman – a shining star in the tiltyard –

THOMAS. You can't fault his manners –

WOLSEY'S GHOST. He speaks reverently to his superiors – is mild with those beneath him – he doesn't slouch around with his jacket off one shoulder, or look in windows to admire himself –

THOMAS. Tell me something I don't know –

WOLSEY'S GHOST. Or interrupt old men.

THOMAS. You're not looking well, you know. I wish you'd prophesy. How long have I left? Twenty years? I suppose I'll see Henry out – then what?

WOLSEY'S GHOST. Well…

THOMAS. The problem that brought you down is mine now. Where do I find the King an heir?

WOLSEY'S GHOST. Ah, well…

THOMAS. There's his bastard son Richmond. Could I legitimise him?

WOLSEY'S GHOST. Hmmm…

THOMAS. No? You mean no. A bastard cannot reign.

WOLSEY'S GHOST. No.

THOMAS. Twenty years married to Katherine – the only child he got was Mary.

WOLSEY'S GHOST. And a churchyard full of dead babies.

THOMAS. All that scandal – all that turmoil to make a second marriage – and for what! For Elizabeth? What use is another girl?

WOLSEY'S GHOST. Well…

THOMAS. What becomes of England if Henry dies?

WOLSEY'S GHOST. Oh, he'll not die just yet. I think he's looking very well. Perhaps a little…

THOMAS. Fatter?

WOLSEY'S GHOST. Putting on a little weight. But that's good living.

THOMAS. He worries that people are watching him – the old families of England with their ancient titles.

WOLSEY'S GHOST. Oh yes, they're watching.

THOMAS. They're waiting to rule again. If he shows any sign of weakness they'll make their move. I can feel them here myself – as if they're lurking in the forests – the living and the dead both.

WOLSEY'S GHOST. Hmmm. Anything else you want to know?

THOMAS. Yes. How am I going to pay for it all – England – the King's great charges – the cost of charity, the cost of justice, the cost of holding the Emperor at bay?

WOLSEY'S GHOST. It's a problem… But no longer my problem.

THOMAS. *Monks* must provide – idle, rich, parasites – monks! Where in the Gospels does it say monks? At Durham they rake in two thousand pounds a year in rents, but they'll take a farthing off some poor beggar to show him –

WOLSEY'S GHOST. St Cuthbert's front tooth.

THOMAS. Down at Maiden Bradley, for a fee, the monks will show you part of God's coat and some leftovers from the Last Supper. They say that if the Abbot of Glastonbury went

to bed with the Abbess of Shaftsbury, their offspring would
be the richest landowner in England.

WOLSEY'S GHOST. Yes – but have you seen the Abbess of
Shaftsbury?

GREGORY (*talking in his sleep*). Am I to be married to the
Abbess of Shaftsbury, Father?

MORE'S GHOST. Where will you strike next, Cromwell? Do
you mean to pull all England down? Your King is destroying
the Church.

THOMAS. He is renewing it. England will be a better country
when her Church is purged of liars and hypocrites. But
because you wouldn't mend your manners, Thomas More,
you're no longer alive to see it. I miss you, you know?
Sometimes I forget you're dead.

WOLSEY'S GHOST. Death comes for us all.

MORE'S GHOST. He came for Wolsey, he came for me – he'll
come for Henry, and he'll come for you –

WOLSEY'S GHOST. Let's not be disagreeable.

THOMAS. Give His Majesty a fine morning's hunting
tomorrow – can you manage that?

WOLSEY'S GHOST. Of course I can.

GHOSTS *fade away. A glimpse of* LIZ *in her white bonnet*.

THOMAS. Liz? Liz…

Scene Three

A glorious morning. KING HENRY *and* JANE SEYMOUR,
dressed for the hunt, stroll in the garden – THOMAS *working
through a pile of papers.* STEPHEN GARDINER *arrives, in
riding clothes, folio under his arm.*

THOMAS. Bishop Stephen? What brings you to Wolf Hall?

STEPHEN. You stole my place as Master Secretary, Cromwell
– you had me sent from Court –

THOMAS. Not I – never think it! While you've been tending
your flock I've missed you every day –

STEPHEN. I've written a book which will bring me back in
favour with His Majesty. In it I show the King's authority is
divine: it descends to him from God –

THOMAS. Not from the Pope? –

STEPHEN. In no wise from the Pope! It descends *directly* from
God. It certainly does not flow upwards from his subjects as
you once asserted.

THOMAS. I wonder what Thomas More would have thought of
your book. Word in Rome is he's to be made a saint.

STEPHEN. Preposterous!

KING HENRY *enters.* THOMAS *stands,* STEPHEN *kneels.*

THOMAS. Majesty.

KING HENRY. Sit, Cromwell… What are you doing here,
Gardiner? I sent you to your diocese.

STEPHEN. I have written a book, Majesty. I call it *Of True
Obedience.*

KING HENRY. Give it to Cromwell.

THOMAS. True obedience, Stephen, true obedience.

THOMAS *drops the manuscript onto a huge pile of work.*
STEPHEN *exits.*

We need an ambassador for the French, Majesty. If you need
someone to break a promise and brazen it out, Stephen's
your man.

THOMAS *waits*. KING HENRY *does not know how to begin.*

KING HENRY. Cromwell…

THOMAS. Majesty?

KING HENRY. I've been walking in the garden. With Jane.

THOMAS. Majesty?

KING HENRY. Wolf Hall has fine gardens… (*Sighs.*) Those
letters – what's the news?

THOMAS. A Medici Cardinal has been poisoned by his brother
– work has stopped on our fortification of Calais – the
builders have downed tools and are demanding sixpence a
day – the Muscovites have taken three hundred miles of
Polish territory – fifty thousand dead –

KING HENRY (*not listening*). Cromwell…

THOMAS. I hope they spared the libraries – and the scholars.
Poland has some fine scholars.

KING HENRY. Mmm…

THOMAS (*probing*). My new coat is coming down to Wiltshire
by the next courier.

KING HENRY *doesn't hear this – he is so lost in his own
thoughts.*

It's a green velvet coat… There are letters from several
foreign rulers… asking if you are going to cut off the
bollocks of all your bishops.

KING HENRY *doesn't react.*

The Abbot of Glastonbury was caught in bed… with the
Abbess of Shaftsbury.

Nothing.

Majesty? The Imperial Ambassador, Chapuys, asks may he
ride up country to visit the Lady Mary?

KING HENRY. No.

THOMAS. I believe –

KING HENRY. No.

THOMAS (*throwing down his pen*). Majesty?

KING HENRY. My mind is still down there in the garden. With Jane… Does it show? On my face? Does it show?

THOMAS. I have seen that expression before, Majesty. (*Confident* KING HENRY *isn't listening.*) You look stunned… Like a veal calf knocked on the head by the butcher.

Scene Four

Whitehall. ANNE *and* LADIES *in her apartments.* THOMAS *and* RAFE SADLER *arrive outside.*

MARK. Welcome to London, My Lord – welcome home.

THOMAS. Mark? I noticed your new stiff doublet. I hadn't realised you were lurking inside it.

MARK (*trying to make himself pleasant*). How are you, Lord Cromwell – how was His Majesty's summer progress?

THOMAS. No 'Lord' – still plain 'Master' – his Majesty needs me in the House of Commons. Ah – you get bonnier each time I see you, Mark. I must go to the Queen.

MARK. Careful – she's in a rage. Brother George is on his way back from France. He went over to arrange a French marriage for Elizabeth and they laughed at him. And the word over there is Katherine is petitioning the Pope to excommunicate our royal master. And you know what that means? Anybody's allowed to kill the King! Any Christian man –

THOMAS. Yes, Mark, I know what excommunication is. I'm doing all I can to prevent it –

MARK. Not just allowed – they ought to do it. They get a blessing from the Pope! And anyone who has an army – like the Emperor – can just come over and conquer us.

THOMAS. You know more of State affairs than I do, Mark. You must stand high in the Queen's favour – to know so much of her mind.

MARK. We lesser men are often most fit for royal confidence. Do you not find it so?

RAFE. Baron Smeaton before long, then?

THOMAS. I'll be the first to congratulate him.

Exit MARK, *smirking*.

I think you should come in with me, Rafe. Time we began to transform you into a politician.

RAFE. Will it hurt? Will there be much pain?

THOMAS. Yes, I should think so – for those around you.

They go in to ANNE.

ANNE. Out – out! You too, Rochford. Out! I don't want you in here.

JANE ROCHFORD. Majesty. (*A deep curtsy – studied insult, gives* THOMAS *a look, points at her belly: 'Who knows?'*)

ANNE. Cremuel. Today I've been making bishops – Gospellers and reformers – my men – all of them. Who'd have thought Hugh Latimer would ever be a bishop? Then, who'd have thought you would be anything at all? But there you are – sworn Councillor, Master of the Rolls, Chancellor of the University of Cambridge, the King's deputy in church affairs and his principal secretary. You wouldn't overreach yourself, would you? Having you at his side suits my purposes – we work well together – for the Gospels, for England – for all the King's interests… But never forget who raised you up so high.

THOMAS. His Majesty has smoothed my path –

ANNE. At my prompting. You owe everything to me.

THOMAS. I know where my loyalties lie.

ANNE. Never forget how low you were – and could be again. (*Looks hard at him.*) Very well. I was promised a French prince for my daughter. Why is the match not yet made?

THOMAS. Ask your brother, Majesty – he's better placed to answer than I. Who knows how he came to fail – in what should have been very simple negotiations?

ANNE. George suspects, Cremuel, that you hinder this match.

THOMAS. I, madam? Why would I do that?

ANNE. Yes – why would you cross me – your benefactor and
protector? You are against a French alliance perhaps? Perhaps.
And you are close to Chapuys – the Emperor's man –

THOMAS. I favour neither France nor the Emperor. I carry out
the wishes of the King.

ANNE. Mine too, I hope?

THOMAS. Your interests chime with his, madam – naturally.
Therefore I am ever your faithful servant.

ANNE. George sent this from Paris – here – read it. (*Thinks
better of it.*) Or… perhaps not. They're saying Katherine stirs
up the Pope and the Emperor to invade England – as does
M'sieur Chapuys – who makes no secret of his hatred for
me. Henry shall banish that man.

THOMAS. If we start throwing out ambassadors, we won't get
to know anything at all. I've just broken his cipher – do you
know how long that takes? If you throw Chapuys out I'll
have to start all over again.

ANNE. Then how shall you put a stop to Katherine's plotting?
Her treason? She should be thrown in a dungeon – she
should lose her head –

THOMAS. The King cannot compromise his honour by any ill-
treatment of the Queen-that-was –

ANNE. Queen-that-*never*-was!

THOMAS. She's the Emperor's aunt. We'd risk a war –

ANNE. Hmmmm. If I were her I too would intrigue – I'd never
give up – never forgive. However… they say she's sick – she
and Mary her bastard both. Up all night puking – down all
day moaning. And I – *I* am the cause of all their pain – all
their misery. Or so they'd have the King believe. I do *not*
believe. So you're to ride to where Katherine is to find out
the truth. Is she feigning? Is she dying? Give her no warning
of your coming.

KING HENRY *enters*.

Henry – I have told him to go.

KING HENRY. To Katherine? I wish you would. There's no
one like Cromwell for seeing into the nature of things.

THOMAS. Majesty.

KING HENRY. Master Sadler.

RAFE. Majesty.

KING HENRY. Whenever the Emperor wants a stick to beat me
with, he tells the world his aunt is dying of neglect, and cold.
Yet she has servants – she has firewood –

THOMAS. Then while I'm gone Rafe here will bring you the
day's agenda.

KING HENRY. Oh no – is there never any escape from your
long lists!

THOMAS. None, sir. If I gave you respite while I'm away,
you'd have me forever on the road.

KING HENRY. I can do nothing without you. Take care – the
roads are treacherous.

THOMAS. England needs better roads – and bridges that don't
collapse. We could give employment to men with no work –
get them out road-mending. It would solve two problems.

KING HENRY. But how would we pay for it?

THOMAS. With a tax on the rich. Rafe – show His Majesty
your figures.

RAFE *produces a bundle of papers.*

I have drawn up this schedule… (*Produces a document.*) We
could call it an income tax.

KING HENRY. Cromwell, I wish to go to bed now. Goodnight.
I shall pray for you.

As KING HENRY *goes* JANE SEYMOUR *enters.*

JANE SEYMOUR. Master Cromwell, when you see Queen
Katherine, tell her I pray for her.

She exits in the same direction as ANNE.

RAFE. Do you think the King has another woman?

THOMAS. What have you heard?

RAFE. Nothing. It's just the way she looks at him. As if…
She's so restless – so angry.

THOMAS. Her sister told me Anne thought every day would be
like her coronation day. Look, Rafe, I must go to the Queen-
that-was. While I'm away, make sure you work him hard. So
hard he'll be glad to see me when I get back. And the income
tax – (*Weighing things up*.) tell him he doesn't have to pay it.
The Crown's exempt.

Enter WESTON.

WESTON. You're to come with me to the King's chamber.

Scene Five

KING HENRY's *chamber*. KING HENRY *in nightgown and
dressing gown*.

KING HENRY. Not you, Weston. Out, boy – shut the door.

WESTON *goes*.

Cromwell, I need to… Dear God – where to begin? What if
I… What if I were to fear…

THOMAS. Majesty?

KING HENRY. What if I were to begin to suspect there's
some… flaw… in my marriage to Anne – some impediment
– something displeasing to Almighty God?

THOMAS. 'Impediment'? What could it be, sir?

KING HENRY. How can I know? Was she not pre-contracted to
Harry Percy?

THOMAS. He swore not –

KING HENRY. Ah, but you threatened him! You trailed him to
some low inn and pounded his head with your fist –

THOMAS. No, Majesty! I would never so misuse any peer – let
alone the Earl of Northumberland.

KING HENRY. Harry Percy said what he thought I wanted to hear – that there was nothing between him and Anne – no promise of marriage – let alone consummation. What if he lied?

THOMAS. On oath, sir? To the Archbishop of Canterbury? Before his King?

KING HENRY. You can be very frightening, you know, Thomas. Now… if she made a contract with Harry Percy it would amount to a marriage. She couldn't then be married to me – not lawfully – not in the sight of God –

THOMAS. But if –

KING HENRY. And I much suspect her with Sir Thomas Wyatt.

THOMAS. No, sir!

KING HENRY. You say 'no', but did not Wyatt run away to Italy because she would not favour him?

THOMAS. Yes – 'because she would not favour him'.

KING HENRY. What if she favoured him at other times? Women are weak – easily won by flattery – and when men write verses to them –

THOMAS. It would still be no lawful impediment to your marriage. Wyatt was married as a boy to Elizabeth Brooke. He was not free to promise Anne anything.

KING HENRY. It would be an impediment to my trust in her! Jesu! She shouldn't have said she came a virgin to my bed if she did not. I'll not have women lie to me… (*Paces*.) Since we left Wolf Hall I can't sleep – turning these doubts over and over in my mind… Do you know, there are those who say Wyatt writes better verses than I do – even though I am the King? (*Paces*.) Bishop Gardiner says if my marriage is not good, and I am forced to put away Anne, I must return to Katherine –

THOMAS. Stephen is wrong –

KING HENRY. I cannot do it, Thomas. Even if the whole of Christendom came against me – I could never again touch that stale old woman.

THOMAS. A King of England cannot be compelled in any matter. You're master of your own household, your own country, and your own Church. Stephen himself has said as much – in that book he's written for you: *Of True Obedience*.

KING HENRY. I must read it. Though I don't want him near me. I know, send him to France. Tell him not to hurry back.

THOMAS. Sir, if I am to ride north at first light –

KING HENRY. Go then... Godspeed.

THOMAS *leaves the chamber.* WOLSEY'S GHOST *is waiting for him.*

WOLSEY'S GHOST. If he wants a new wife, fix him one. I didn't, and I'm dead.

THOMAS. Are you? How can one tell?

ACT TWO

Scene Six

Kimbolton. Outside KATHERINE OF ARAGON*'s chamber.*

CHRISTOPHE. Be careful, master, the city wives say this Katherine put a curse on Anne Boleyn so she won't have a boy – or if she does it won't be Henry's.

THOMAS. Whose will it be then?

CHRISTOPHE. Anne cuckolds the King to pay him back – she means to put a bastard on his throne just to spite him – because he has other women. She chases him with a pair of shears shouting she'll geld him –

THOMAS. Londoners say anything –

CHRISTOPHE. The gentlemen of the Privy Chamber do her one after another – they stand in line frigging their members till she shouts 'Next!'

THOMAS. Then things must have slipped a bit since Queen Katherine's day.

THOMAS goes in to KATHERINE, *who is sick, sitting by a good fire, swaddled in an ermine cape.*

KATHERINE. Well, Cromwell – how am I looking? I've not seen myself in the mirror these many months. (*Laughs.*) The King once thought me beautiful – like an angel… How is his concubine? I hear she's always on her knees… Praying to her reformed God?

THOMAS. She's much admired by her scholars and bishops.

KATHERINE. True churchmen would shrink from her in horror. She prays for a son. She lost the last child – I know how that is… I pity her.

THOMAS. She has hopes of another.

KATHERINE. While Henry has hopes of another woman, I hear? The concubine will be looking at her ladies, wondering

'Is it you, madam? Or you – or you?' They say when she's
crossed she carps like a common scold. A queen must learn
to live and suffer under the world's eye. No woman is above
her but the Queen of Heaven. If she suffers, she must suffer
alone – and she needs a special grace to bear it. Boleyn's
daughter has not received that grace –

THOMAS. You're in pain –

KATHERINE. It's nothing… The King's gentlemen will swear
they'll lay down their lives for her – they once offered me
the same devotion – because I was the King's wife. It had
nothing – *nothing* – to do with my person. But *la Anna* takes
devotion as a tribute to her own charms. Foolishness…
(*Pause.*) I want to see my daughter before I die.

THOMAS. Were it in my power, madam, I…

KATHERINE. What harm can it do?

THOMAS. The King is advised that if he permits Mary to make
the journey, she might take ship for the territories of her
cousin the Emperor –

KATHERINE. And come riding back with a foreign husband at
her side, an Imperial army at her back, and chase him out of
his kingdom? You can assure Henry, our daughter has no
such intention. I will answer for her with my life.

THOMAS (*considers her*). You are dying, madam.

KATHERINE (*straight back, she knows*). I wish my death
might do him some good. Set Henry an example when the
time comes for his own.

THOMAS. Do you often think about the King's death?

KATHERINE. I think often about his afterlife. I pray for him.

THOMAS. So you work for the good of his soul? Why then do
you obstruct him? If you had entered a convent and allowed
him to remarry, he would never have broken with Rome.
Henry was a faithful son of the Church. You drove him to
this extremity. The Defender of the Faith threatened with
excommunication? You, not he, split Christendom. But I
expect you often think about that too? In the darkness –
silence of the night –

KATHERINE. You are... contemptible! (*A long look*.) A state such as mine usually buys kindness.

THOMAS. I wish to be kind but you'll not see it. Madam, put your own will aside for the sake of your daughter – reconcile with the King. If you leave this world at odds with him, blame will be visited on Mary. She is young – she has a life to live –

KATHERINE. I know the King. He'll not harm Princess Mary. You won't let him. (*Silence*.)

THOMAS. He might permit her to visit you. If you'd advise her to be conformable to his will – and recognise him – as now she does not – as Head of the Church –

KATHERINE. No! In that matter the Princess Mary must consult her own conscience... (*Studies him*.) Do not pity me, Cromwell. I have been preparing for death a long time.

THOMAS. Is Mary also ready to die?

KATHERINE. She has meditated upon Christ's Passion since she was an infant in the nursery. She'll be ready when He calls.

THOMAS. You are unnatural. What parent would risk her child's death?

KATHERINE. What mother would risk her daughter's soul?

THOMAS. For the love of God – advise Mary to obey the King!

KATHERINE. The *Princess* Mary. (*She is exhausted*.) I have often wondered, Master Cromwell... You know many languages – fluent in so many tongues – and you lie as fleetly in all of them. In what language do you confess?

THOMAS. God knows our hearts, madam. I may need forgiveness – I do not need absolution.

Scene Seven

Going to KING HENRY, EUSTACHE CHAPUYS *intercepts*
THOMAS.

THOMAS. Ambassador Chapuys!

CHAPUYS (*on the attack*). Cremuel, where have you been? I
am kept waiting here hour after hour, while the King's with
her, the woman. How much longer will they be?

THOMAS. All day. He's in love. You know how that is,
Eustache. Or do you?

CHAPUYS. Mother of God. My master the Emperor says, put
these letters into the King's own hand.

THOMAS *holds out his hand.*

Are you the King? Oh no! You think I am new to this game?

THOMAS. Come in, then. I'll introduce you to the Queen.

CHAPUYS. I cannot breathe the same air as the concubine! My
master will never forgive it. Are you trying to ruin me?

THOMAS. Ambassador. (*Walks away, smiling.*)

CHAPUYS. Cremuel! Come back! Come to supper.

THOMAS (*calling*). No – you come to me. The food's better.

He goes in. KING HENRY *and* ANNE *are at a table with*
BUILDERS *and* ARTISTS, *happily working together on
plans for another new palace.* ANNE *ignores him.*

(*To* KING HENRY.) Majesty. Katherine is sick. Her doctors
say she'll soon be in her grave –

ANNE. She'd come out of it – flapping in her shroud – if she
saw her chance to thwart me!

KING HENRY. Sweetheart –

ANNE. We should bring her bastard Mary here – make her,
on her knees, beg pardon for her treasonous obstinacy,
and acknowledge my daughter – *my* daughter – England's
only heir!

THOMAS. Building again, are we, sir?

KING HENRY (*guiltily*). See for yourself. (*Pushing plans across the table*.) I'm thinking of a new palace in the French manner –

ANNE. A deer park – fountains –

THOMAS. It would cost a great deal –

ANNE. Cost, expense – that's all Cromwell ever thinks about.

THOMAS. I need money for –

ANNE. For what?

THOMAS. Gunpowder – fortification along the south coast – for when the Emperor comes over.

ANNE. Pah! He won't come here if we make allies of the French.

THOMAS. Or if he hears we're fortifying our seaports, and laying in great supplies of gunpowder.

ANNE *sulks*.

KING HENRY. Sweetheart… (*Raises his eyes at* THOMAS.) Can Katherine die? What use is life to her now? Sure – she must be tired of contention. God knows I am! Better to join the saints and holy martyrs –

ANNE. She's kept them waiting long enough. (*False laugh*.)

KING HENRY. She's forever forgiving me. It is she who needs forgiveness. For her blighted womb.

THOMAS *bows out*. JANE ROCHFORD, MARY SHELTON, *and* ELIZABETH, LADY WORCESTER *are in playful mood and waiting for him*.

JANE ROCHFORD. Bishop Gardiner is furious.

THOMAS. Oh, that's old news –

JANE ROCHFORD. What have you done to him this time?

THOMAS. The King is sending him back to Paris as ambassador. Stephen will be away from Court for many months. Now tell me about Anne. Is she or isn't she?

JANE ROCHFORD. Ah! Has she said nothing?

THOMAS. I must know! Tell me plainly – is she with child? Lady Worcester – I'm sure you know?

JANE ROCHFORD. There you are, Beth. I told you you're his little favourite.

LADY WORCESTER. Some people would give a great deal for the information.

THOMAS. I'll give you...

LADY WORCESTER. What? What will you give me?

THOMAS. An almond tart.

LADY WORCESTER. Not enough.

THOMAS. Oh, very well... Two almond tarts. Will you tell me?

LADY WORCESTER (*takes his hand and whispers in his ear*). No.

THOMAS. Mary Shelton, then – be kind to me?

JANE ROCHFORD. Shelton knows. She's had to let out her bodices.

MARY SHELTON *dissolves in giggles*.

THOMAS. She's pregnant then?

MARY SHELTON. Mmmm.

THOMAS. Sure?

MARY SHELTON. That much. (*Holding her finger and thumb an inch apart*.)

LADY WORCESTER. Hardly unexpected – she was with the King most of the summer.

JANE ROCHFORD. And when she wasn't with the King she was with Harry Norris.

LADY WORCESTER. Shhhh! (*Laughs – gives her a dig to shut her up*.)

JANE ROCHFORD. What did I say? Only that when the King wasn't with her, Norris was. Carrying Henry's love letters. Where's the harm in that?

THOMAS (*laughing*). Lady Rochford, if somebody said to you, 'It's going to rain,' you'd turn it into a conspiracy.

He hurries away. RAFE *falls in with him.*

Scene Eight

THOMAS. Rafe, we need Edward Seymour – and his father –

RAFE. Something's happening. (*Exits.*)

THOMAS. Something's happening.

　　EDWARD *and* SIR JOHN *materialise around* THOMAS.

SIR JOHN. Where's my daughter – where's Jane?

THOMAS. Walking in the garden with the King.

SIR JOHN. But there's nothing to see in the garden? It's winter.

THOMAS. How shall I put this, Sir John? (*Hesitates.*) The King wants a new woman in his bed. He'll not touch Anne until she's given birth – he dare not.

EDWARD. This is Jane's chance, Father.

SIR JOHN. Well, if she's to start earning her keep at last… Good! I don't know what he can see in her. Why would any man want Jane in his bed? It would be like kissing a stone – the very thought numbs my parts with cold.

EDWARD. No one who calls himself a Christian should imagine his daughter or his sister in a man's embrace.

SIR JOHN. No indeed… Oho! Though they say George Boleyn –

EDWARD. Father! How best may this be managed?

THOMAS. Henry has made his choice. Now Jane must keep her distance. If Anne catches Henry looking at Jane I'm afraid her sufferings will increase –

SIR JOHN. Oh, it will be nothing – only a pinch or a slap – Jane knows how to bear herself patiently. Look what those two chits Mary and Anne did for the Boleyns! They were in trade, you know – look at them now – the father's Earl of Wiltshire – and all the jewels young George wears – he jangles as he walks. Henry had to make Anne Boleyn a Marquise before she let him have her.

EDWARD. And you know what he made her next, Father.

SIR JOHN. What? What did he make her?

EDWARD. He made her Queen.

> JANE SEYMOUR *enters suddenly*.

What has the King said to you, sister?

JANE SEYMOUR. He asked me to be his good mistress.

THOMAS. He said 'good mistress' not 'mistress'? You're sure?

SIR JOHN. Is there a difference?

THOMAS. 'Mistress' would have been a summons to his bed. 'Good mistress' means he's offering a chaste and prolonged courtship –

SIR JOHN. Not too prolonged or Anne will drop her litter and Jane will miss her chance.

JANE SEYMOUR. He asked me if I would look kindly on him.

EDWARD. 'Kindly'?

JANE SEYMOUR. For instance, if he wrote poems – praising my beauty – I said I wouldn't laugh at them – even behind my hand.

SIR JOHN. I don't understand –

JANE SEYMOUR. Nor find fault – even if he exaggerates. In poems it's usual to exaggerate.

THOMAS. If he sends you a jewel you must wear it.

JANE. Yes – I see.

THOMAS. If he sends you money –

JANE. I must give it to the poor.

THOMAS. No – send it back.

EDWARD. But if he attempts anything on your person, you must scream.

JANE SEYMOUR. What if nobody comes?

THOMAS. Don't scream, Jane. Pray aloud to the Blessed Virgin – something that will appeal to His Majesty's piety – and... er...

EDWARD. And put him in mind of every Christian man's need for restraint.

THOMAS (*grateful*). Thank you, Edward.

JANE SEYMOUR. Have you a prayer book on your person, Master Secretary? Father? No – I thought not.

EDWARD (*grimly*). Here's mine. (*Offering his prayer book.*)

JANE SEYMOUR. I'm sure I'll find something to put the fear of God in him. I thought, when you sent for me, Master Cromwell, I was to be married at last to your sweet son Gregory. Or to you.

THOMAS. I'm too old for you, Jane – I could be your father.

JANE SEYMOUR. Could you? I'd no idea. My mother's never mentioned it. Well, stranger things happen at Wolf Hall...

She goes.

Scene Nine

The Queen's chamber. JANE ROCHFORD *comes out.*

Funereal atmosphere. JANE ROCHFORD, *grave and serious, approaches, stops* THOMAS *at the door of* ANNE's *apartments.*

JANE ROCHFORD. Master Secretary. Something terrible has occurred. (*Crosses herself.*) There has been a death in the royal household.

THOMAS *crosses himself.*

A young life cut short –

THOMAS. God have mercy, who is it?

JANE ROCHFORD (*folds her hands in prayer*). Anne's little doggie. He fell out of a window. (*Yells with laughter – bunches her hands into paws and squeaks*.) Wait till you see her. She's cried her eyes to mean little slits. When she miscarried her child she never shed a tear?

He goes to ANNE.

ANNE. Cremuel? Out! Out! (*Dismisses her* LADIES *with angry, crow-scaring gestures*.) They found him… down there in the courtyard. The window was open above. (*Sobs*.) Who would do such a thing?

THOMAS. It was an accident. Surely.

ANNE. No! It was done to frighten me. (*Wipes away tears with her knuckles*.) There's bad news from Kimbolton.

THOMAS *offers a handkerchief*.

Katherine could linger on another six months. And the French never meant to make a marriage with Elizabeth. No! They offer a match for their Dauphin with Henry's Spanish bastard. It's as if I don't exist – as if my daughter had never been born – as if Katherine were still Queen. Well, I shall be revenged on Lady Mary.

THOMAS. What will you do?

ANNE. Marry her off – to someone of no consequence. Or disgrace her. You've handsome boys in your household, Cromwell. Loose them to her. Flatter her. The sad little wretch has never had a compliment in her life. She's eighteen now. She wants boys – to write her verses – to flutter their eyes at her – to sigh when she enters a room. (*Illustrates the sigh*.) How do I know this? Because I was once as foolish as any other girl. (*A hard, dry laugh*.)

THOMAS. The King will kill any man who goes near her.

ANNE. They've no need to bed her. Just make a fool of her – in public. I wish to destroy her pious reputation.

THOMAS. No. That is not my aim.

ANNE. *Your* aim?

THOMAS. Those are not my methods.

ANNE. You refuse me? You think you're grown so great you no longer need me? I know you're talking to the Seymours – Ha! You thought it a secret? I'll make you sorry. Nothing is secret from me – nothing! What does Jane Seymour have but her maidenhead? What use is a maidenhead the morning after? Queen of his Heart – then just another drab who can't keep her skirt down. She has neither looks nor wit – she won't hold Henry a week! (*Laughs.*)

THOMAS (*gentle and genuine*). Let me advise you. Keep yourself in quietness until your son is born. Strife and contention can mark a child even before it sees the light. You say Jane won't hold your husband a week? Then pretend you don't see her. Turn your head from sights that are not for you.

ANNE. And I advise you, Cremuel. Make terms with me before my son is born.

THOMAS (*wanting reconciliation*). Things were once happier between us, madam –

ANNE. Henry will never abandon me. He will not turn his back on the great and marvellous work I have done in this realm – my work for the Gospel. And he'll never again bend his knee to Rome. Since I was crowned I have made a new England – an England that cannot subsist without me.

THOMAS. If there is anything I can do for you, tell me, and I will do it. (*Studies her for a moment.*) But do not threaten me, madam. Do not threaten me.

ANNE (*reconciliation refused*). Those who are made can be unmade.

THOMAS. They can. I know it, madam. (*Bows and leaves.*)

Scene Ten

Christmas at Austin Friars. 'Pastime with Good Company.'

THOMAS. Rafe, make them sing something else.

RAFE. But it's the King's song, sir.

THOMAS. I know. Make them sing something else.

> RAFE *speaks to the band. A different song.* THOMAS *moves among his guests. Enter* CHAPUYS *very distressed.*

> That's a very jaunty hat, Eustache – it suits the festive season.

CHAPUYS. Queen Katherine is near her end. She can't even take water. In six nights she's not slept two hours together. (*Through tears.*) She cannot live, and I do not want her to die alone… The King will not let me go. Will you speak to him?

THOMAS. He's at Greenwich. (*Moved.*) Come on then.

Scene Eleven

Greenwich.

NORRIS. Ambassador Chapuys, Cromwell – a Merry Christmas to you. What brings you to Greenwich?

THOMAS. The Imperial Ambassador wishes to see His Majesty.

NORRIS. But… His Majesty is with the French Ambassador.

CHAPUYS. I'll wait.

NORRIS. Very well, I'll inform him you're here.

THOMAS. How is His Majesty?

NORRIS. Cheerful enough. Well… he was…

THOMAS. Unusual attire.

NORRIS. We are dressing for the masque. (*Exits.*)

CHAPUYS. Unctuous? Is that the word? Norris does oil around, does he not?

THOMAS. I remember the Cardinal kneeling in the mud to him. I can never wipe it from my mind.

NORFOLK enters with ANNE on his arm. She's angry that THOMAS is here – even angrier he's brought CHAPUYS, who refuses to acknowledge her as Queen, with him.

CHAPUYS (*pointedly ignoring ANNE*). My Lord Norfolk.

NORFOLK. Ambassador Chapuys.

CHAPUYS turns his back deliberately on ANNE who rushes out, angry, followed by NORFOLK. KING HENRY, with the FRENCH AMBASSADOR, enters. A black look at THOMAS.

KING HENRY. Ah! Merry Christmas, M'sieur Chapuys – you're very welcome. You know the French Ambassador?

The AMBASSADORS nod curtly to each other.

FRENCH AMBASSADOR. Majesty, farewell. King Francois will be highly gratified to hear that we have been able to bring matters to such a happy conclusion. He has knit his heart to yours. With the friendship of France, no power in Europe will threaten you, and my King will argue your case in Rome. Ambassador Chapuys. (*Curt nod. Exits.*)

CHAPUYS. Katherine, the Queen –

KING HENRY. The Dowager Princess of Wales? Yes, I hear the old woman's off her food.

NORRIS (*to THOMAS*). Will you excuse me? I have to dress up as a Moor.

KING HENRY. Now the Duke of Milan is dead, France and your master the Emperor both lay claim to his duchy – unless they can resolve it there'll be war. You know I've always been a friend to the Emperor, but the French are promising me castles, towns – a seaport even –

CHAPUYS (*snaps*). The French will give you nothing. Poor friends they have been to you these last months while you have been unable to feed your people! If it were not for the shipments of grain the Emperor permits, your people would be corpses piled from here to the Scots border.

A difficult moment – then KING HENRY *laughs.*

KING HENRY. Some exaggeration there – surely!

CHAPUYS. My mission will brook no delay. I beg permission
to ride to the… to where Katherine is. And I implore you to
allow her daughter to visit her. It will surely be for the last
time.

KING HENRY. I can't move Mary around without my
Council's advice. No hope of summoning them today. Icy
roads, you know. So how are you proposing to travel north?
Have you wings?

KING HENRY *winks at* THOMAS, *taking* CHAPUYS
apart, THOMAS *starts to follow.* KING HENRY *waves him
back.* NORRIS, *dressed as a Moor, intercepts him. A dragon
hurries past.*

THOMAS. Who's in that dragon?

NORRIS. Young Weston – he's going to waggle, waggle to the
Queen's apartments to beg for sweetmeats.

THOMAS. Are you jealous of Weston, Harry?

BRERETON *joins them.*

NORRIS. Ha! She'll fondle him and pat his little rump. She's
partial to puppies.

THOMAS. Who killed her little dog?

NORRIS. Don't say that – she goes on and on about it – she
won't accept it was an accident. But it was.

BRERETON. Has Weston gone to the Queen?

THOMAS. A fine leopard skin, William. Is it real? (*Lifts it up,
revealing* BRERETON'*s genitalia.*) Dear God, man –
you're naked!

BRERETON. It's the season of licence.

THOMAS. As long as Queen Anne is not treated to the sight of
your *attributi*.

NORRIS. He wouldn't be showing her anything she hasn't seen
already! (*Laughs.*)

THOMAS (*a chill descends*). What are you suggesting?

NORRIS. You... You know what I meant. I didn't mean William's – I meant the King's.

BRERETON. I do believe you're blushing, Norris.

NORRIS *puts his hand to his blacked-up face*.

NORRIS. Cromwell, you don't –

BRERETON. What's he doing here anyway? Shouldn't you be busy with the King's affairs? I've heard that when you bring him papers he doesn't like, he smacks you about the head. Just so you'll remember your place from time to time. I'll go slay my little dragon.

The DUKE OF SUFFOLK, *in tilting armour, drunk, heads for* KING HENRY. NORRIS *tries to stop him*.

SUFFOLK. Harry! Harry!

NORRIS. My Lord Suffolk, the King is not to be interrupted –

SUFFOLK. Ha! (*Pushing past*.) By God, Harry, you're quit of the old lady! Rejoice – she's coughing blood! So now you can rid yourself of the other one and get yourself a French girl! By God, they'll give us back Normandy as a dowry!

CHAPUYS *approaches*.

And you, Emperor's man – take yourself off!

KING HENRY (*white with fury*). Suffolk! My wife is carrying my son –

SUFFOLK. I know that, Harry – but you said you wanted rid –

THOMAS. My Lord! (*Dragging* SUFFOLK *away*.)

SUFFOLK. Think you know everything, Cromwell? Wrong! Harry makes plain his intentions only to his friends – to *me* –

THOMAS. You're mad if you think he'll turn Anne out – she's carrying his child –

SUFFOLK. He's mad if he thinks it's his!

THOMAS. Suffolk!

Damage limitation. THOMAS *shoves* SUFFOLK *away before he can say more.*

If you know anything against the Queen's honour… then, for God's sake, My Lord – come to me in confidence –

SUFFOLK. I spoke to Harry *in confidence* – I told him about her and Wyatt and he threw me out. Oh, piss off back to your counting house, Putney boy! Fetch in more money, that's what we keep you for! You're not fit to talk to princes –

He shoves THOMAS *back – makes for* KING HENRY *again.* CHAPUYS *steps between them.*

CHAPUYS. Majesty, I take my leave. The Emperor will find it a consolation to have news of his aunt's final hours from the hand of his own envoy.

KING HENRY. I can do no less. Ambassador Chapuys, godspeed.

CHAPUYS *and* THOMAS *return to the landing stage.*

THOMAS. I'm sorry you had to hear that.

CHAPUYS. When the Duke of Suffolk bawls in Greenwich, trees fall in Germany. For what it is worth, Putney boy, I believe you are fit to talk to princes and I would back you in any court this side of Heaven. If I wanted an advocate to argue for my life, I'd give you the brief.

THOMAS. Eustache… You dazzle me. You know… when Katherine dies it will clear the way for an alliance with your master. A lasting peace is what you and I have always worked for. Katherine has come between us.

CHAPUYS. What of this French marriage?

THOMAS. That will never happen.

CHAPUYS. Here. Will you look after my hat? Where I'm going it will hardly be thought… suitable.

THOMAS. Godspeed, my friend. (*Takes the hat.*)

CHAPUYS. Pray to Our Lady I'll be in time…

CHAPUYS *is rowed away.*

Scene Twelve

Darkness. Then a flame. Darkness. More flames. A scream –
chatter of women – confused noise. The flames take hold. Panic.
A naked young man – we mustn't know who – beats out the
flames with a pillow. Semi-naked female and male figures –
some in nightshirts, some hiding their nakedness with whatever
comes to hand – sheets, prayer books, etc., come and go
confusedly. Smoke. KING HENRY *is heard in the darkness*
getting more and more agitated: 'What's happening – where's
my wife – bring me some lights – who's there – where are my
people?', etc. Voices trying to calm him. Noise increases. Light
increases. WESTON *and* MARY SHELTON *come out – then*
THOMAS *with* LADY WORCESTER. *People distance*
themselves guiltily from each other. NORRIS *brings on* ANNE,
who is heavily pregnant. LADIES *wrap her up as it's winter*
and cold. As much confusion as possible – Who was where?
Who saw what? Who knows what happened?

ANNE. Who has my gown? Is the fire out? It was a candle…
   Don't let them wake my husband –

JANE ROCHFORD. Too late!

KING HENRY (*bellowing, off*). Nan! Nan – where is she?

JANE ROCHFORD. It was nothing – who overturned the
   candle? Who was –

   KING HENRY *charges in, very emotional.*

KING HENRY. Nan – Nan! Are you hurt? Is my child
   unharmed? Oh, Nan!

   In tears. He falls to his knees – holds her – resting his head
   against her pregnant belly.

ANNE. My Lord –

KING HENRY. My son! Oh, my son, my son! –

ANNE. The boy is unharmed –

KING HENRY. Oh –

ANNE. Our Prince is safe – *I* am unharmed –

THOMAS. Bring her some wine. Who's there? Give her air –
   let her breathe –

NORRIS *glares at* MARY SHELTON. WESTON, *nakedly brazen, finds it all hilarious.* LADY WORCESTER *is trying to look as if she's not there.*

KING HENRY. Who was with you? Which of your ladies –

ANNE. My Lord –

KING HENRY. Which ladies are in attendance today? Whose office is it to wait upon the Queen?

MARK, *almost naked, hurries across the stage.*

ANNE (*to* KING HENRY, *in an attempt to distract him*). My Lord – help me up – let me get up –

KING HENRY *goes to her, but* NORRIS *is quicker. He slides behind her and lifts her up. Very gently. This poor man adores her. Will* KING HENRY *notice?* KING HENRY *eyeballs him.*

KING HENRY. Oh, Nan – I should have been with you. Norris – Harry – dear friend – do I owe you my son's life?

NORRIS. There was no danger – an unattended candle –

KING HENRY. Unattended by whom?

JANE ROCHFORD. She needs to lie down. Mary Shelton – wake up! Make up my bed for the Queen – I'll stay with her –

KING HENRY. Why was she alone?!

WESTON (*downstage. Aside*). She wasn't!

MARY SHELTON. Shhh – (*Exits.*)

Enter GEORGE *in his nightshirt looking shifty.*

GEORGE. Sister!

ANNE. Where did you go? Where were you?

NORRIS (*to* GEORGE). There was no danger –

KING HENRY. Thank God –

ANNE. One corner of the tapestry caught fire – that's all – My Lord, go back to your chamber –

KING HENRY. No – I'll see for myself. Come with me.
Brereton. (*Starts to exit*.)

ANNE (*glaring at* WESTON). Francis, were you with Shelton?

KING HENRY. Nan!

KING HENRY *and* ANNE *exit together.*

NORRIS. This is not the time – nor the place. But you'll hear
from me, boy!

WESTON. Not the place – surely! The King told us you were at
Hampton Court. Who can have lured you back so suddenly?

NORRIS. Boy!

WESTON (*laughing, flashes at him*). Hardly! (*Exits, chased by*
NORRIS.)

JANE ROCHFORD. I could have been burned up too, husband.
Would you have rushed to save me?

GEORGE. Jesus! I'd have brought more logs. (*Exits*.)

JANE ROCHFORD, *exiting after* GEORGE, *stops as*
THOMAS *comes in, dressing.*

THOMAS. Beth – where's –

LADY WORCESTER *runs to him with his hat.*

LADY WORCESTER. And where did you go? Here. (*Putting
his hat on straight*.) There. (*Kisses him*.) Now anyone would
think you'd been in bed with a couple of your account
books!

They realise JANE ROCHFORD *is watching them.*

JANE ROCHFORD. Lady Worcester?

LADY WORCESTER. Not the place – not the time… (*Hurries
off*.)

JANE ROCHFORD. Not like you to be caught in the wrong
bed, Cromwell. Her husband's a dangerous man they say.

THOMAS. Goodnight, Lady Rochford.

JANE ROCHFORD (*smirking*). Goodnight, Master Secretary.

ACT THREE

Scene Thirteen

Solemn music. MONKS. *An effigy of* KATHERINE'*s body on a bier carried to Peterborough – turns into preparations for a tournament. Music becomes celebratory –* KING HENRY *holding baby Elizabeth,* ANNE *very pregnant.*

Enter, armed: NORRIS, BRERETON, WESTON – *then* GREGORY, THOMAS WYATT, EDWARD, *others. Heraldry. Exeunt Royal Party.*

WYATT. Everyone expected the King to bring Katherine's body to St Paul's. Now they're saying she's to be laid to rest in Peterborough.

THOMAS. Well… Peterborough is as good a place as any. If you're dead.

NORFOLK. Damned if I'll go to Peterborough. Is anybody organising anything?

THOMAS. The King's been fully occupied planning this tournament. Gregory's in a sweat of preparation about it – my house has been full of armourers and horse dealers for weeks.

RAFE. The bills are coming in thick and fast.

GREGORY (*who is still putting on his armour*). Father, I hope I'm not drawn against the King. Suppose I unhorse him? Imagine if he came down? And to a novice like me –

NORFOLK. I wouldn't worry, lad. Henry was jousting before you could walk.

GREGORY. That's just it – he's not as quick as he was.

NORFOLK. Then get yourself drawn on the King's team from the start. That avoids the problem. (*Exits.*)

GREGORY. How do I do that?

THOMAS (*wondering at his innocence*). I'll have a word.

GREGORY. No! How would that stand with my honour? Some things I must do for myself.

THOMAS. As you please.

GREGORY *goes*.

Clank away – my tender son.

RAFE. You've no need to worry.

THOMAS *goes to* KING HENRY*'s tent. He is arming.*

KING HENRY. Cromwell, how much does the lordship of Ripon bring in?

THOMAS. To the Archbishop of York? A little over two hundred and sixty pounds, sir.

KING HENRY. Do you speak Turkish?

THOMAS. No, sir.

KING HENRY. Oh? Why don't you?

THOMAS. I was never in those parts. Majesty, if you run against my son Gregory, will you forbear to unhorse him? If you can help it?

KING HENRY. Once you are thundering down at a man, you cannot check. It's quite a rare event, you know, to bring your opponent down. Don't be concerned about Gregory – he's very able. Or is it me you're worrying about? I know you Councillors think I should retire to the spectators' bench – and I will, I promise. A man my age is past his best. (*Laughs.*) You've turned your boy out beautifully – no nobleman could do more. He's a credit to your house. Put that on the table there. (*Handing him an ornamental dagger.*) I have it in mind to promote Edward Seymour into my Privy Chamber. (*Looking across at* EDWARD.)

THOMAS. A good man, I think. Serviceable.

KING HENRY. And I shall have your boy Rafe Sadler among my grooms. He's a gentleman born, and a pleasant young man to have near me. It would help you, Cromwell, would it not?

THOMAS. It would, sir.

KING HENRY. And I shall do something for Jane. She has no guile in her – and she has nothing… She asks nothing… (*Wipes away a tear.*) I've written her this letter. I'll send a purse with it, for she'll need money now the Queen has removed her from her chamber.

THOMAS. Delicately expressed, sir. She's very innocent.

KING HENRY. Give it back. I'm still working on it. Coming to watch me joust?

THOMAS. Alas! The Emperor's fleet is set for Algiers, and the Abbot of Fountains Abbey, who keeps six whores, has been plundering his own treasury – all matters that need my attention –

Enter SUFFOLK *in armour – behaving as usual like* KING HENRY'*s big brother.*

SUFFOLK. Hurry up, Harry – everybody's waiting.

KING HENRY. I know – it's this new armour. Feels tighter than at the last fitting –

SUFFOLK. It's not the armour that's tighter, Harry, it's you that's –

KING HENRY. Yes, yes! (*Starts to go.*) Six whores? Did you say six? Jesu! How do you think he manages it?

The tournament – soundscape. Then an ominous note. RAFE *appears, not knowing how to begin.*

THOMAS. Rafe? (*Wrapping his fur robe around him – expecting a blow.*) Is it Gregory?

RAFE. Gregory is unhurt.

WYATT *arrives.*

THOMAS. Why the silence?

WYATT. It's the King… King Henry is dead.

GREGORY *arrives, with* CHRISTOPHE.

THOMAS. Ah. (*Draws the ornamental dagger.*)

Scene Fourteen

Confusion – panic – shock – noise. Frantic COURTIERS.
KING HENRY*'s corpse on a makeshift bier.* NORRIS *kneeling,*
weeping, and praying to Our Lady.

THOMAS. Where were his surgeons? (*Aside to* RAFE.) Rafe –
we have to keep this hidden. (*Examines* KING HENRY.)
Still warm.

NORFOLK *arrives.* RAFE *goes.*

NORFOLK. By God, Cromwell!

THOMAS (*under his breath*). Christ Jesus! Norfolk –

NORFOLK. Laying hands on… Off – off!

Shoves THOMAS, *who just shrugs him off.*

WYATT. My Lord Norfolk – he is beyond help –

THOMAS. Norfolk – MY LORD NORFOLK! My Lord – who
is with the Queen?

NORFOLK (*rambling*). I told her – I'm her uncle, God damn it
– who else should do it? She's fallen into a fit. God – God!
Who governs now for her unborn son?

WYATT. God help us – Anne will be Regent –

NORFOLK. Never! No big-bellied woman can rule! It must be
me, me, me!

RAFE *brings* SUFFOLK – *in despair – he's lost his 'young*
brother'.

THOMAS. We have to get Princess Mary –

SUFFOLK. Her keepers are the Boleyns. They'll never yield
her. Dear God, Harry! What have you done to us!

THOMAS. If news gets up country before we do, we'll never
see Mary alive –

SUFFOLK. The bitch will have her head –

NORFOLK *tries to pull* THOMAS *away. Reliquaries*
rattling.

NORFOLK. Cromwell, take your hands of His Majesty's
sacred person –

THOMAS *bats him away* – KING HENRY *takes a faint
breath* – THOMAS *puts a hand on* KING HENRY*'s chest.*

THOMAS. Wait! (*Slaps down his other hand on* KING
HENRY*'s chest.*)

NORFOLK. God's blood and nails!

SUFFOLK. Harry, Harry! Now God be thanked –

THOMAS. Fetch Dr Butts – fetch any man with skill. If he dies
again they'll not be blamed – my word on that. Air! Let the
King have air!

KING HENRY *takes a deep sucking breath that might turn
into a death rattle. Then tries to sit up.*

Majesty?

GREGORY *goes to* KING HENRY *to help him sit up.*

SUFFOLK. Don't touch him! Lay him down! Let him lie down!

GREGORY, *ignoring them, lifts* KING HENRY *into a
sitting position.*

KING HENRY. Cromwell? Where's Cromwell?

THOMAS. Majesty.

KING HENRY. I hit the earth and smelled it – damp like the
grave. I heard voices – very distant. I couldn't make out the
words – I felt myself borne through the air. I did not see God
or His angels.

THOMAS. You must be disappointed to see only Thomas
Cromwell.

KING HENRY. Never was sight more welcome! Clear
everybody out of here.

RAFE, SUFFOLK *and* GREGORY *clear the tent.*

Help me up. I must show myself – let nobody rumour it I am
mauled or dead.

ANNE *approaches nervously, frail, supported by* JANE
ROCHFORD, SIR THOMAS BOLEYN *and* GEORGE.

ANNE. My Lord. I pray, all England prays, you'll never joust again.

> KING HENRY *beckons her to come close. He stares into her face.*

KING HENRY. May as well geld me while you're at it. That'd suit you, would it not?

> *Shock.* BOLEYNS *whisk* ANNE *away.* SUFFOLK *and* GREGORY *help* KING HENRY *out. Cheers.* THOMAS, RAFE *and* CHRISTOPHE *remain.*

THOMAS. My first thought was 'Thank God it's not Gregory.' Then I thought – with Henry gone, if I stay I'm a dead man. With Anne as Regent; she'll kill me. If they make Mary Queen, her people will kill me too.

RAFE. There'd have been civil war.

> SUFFOLK *returns.*

THOMAS. This incident never happened, Your Grace. Or if it did it was of no importance.

SUFFOLK. I know how to keep my mouth shut, Cromwell – do you think I'm stupid or something? (*Exits.*)

> THOMAS *and* RAFE *share a smile at* SUFFOLK*'s expense.* RAFE *opens his folio, ready for a bit of team-writing.*

THOMAS. The King came down –

RAFE. His horse came down?

THOMAS. He hit his head – was stunned –

RAFE. Dazed –

THOMAS. Dazed for ten – no, five minutes – and is now perfectly restored to full health…

RAFE. *Mens sana in corpore sano?*

THOMAS. Yes – why not? (*Working hard to make this disaster a triumph of public relations.*) I think… it may have done him good.

RAFE (*catching on*). Sharpened him up. (*Scribbling.*) *Deo gratias!* (*Closes his file.*)

THOMAS. That should do it. Get that out first thing tomorrow
– to the ambassadors.

RAFE. I'll get it to them tonight.

Scene Fifteen

Fateful music. Gloom. Court.

JANE ROCHFORD. On the day of Queen Katherine's burial, I
was with Anne when she broke off her merriment at the
thought of Katherine going under the ground. I was with her
when she put down her book – when Mark Smeaton put down
his lute. I watched her face turn white – like wax. We swept
her to her chamber and bolted the door. It was a boy,
Cromwell. She had carried it less than four months, as we
judge. Conceived early October then.

THOMAS. On our summer progress.

JANE ROCHFORD. Who was she with when her child was
conceived? Consult your itinerary. Was she with the King?
Or was Harry Norris with her – or some other gentleman?
Who was here and who was there –

THOMAS. Lady Rochford –

JANE ROCHFORD. Another child lost – another chance missed.

THOMAS *goes in to* KING HENRY. THOMAS
CRANMER *is with him.*

KING HENRY. This is the second boy she's lost. I am run ragged
by the dead. Though who knows how many other of my sons
have bled away? Women keep silence until their bellies show.
What does God want of me, Cranmer? What more can I do to
please Him? I see He'll never give me male children.

CRANMER. We much misconstrue our Creator if we blame
Him for every accident of fallen nature.

KING HENRY. Oh? I thought he regarded every sparrow that
falls? Why then has he so little regard for England? (*Sulks.*)
Anne blames Norfolk – who burst in on her shouting I was

dead. She blames me because she says I am mooning over Seymour's daughter – because from time to time I send Jane sweetmeats from my table – but I said to her – to Anne my wife – 'Just be clear on this, madam, if any woman is to blame, it is you. I'll speak to you when you are better – when you are restored to health – As I fear *I* shall never be…' She says she will quickly give me another son now Katherine's dead – though I can't see how that will speed the business. If a king cannot have a son, it's no matter what else he can do. The triumphs, the spoils of victory, the just laws he makes, and the famous courts he holds… all these are as nothing… And my leg hurts. My fall opened an old wound – the ulcer will not mend. Without an heir, the country will fall into doubt, confusion, faction and conspiracy. When I think what I did for this Queen – how I raised her from a gentleman's daughter. I can't imagine why I did so. It seems to me… I was somehow dishonestly led into this marriage.

CRANMER. How dishonestly?

KING HENRY. I was not in my clear mind. It's clear enough now.

CRANMER. Your mind cannot be clear. You've suffered a great loss.

KING HENRY. I believe I was seduced – practised upon by charms and spells. And if it were so the marriage would be unlawful, would it not?

CRANMER. Sir, sir… Majesty –

KING HENRY. Oh, peace! Give you goodnight. For I supposed even this day must end.

THOMAS *and* CRANMER *come out of* KING HENRY's *chamber.*

CRANMER. Charms and spells. He was speaking figuratively, surely?

THOMAS. A man in pain will say anything.

CRANMER. We should not take any notice.

THOMAS. No.

CRANMER. No. (*Goes.*)

WOLSEY'S GHOST (*ambling on*). If I were you, I'd take
notice… Oho – here they come! Tread carefully, Tom.

NORFOLK *and* SUFFOLK, *who have been lying in wait,
draw* THOMAS *aside*.

NORFOLK. Cromwell. We want rid of her.

THOMAS. 'We'?

SUFFOLK. Harry wants rid of her – we know you want it too.

NORFOLK. The old Queen's people are with us – they want
Mary next in line – they'll not stand by and see her
insulted –

SUFFOLK. Nobody outside this realm accepts Anne Boleyn
as Queen –

NORFOLK. Not even the French –

SUFFOLK. She has her foot on our necks. Yet she's not done
her duty – there's no son –

NORFOLK. She's no wife to him –

SUFFOLK. The common people say she witched him into it –

NORFOLK (*crossing himself*). I can believe it – it's why God
took the child.

THOMAS. Oh, you know the King – one day they fall out, the
next he can't do enough for her –

NORFOLK. She's failed.

SUFFOLK. Harry hates failure – you should know that.

WOLSEY'S GHOST. Listen to the Duke, Tom.

THOMAS (*laughs*). *Interdum stultus bene loquitur.*

NORFOLK. What – what's that!

THOMAS. Nothing – just a Latin tag of the Cardinal's.

WOLSEY'S GHOST. 'Sometimes even a fool talks sense.'

SUFFOLK. What?

THOMAS. The Boleyns are a force to be reckoned with –

NORFOLK. Thomas Boleyn? I'll put him in terror of his life –

SUFFOLK. And the son's a wilting violet –

THOMAS. And what about me? What do I get?

NORFOLK. You get your treaty with the Emperor – no more threat of his troops burning and raping their way down Cheapside and Whitehall as they did in Rome – think of the money you'll save.

THOMAS. That's what England gets. It's time I had something out of this too. I need a seat in the House of Lords.

NORFOLK. I'll see you hanged!

THOMAS. No – Norfolk, I'll see you hanged first. You think I couldn't do it?

NORFOLK. You want to bully the Lords as you bully the Commons –

THOMAS. Yes – yes! That's exactly what I want.

SUFFOLK. Jesus – that's plain enough.

NORFOLK. Hmmm. (*More of a politician than we thought him*.) Nothing higher than a barony.

THOMAS. That will do for now.

NORFOLK (*grim. Spitting on his hand*). Agreed.

SUFFOLK (*not spitting*). Baron Putney Boy then.

Handshakes all round.

Interval.

Scene Sixteen

Whitehall. The Court. Cheerful music. THOMAS *and*
CHAPUYS. CHAPUYS *moves away – talks to* SUFFOLK.
JANE SEYMOUR *timidly takes* THOMAS *aside.*

JANE SEYMOUR. Here's my difficulty… (*Pause.*) The more
the King says, 'Jane, I am your humble suitor,' the less
humble he seems. I mean – he's *the King*, isn't he? I'm
thinking what if he stops talking and I have to say
something? I'm like a scalded cat. Have you ever seen a
scalded cat, Master Secretary? – I haven't. But if I'm so
frightened of him now… What must it be like to see him
every day? You see him most days. Still…

THOMAS. Not the same.

JANE SEYMOUR. What does he like to talk about?

THOMAS. Well… We speak mostly of State affairs… Horses?
He likes to know about trades and crafts – simple things. In
my youth I shoed horses – he likes to hear about smithing –
the right shoe for the job, so he can confound his own smiths
with secret knowledge.

JANE SEYMOUR. 'The right shoe for the job'? Anything else?

THOMAS. Dogs – hunting dogs, their breeding and virtues.
Fortresses!

JANE SEYMOUR. Dear God!

THOMAS. Artillery – iron foundries… We sometimes say we'll
have a day out – ride down to Kent together – to the Weald –
to visit the iron masters – discover new ways of casting
cannon…

JANE SEYMOUR. Well, that's that then. I couldn't cast a
cannon to save my life. He sent me a purse of money.

THOMAS. What did you do with it?

JANE SEYMOUR. What you told me. I sent it back.

THOMAS. You mustn't give in to him.

JANE SEYMOUR. Why would I?

THOMAS. You might be seduced by his honeyed words.

JANE SEYMOUR. His *what*!

> *She goes to* EDWARD. CHAPUYS *comes forward.*

CHAPUYS. The Emperor wants Anne Boleyn gone, and Mary back in the line of succession. Then you'll get your treaty, and there'll be peace in Europe.

THOMAS. I have influence, but I cannot speak for the King. No man can.

> CHAPUYS *moves away – talks to* SUFFOLK. KING HENRY *takes* THOMAS *aside.*

KING HENRY. Jane returned my letter and my purse, but with very tender words – I'm told she pressed her lips to my seal. I was wrong to send it. You have spoken to me of her innocence and her virtue – with good reason, it appears. I would do nothing to offend her honour.

THOMAS. Now that Edward Seymour there is of your Privy Chamber – if he were to bring his wife to Court, Your Majesty could take supper with the family without any affront to Jane's modesty. Perhaps Edward should have a suite in the palace?

KING HENRY. He should. (*Beams.*) Good man, young Edward – grave and serious. (*Smiles at him.*) I'm sure you'll turn him into a useful one.

THOMAS. Yes, Majesty – I believe I can work with Edward.

> KING HENRY *goes to* JANE SEYMOUR. THOMAS *moves away to* EDWARD.

EDWARD. He talks to her quite openly now.

THOMAS. But as long as the King stands by Anne, I must too.

EDWARD. You've no interests of your own?

THOMAS. I represent the King's interests. It's what I am for. Don't raise your hopes, Edward – not yet.

> *A commotion.*

KING HENRY. Do not presume to know my mind! Who told you I acknowledge the Emperor's claim to Milan? King Francis has as good a claim – or better! Do you take me for a

fool? Am I his lapdog? 'Come to Charles! Come to your kind
master!' First he whips me, then he pets me, then it is the whip
again. (*Shoves aside* CHAPUYS *with his fist. The effect of his
exit is lessened by his limp.*) I'm no dog – I am no child!

Roar of conversation. BOLEYNS *smirk.* CHAPUYS *hurries
to* THOMAS, *others gather.*

CHAPUYS. He attacked me! Says he'll send soldiers to fight
for France – Ha! Where are these troops? Pooh! I have eyes
– I see no soldiers – he has no army –

NORFOLK. Peace, Amabassador. Let the King cool down.

THOMAS. Hold back your dispatches to the Emperor – do not
write tonight.

NORFOLK. In Council tomorrow all will be put right – is that
not so, Master Secretary?

THOMAS. Oh, I'm sure. Ambassador – here's an opportunity
for you to meet Edward Seymour –

EDWARD. Ambassador Chapuys –

KING HENRY. Cromwell! (*Charging back.*) Make him
understand. It's not for the Emperor to make conditions to
me. How dare he threaten me with war!

CHAPUYS. I? I threaten *you*? –

KING HENRY. What were you saying to him? 'Oh, I'm sure of
King Henry – I keep him in my pocket' – don't deny it – I
heard you, Cromwell! Would you train me up like one of
your boys at Austin Friars? Touch my cap when I come
down in the morning, walk half a pace behind you with your
inkhorn and your seal. And why not a crown, eh, carried
behind you in a leather bag? You think yourself the King,
and me the blacksmith's boy!

THOMAS *raises his palms and crosses his wrists.* KING
HENRY *backs off, confused.*

THOMAS. God preserve Your Majesty.

KING HENRY *goes.*

CHAPUYS. Mother of God! I thought you were going to forget
yourself and hit him.

THOMAS (*smiles*). I never forget myself.

> THOMAS *is alone. Out of the darkness, the Council gathers around him – we blend into Scene Seventeen.*

Scene Seventeen

Council assembles. Next morning. As many as possible – a few BISHOPS. *Not* STEPHEN.

BOLEYN. Can we come to order?

NORFOLK (*to* THOMAS). All right, lad? It's what he does, you know? You're balanced just so, then he blows the pavement from under your feet. Who's chairing this Council?

BOLEYN. I am. (*Sits in the chair as if it's the throne, smirking.*)

SUFFOLK (*aside-ish*). God help us.

BOLEYN. His Majesty has charged me with…

> KING HENRY *arrives – a great sulky baby, meeting nobody's eye.* BOLEYN *leaps from the throne as if it's red hot and* KING HENRY *sits.*

KING HENRY. Get on with it.

> *Fraught pause – they all look at* THOMAS *who stares into the middle distance. Panic. Then all except* THOMAS *talk at once:* 'Majesty. If it please you. Would Your Majesty graciously please. The business is…' *etc.*

Sweet Jesu! Bleat, bleat, bleat! Is this my Council or the farmyard?

BOLEYN. If it please you, Majesty, for the good of the commonweal, look favourably on the Emperor's –

KING HENRY. For the good of the commonweal, I must receive Chapuys, continue our negotiations, and swallow any personal insults I receive.

NORFOLK. Like a draught of medicine, Henry. Bitter – but, for the sake of England, don't spit.

KING HENRY. Next?

SUFFOLK. We should discuss the marriage of the Lady Mary.

KING HENRY. Oh? Why?

BOLEYN. Her doctors say congress with a man would be good
for her health. If a young woman's vital spirits are bottled,
her appetites wane and she begins to waste. Marriage will
cure her.

SUFFOLK. Is marriage the only cure?

BOLEYN. That, or strenuous exercise on horseback.

SUFFOLK. Difficult for somebody under house arrest.

KING HENRY. The Emperor wants my daughter married to one
of his relatives. That will not occur. Mary will not go out of
this realm. She'll go nowhere while her behaviour to me is
not what it ought to be.

THOMAS. Her mother's death is raw with her. No doubt she
will see her duty over these next weeks.

BOLEYN. Ah! Finally we hear from Cromwell. You usually
speak first, last, and in the middle – so we, more modest
Councillors, are obliged to speak *sotto voce*, or not at all.
Does your reticence relate in any way to the check His
Majesty gave you?

KING HENRY (*icily*). Thank you for that, Boleyn.

NORFOLK. If Mary refuses to swear loyalty to the King and his
daughter Elizabeth, I'd plant her hand on the Gospel and beat
her head against the wall till it were as soft as a baked apple.

KING HENRY. And thank you, Lord Norfolk. I'm sure you
would. We have not so many children that we can well afford
to lose one. In time she will, I hope, be a good daughter to me.
(*Stands suddenly.*) Master Secretary, walk along with me...

THOMAS *follows*.

You know... I wish we could go down to the Weald one day,
to talk to the ironmasters.

THOMAS *waits*.

I've had drawings made – mathematical drawings, and taken advice as to how our ordnance can be improved, but – to be truthful – I can't make as much of it as you would.

THOMAS *waits respectfully.*

One must study the process from the beginning, I think – whether it's making ordnance, or armour. (*Pause.*) I've never been too proud to sit down for an hour with the gauntlet maker who armours my right hand. We must study, I think, every pin – every rivet.

Still nothing.

And… And so… as you are my right hand, sir…

THOMAS *nods, sympathetically.*

So, to Kent – to the Weald – will we go?

THOMAS (*smiling*). Not this summer, sir. No. You will be employed otherwise. Besides, the ironmasters need their holiday. They must lie in the sun. They must pick their apples.

KING HENRY (*mild, beseeching*). Give me a happy summer. I cannot live as I have lived, Thomas. Get me Jane. Deliver me from this bitterness and gall. (*Pause.*)

THOMAS. An annulment, Majesty?

KING HENRY. Yes… An annulment.

THOMAS. I shall consult the canon lawyers. I shall speak to Archbishop Cranmer. What reasons shall we cite?

KING HENRY. If the pre-contract with Harry Percy won't run… you know that I was… before I was with the Queen, I was, on occasion, with her sister Mary, who gave me a…

THOMAS. Yes, Majesty – I remember Mary Boleyn.

KING HENRY. Do what you have to do. I will back you. But be very secret. I don't want…

Exit KING HENRY.

THOMAS. You don't want history to make a liar of you.

Enter EDWARD.

Before your Council you had me state you had never had to do with Mary Boleyn – while you sat there and just nodded. You removed all impediments – Mary Boleyn – Harry Percy – you just swept them aside. Now times have changed – our requirements have changed – and the facts must change behind us. Edward, get your sister out of here – send her back to Wolf Hall. We're going to try for an annulment. I don't know yet on what grounds.

EDWARD. We'll be placing ourselves in great danger. If the Boleyns come down – they'll fight – they may take us with them. The Queen must not suspect –

THOMAS. Well, we can't keep it from her for ever – can we? If there's going to be a fight I'll not run from it.

EDWARD. What if you lose?

THOMAS. Oh, it wouldn't be so bad. They'll only cut off my head.

EDWARD. If you're lucky.

THOMAS. There's something I must do, Edward. Come with me.

Scene Eighteen

Country scene – birdsong.

CHRISTOPHE. So where are we? I've never been here.

THOMAS. Drink in all that wonderful country air, Christophe! This is Stoke Newington. If I can persuade Harry Percy to consider his best interests, the King's difficulties may be over.

THOMAS *and* RAFE – *who is now very much a gentleman – go in to* HARRY PERCY, *who is ill.*

My Lord, you're looking very sick. I hope it's not because I've come to visit you?

HARRY PERCY. No, Cromwell – it's my liver.

THOMAS. I stand before you a poor suitor. You'd never guess my errand.

HARRY PERCY. Oh, I believe I would.

THOMAS. I put it to you, My Lord – you are married to Anne Boleyn.

HARRY PERCY. I'm not.

THOMAS. I put it to you that in or about the year 1523, you made a secret contract of marriage with her, and therefore her so-called marriage with the King is null.

HARRY PERCY. Cromwell, you dragged me before the Council and made me swear on the Bible I'd had no contract with Anne. You saw me – you heard me. How can I take it back?

THOMAS. On that occasion you'd been drinking heavily – I put it to you that your memory failed you.

HARRY PERCY. I did marry Anne but had forgotten it?

THOMAS. You were always a drinker, My Lord – drink has reduced you to your present condition. When you swore your oath –

HARRY PERCY. Before the Council – to the King and the Archbishop of Canterbury –

THOMAS. Yes, on that occasion you were confused – still drunk.

HARRY PERCY. Never more sober.

THOMAS. You weren't paying attention to the questions put to you.

HARRY PERCY. Never more attentive.

THOMAS. Archbishop Warham was old and infirm – perhaps there was some defect in the form of the oath he administered.

HARRY PERCY. He was old – he was infirm – but he was competent.

THOMAS. But if there were some defect in the procedure…

RAFE. How do you know, for example, that the book was, in fact, a Bible?

HARRY PERCY. It looked like a Bible.

THOMAS. I've a book on accountancy that looks like a Bible. It's often mistaken for one.

HARRY PERCY. Especially by you. I swore on the Bible – then the King made me swear again on the Sacred Host – the very body of Christ. I'll not take back such an oath.

RAFE. Don't you want to help Anne?

HARRY PERCY. How can it help her?

EDWARD. If she's married to you, she was never married to Henry. That makes her daughter Elizabeth a bastard. And it clears the way to the throne for the children of the King's new marriage.

THOMAS. If Henry is sure Anne can lawfully be set aside, he'll treat her kindly. Convents can be comfortable…

HARRY PERCY. No.

THOMAS. You won't help her?

HARRY PERCY. I can't. On peril of my soul, I can't perjure myself. Not again… What's Anne Boleyn to me? She is a stranger now. Wolsey was right. Love has run its course.

THOMAS. You're heartless.

HARRY PERCY. I'm dying.

THOMAS. Listen. If the King were to offer –

HARRY PERCY. What? Rewards, honours, favours? Can he add years to my life? Too late, Cromwell. See yourself out.

THOMAS *and* RAFE *leave*.

RAFE. Well… We'll just have to find some other way.

THOMAS. I think we must let the Boleyns direct this. Open a space for them.

RAFE. Let them ruin themselves?

THOMAS. If I can just set the mill wheels turning –

RAFE. They might fall into the machinery? I don't like it. Suppose you start the process and the King changes his mind? Suppose Anne gets pregnant again? Suppose she gets him back – she always has in the past – Henry would destroy you.

THOMAS. No – I'd go find myself some German prince to play with.

RAFE (*taken aback*). You don't speak German.

THOMAS. I know, but give me a week.

RAFE. You'd never get out of England – they'd block the ports.

THOMAS. I'll fly then. Look – the Cardinal's magic ring.

RAFE. This is no time for light answers, sir. You're risking everything – your life –

THOMAS. Not for the first time. Make or mar all. You could get Gregory out, couldn't you?

RAFE. Yes, sir.

THOMAS. And yourself too? That leaves Tom Wyatt.

RAFE. Oh, for the love of God, sir, don't fail – I beg you!

ACT FOUR

Scene Nineteen

THOMAS*'s office. Bustle.* GEORGE *is shouting, off.*

CHRISTOPHE. Brother Georges is here – and your Lady Worcester.

THOMAS. Is she? I haven't seen her for weeks. Bring her in – George can wait.

CHRISTOPHE. When you see her you will have a surprise. Ho, ho!

LADY WORCESTER *sails in, pregnant and smiling.* THOMAS *takes this in.*

THOMAS (*recovering*). If I'd known, I would have come to you, Beth. Christophe – a cushion for Lady Worcester. And bring the cakes.

LADY WORCESTER. Yes, lots of cakes. I am feeling particularly greedy today.

CHRISTOPHE *brings a plate of almond creams.*

Is that boy a waiter?

THOMAS. He makes himself useful to me in all sorts of ways.

LADY WORCESTER. I shouldn't have come. The Earl's very jealous. He suspects this little creature – (*Her belly.*) is not his own.

THOMAS. But it is? Isn't it?

LADY WORCESTER. Ah well… (*Smiles and shrugs.*)

THOMAS. Are there other possibilities?

LADY WORCESTER. Apart from?

THOMAS. Apart from… your husband?

LADY WORCESTER. I should think so. Wouldn't you? Wives enjoy a change from time to time.

THOMAS. Do you think the Queen enjoys a change?

LADY WORCESTER. Yes, well, it did look bad for her, didn't it – the night of the fire?

THOMAS. Gallant Harry Norris – on hand to extinguish the flames.

LADY WORCESTER (*stares*). Is that what you've heard? No. Young Mark Smeaton smothered the fire. With her pillow.

THOMAS (*wrong-footed*). But… What would Mark be doing there?

LADY WORCESTER. Fingering his lute?

THOMAS. He's looking very pretty in his silk damask and gold fringe.

LADY WORCESTER. And Francis Weston looks like the Cornhill Maypole.

THOMAS. Where does the money come from?

LADY WORCESTER. Oh, Anne's boys must have their presents – for all the little services they perform – the Queen is very generous. Is this almond cream? Busy all day and all night too – they are so ambitious – nakedly so. Why speak of 'idle youth'? They must have jewels for their caps, gilt buttons for their sleeves, fees for their tailors – I know – I have debts myself because of those… boys.

Pause.

THOMAS. I'll settle them.

LADY WORCESTER. A hundred pounds and my husband must never know.

CHRISTOPHE. Jesus!

THOMAS. Out, Christophe.

He goes.

The Cardinal used to say, 'Your instincts will always warn you when something is happening behind closed doors. Make it your business to find out what it is.'

LADY WORCESTER. The Queen's doors are often closed.

THOMAS. And who is behind them? Norris? Weston?

LADY WORCESTER. William Brereton?

THOMAS. But not Mark – never Mark? What would she want with such a… such a…

LADY WORCESTER. We all know the King is tired of her. He wants… another. If a closed door would give him what he wants… Well, I could go so far. But I don't want her harmed – none of us wants her harmed.

THOMAS. What do you think should happen to her?

LADY WORCESTER. I don't know. Convents can be comfortable. The whole thing was a mistake – she's really married to Harry Percy, isn't she? Now I must go – the Earl's spies are everywhere. When will you send me the money?

THOMAS. Today. Now. The Bank of Cromwell offers the best rates for useful information. Christophe!

He comes in.

Tell Rafe I need a hundred in gold.

LADY WORCESTER. A hundred for the moment. I like your cakes. (*Sweeps out, taking a handful.*)

CHRISTOPHE. A hundred! Jesus! What's that by the hour, master?

THOMAS. Christophe – take the plate.

CHRISTOPHE. Look at that! She's licked out the cream and left the crumb.

THOMAS. George now. And his father, when he comes.

RAFE *shows in* GEORGE.

GEORGE. You keep me – a lord – waiting? Cromwell, though you are of the King's Council, you are no gentleman born. His Majesty is pleased to bring you often into his presence, but never forget who placed you where he could see you.

THOMAS. I shall remember – and profit by your advice.

GEORGE. See you do.

RAFE *brings in* BOLEYN.

THOMAS. Ah – My Lord.

BOLEYN. Cromwell.

THOMAS. Matters have come to the King's attention that, had he known them, would have prevented his marriage with your daughter.

GEORGE. What 'matters'? There are no 'matters'. Harry Percy stands by his oath.

THOMAS. Then what am I to do? Perhaps, George, you can help me – and the King – with some suggestion of your own?

GEORGE. We'll help you to the Tower.

THOMAS. Minute that, Rafe. My Lord, in the matter of your daughter and Harry Percy, the late Cardinal warned you there could be no match between them because of the high estate of the Percy line and the lowness of your family. You answered you were not responsible for what Anne did – you could not control your own children. You asserted your daughter and Harry Percy had 'gone far' in the matter. You implied their liaison was consummated and by pre-contract a true marriage.

BOLEYN (*smirks*). But then the King made known his feelings for my daughter –

THOMAS. So you rethought your position. As one does. Rethink it once more. It would be better for Anne if she *had* married Harry Percy. Then her marriage to the King could be proclaimed null. And His Majesty is free to marry another lady.

BOLEYN. Ah, well… So what happens to Anne?

THOMAS. Convent?

BOLEYN. I'll want a generous settlement. For the family.

GEORGE. Wait! My Lord – Father!

BOLEYN. George, things are as they are. Calmly! She'll be left in possession of her estates?

THOMAS. The King would prefer it if she withdrew from the world… Some godly house – well-governed – where her beliefs and faith will be a comfort to her.

GEORGE. You disgust me! Both of you!

THOMAS. Rafe, minute Lord Rochford's disgust.

BOLEYN. And our Offices of State? I'll continue as Lord Privy Seal – surely? And my son here –

GEORGE. Cromwell wants us out! That's what's behind this –

RAFE. Oh, do sit down, George! (*Laughs.*) Or, of course, My Lord – stand if you please.

GEORGE. Blacksmith's boy! Force my sister out and your new friends will make short work of you. And if you fail – if she and the King are reconciled – *I'll* make short work of you. Whichever way you turn, Cromwell, you're a dead man.

BOLEYN. I'll talk to her. I'll talk to Anne. I marvel, George, that you cannot see which way this is tending.

GEORGE. What? What!

BOLEYN. Come. Shh – shh. (*Ushers* GEORGE *out, turns and bows.*) Master Secretary. Master Sadler.

RAFE. Which way is it tending?

THOMAS. Ah! (*Collects his papers.*)

RAFE. I remember – when the Cardinal came down – a masque at Court. I remember Mark Smeaton dressed in Wolsey's scarlet robes... And how four devils bore him off to Hell – four masked devils. One at each foot – one at each –

THOMAS. George was the right forepaw.

RAFE. You've never forgiven.

THOMAS. The whole Court laughing, hissing and jeering as the Cardinal was dragged and bounced across the floor. Except for one voice that called out 'Shame on you! Shame on you...'

RAFE. It was Thomas Wyatt.

THOMAS. It was...

Scene Twenty

THOMAS*'s office.* MARY SHELTON *arrives. She is baffled, frightened, distressed – on the point of tears – she hardly knows where to begin so she tries the middle.*

THOMAS. Mary Shelton… (*Steering her to a chair.*) Mary, what's the matter?

MARY SHELTON. I pray I may never see another day like this! You know Harry Norris and I – you know we were to be married? Well, he's been quarrelling with me –

THOMAS. Over Francis Weston?

MARY SHELTON. Weston – yes – that boy is always in the Queen's rooms – and Harry suspects he comes for me.

Flashback:

NORRIS. I'll give that young puppy a kicking he'll not forget.

ANNE. No kicking in my chamber, if you please.

NORRIS. Then I'll take him into the courtyard and kick him –

WESTON. You know who I come for – it's not your Mary Shelton.

ANNE. Don't tell us – let's guess! Whom do you love, Francis? Lady Rochford? Lady Worcester?

WESTON. You know very well – it's yourself.

ANNE. Then my brother George will kick you too! (*Laughs.*)

Enter BRERETON.

William Brereton! Now, here's the man for me!

THOMAS. Jesus! William Brereton – who would have believed it possible?

MARY SHELTON. One minute she's reading Tyndale's Gospels, next moment… you'd swear a demon gets into her. She torments them all.

THOMAS. What of today? You were praying you'd never see another day like this one.

MARY SHELTON. Mark began it.

THOMAS. Mark Smeaton?

MARY SHELTON. The Queen was tousling him and pulling his ears.

ANNE. Oh, look at this poor little doggie!

MARK, *weeping, kneels*.

MARK. Lady, I beg you –

ANNE. Oh, for Mary's sweet sake, get up – and think yourself favoured that I notice you at all. A lover, and struck dumb? Come on! Praise my eyes – are they not lodestars?

MARK. Farewell.

MARK *turns his back and hurries away.* ANNE *laughs at him.*

ANNE. Does he imagine I'm some night-walking slut from Paris Garden?

JANE ROCHFORD. Mark should be dropped from a great height… like your other lapdog. (*Laughs.*)

ANNE. Oh! (*Slaps* JANE ROCHFORD – *bursts into tears.*)

JANE ROCHFORD. Do that again and I'll buffet you back. You – a queen? You're a mere knight's daughter – and your day's nearly over!

ANNE. Norris, you swore you'd do anything for me –

NORRIS. Majesty?

ANNE. Then take away my brother's wife and drown her –

NORRIS. But –

ANNE. Do it! You swore you'd walk barefoot to China for me.

NORRIS. I believe it was barefoot to Walsingham.

ANNE. To Walsingham then – confess your sins there! You pray the King will die, don't you – so you can have me in your bed? Hoping for dead men's shoes! Norris won't marry you, Shelton, because he swears he'll be mine! But he'll do nothing for me – not one simple thing! – like putting Lady Rochford in a sack and carrying her to the riverbank.

JANE ROCHFORD *exits in tears*.

NORRIS. Will you spill all our secrets? Are you mad?

He hurries away.

ANNE. Harry! Harry!

THOMAS. 'Spill all our secrets'? You're sure he said 'our' and not 'your'? Who heard this?

MARY SHELTON. All of us. Anne's terrified Jane Rochford will go to the King.

THOMAS. It's treason, you know – to imagine the death of a king.

MARY SHELTON. Harry Norris won't marry me now.

THOMAS. I'll marry you, Mary.

MARY SHELTON. Never! You think yourself too great a prize.

She goes. Enter JANE ROCHFORD.

JANE ROCHFORD. The whole of England knows about it now – the Queen and Harry Norris. The King's beside himself – face crimson – he's convinced she's cuckolded him – and Anne holding up her little ginger pig to him, 'Husband – how can you doubt she is your daughter?' (*Laughs*.)

THOMAS. Why come to me?

JANE ROCHFORD. All her women want to speak out – to save ourselves. If Anne's been playing the whore we'll be blamed for concealing it.

THOMAS. You once told me she was desperate to have another child but believed the King no longer capable of fathering one. Would you repeat that before a court?

JANE ROCHFORD. Well... Now it's come out about Norris and Weston –

THOMAS. But surely – these expressions of love? Isn't it just a form of courtesy?

JANE ROCHFORD. You think so? It's been going on for years. Norris and Weston aren't the only ones. Men come and go by night. If anyone queries why, they say they're on His

Majesty's business. Before Henry married Anne she used to work him in the French fashion. You know what I mean? Oh, come – you've been in France! She made him spill his seed otherwise than he should. He calls it a filthy proceeding – and he blames her for his sin. God love him, Henry does not know where filth begins! My husband George does – he's always with Anne –

THOMAS. He's her brother. Lady Rochford, I know you'd have it a crime to be a fond brother and a cold husband – but no statute makes it so –

JANE ROCHFORD. He'd go to it with a terrier bitch if she wagged her tail at him and said 'bow-wow'. He's given me a disease – I'm afraid I'll die of it… He spends time in her chamber. Alone with her – the door closed –

THOMAS. In conversation?

JANE ROCHFORD. I listen at the door and hear no voices.

THOMAS. Perhaps they join in silent prayer –

JANE ROCHFORD. I've seen them kiss –

THOMAS. A brother may kiss his sister –

JANE ROCHFORD. His tongue in her mouth – hers in his?

THOMAS. Why would she do that?

JANE ROCHFORD. Work it out. If she gets a boy and it has Weston's face – if it looks like Norris or Brereton – what then? But they cannot say it's a bastard if it looks like a Boleyn. It would kill Henry if he knew how they laugh at him. How they talk of his member. (*Laughs.*)

THOMAS. Does George ever speak of the King's death? Think before you answer. If you give evidence against your husband in court or in Council, you may find yourself a lonely woman in years to come. And be advised by me. Talk to no one.

JANE ROCHFORD. Be advised by me. Talk to Mark Smeaton.

Exit JANE ROCHFORD. *It grows dark.* WOLSEY'S GHOST *comes forward – he's been there all through the scene. Other* GHOSTS *and shapes only half-seen.*

WOLSEY'S GHOST. I see what you're up to – turning over stones, prodding rotten logs – waiting to see what crawls out.

THOMAS. Have you any better ideas?

WOLSEY'S GHOST. Thomas… You're in our world now. You're walking with the dead. Don't lose your soul for Henry.

THOMAS. Did you lose yours?

WOLSEY'S GHOST (*gently*). Can't you smell the scorching?

Scene Twenty-One

Scene grows darker.

CHRISTOPHE. It's cold – I'll light the fire?

THOMAS. No, Christophe – not yet.

> RAFE *brings in* MARK.

RAFE. Here's Mark. He's brought his instrument.

THOMAS. It won't be needed.

MARK. Sir? I thought I was here to entertain you.

THOMAS. You are. I must ask your charity, Mark. My master the King and my mistress the Queen are at odds. My dearest wish is to reconcile them. What bitter days these are! I can't remember such a time of tension and misery – not since the Cardinal came down. I've asked you here because you're close to the Queen. Can you tell me why she's so unhappy?

MARK. Is it any wonder she's unhappy? She's in love!

THOMAS. Is she?

MARK. Of course.

THOMAS. With whom?

MARK. With me… I see I've amazed you?

THOMAS (*caught off-guard*). Not so! I've seen you together, Mark – observed the eloquent looks that pass between you… If these may be seen in public, what then in private?

RAFE. You're a very handsome young man.

THOMAS. Any woman would be drawn to you.

RAFE. Though everyone thinks you're a sodomite.

MARK. Not I, sir! I'm as good a man as any of them.

THOMAS. So the Queen would give a good account of you...
as a man? She's tried you and found you... to her liking?

MARK. I can't discuss it.

THOMAS. Quite right. Nor should we.

RAFE. So we must draw our own conclusions.

THOMAS. She's not an inexperienced woman. Would she be
interested in a less than masterly performance?

RAFE. I think not.

MARK. We poor men – poor men born – are in no wise inferior
in that way.

THOMAS. And often superior.

RAFE. To her more noble young lovers?

THOMAS. She does have other lovers?

MARK. Ha! They're all jealous of me.

RAFE. Ah! She has tried them all –

THOMAS. And Mark takes the prize. Oho – we must
congratulate you, Mark.

RAFE. How many times have you fucked her?

Chill descends.

THOMAS. It can't be easy to manage – to lie with the Queen –
even though her ladies are complicit.

MARK. Ha! Her ladies are no friends to me! They'd never
admit what I've told you is true. They're friends to Norris
and Weston – those gentlemen. I'm nothing to them – they
ruffle my hair and call me 'waiting boy'. And...

THOMAS. The Queen's your only friend. But such a friend!
Now... you've given us two names: Norris – Weston... Tell

us who the others are. And answer Master Sadler's question: how many times?

MARK *freezes*.

Well… it doesn't matter. The Council will be astonished to hear of your prowess, Mark – there'll be many lords who will envy you. But now you'll want your supper, won't you? – We all want our supper, so let's get on. Let's get everything down in writing. Ink and paper, Rafe.

MARK. I can mention no names.

THOMAS. Perhaps she tells you she has no other lovers? She's yours alone? Oh, Mark – she's deceiving you! Don't you see? She could do that, don't you think? Look how easily you and she deceive the King.

MARK. No! I don't know how I came to say what I said.

THOMAS. Nor do I. No one hurt you, did they? You spoke freely.

RAFE. You said all her other lovers were jealous of you?

MARK. I take it back.

THOMAS. It's turned chilly in here.

RAFE. We should have a fire lit.

A BOY *appears and lights the fire. This takes time.* MARK *stands. Nobody stops him. He goes to the door. Nobody stops him.* MARK *tries to speak, and then bows, and goes out, closing the door behind him. After a while,* CHRISTOPHE *leads* MARK *back into the room, pulling him in gently by the hand.*

CHRISTOPHE. Come – seat yourself again, pretty boy.

THOMAS. Ambition is a sin, Mark. Or so they tell me. Whom did you displace in the Queen's bed? Norris?

RAFE. It was – wasn't it? Harry Norris?

THOMAS. If your confession is prompt and full, clear and unsparing –

MARK. Confession! –

THOMAS. It's possible that the King will show you mercy.

MARK (*terrified*). I don't know!

THOMAS. The others are more culpable – trusted, educated gentlemen – raised to greatness by the King. Whereas you are very young – more to be pitied than punished.

MARK. I dare not name names.

RAFE. Then tell us first about your own adultery with the Queen. No? Do you need time to think it over – time alone? Why not go and spend ten minutes – with Christophe here?

CHRISTOPHE. Five would do it.

MARK. Mother Mary help me!

THOMAS. No one wants your pain, Mark. I've no use for your screams. I need words that make sense – words Master Sadler can transcribe –

RALPH. You've already spoken them –

THOMAS. Why is it so difficult to speak them again?

Pause.

MARK. Tell me again… what I must say – what my confession must be… Clear and… what was it? But, you understand me, sir, I cannot tell you what I do not know?

THOMAS. Can you not? Then you must be my guest tonight. In the morning, Mark, your head will be clear and your memory perfect. Why protect the gentlemen who share your sin? Believe me, if your positions were reversed, they'd not spare a thought for you.

RAFE. So. Harry Norris? (*Writes.*)

MARK. Yes.

THOMAS. William Brereton?

MARK. Yes.

THOMAS. Francis Weston?

MARK. Yes.

THOMAS. Her brother George – Lord Rochford?

MARK. Yes – that's well known. And Thomas Wyatt –

THOMAS. No. Not Wyatt.

CHRISTOPHE *playfully slaps* MARK *across the head.*

MARK. No – not Wyatt.

THOMAS. And you have had to do with the Queen how
many times?

MARK. A hundred.

Another slap.

A thousand.

Another slap.

RAFE. Three or four?

MARK. Three or four.

THOMAS. Thank you.

MARK. What will happen to me?

THOMAS. That rests with the court that will try you.

MARK. What will happen to the Queen?

THOMAS. That rests with the King. Go and sleep now, Mark.
Christophe will stay with you.

CHRISTOPHE *leads* MARK *away gently, by the hand.*

In the morning who will he not give us? Kitchen boys,
cooks, and Archbishop Cranmer if we want them…

RAFE. You should bring in Wyatt too, sir. For years there's
been talk. I don't see how you can go on protecting him.

THOMAS. It's not Wyatt who stands in my way with the King.
It's not he who drops slanders against me like poison into
Henry's ear. Any more worries?

Scene Twenty-Two

Night, confusion, NORRIS, MARK, BRERETON, GEORGE *and* WESTON *are carried off to the Tower.* SIR WILLIAM KINGSTON *and his* MEN *receive them and lock them in separate cells.*

KING HENRY. Norris denies everything. The Lord Chancellor questioned him and he went so far as to admit he loves her. But when it was put to him that he's an adulterer who wishes me dead so he can marry her, he says, 'No, no – and no.' So now *you* must put questions to him. If he confesses – if he names the others – there can be mercy.

THOMAS. Mark Smeaton has named the others.

KING HENRY. Cromwell, these are men I have called my friends. I'll not trust the word of some scoundrel with no family or breeding. You know when a man and a woman are together in matrimony, one way is apt for the getting of children – it is sanctioned by the Church. The man lies on her and... Well now, what does it mean when a woman turns herself about, and about in bed? Offering herself this way and that? Where would any woman, not bred in a whorehouse, get such knowledge? A sober, godly matron whose only duty is to get a child?

THOMAS. I've no answer, sir.

KING HENRY. Cramner cannot believe it – and yet he must. She deceived that godly man – a man who sees into the truth of things. Is it any wonder she deceived me? I'm a simple man. She swore she was untouched – I believed her. I believe she has committed adultery with a hundred men. Some of these acts alleged against her are not fit for discussion among decent people. Her brother? Her own brother? Is it possible? Why not? Why not drink the filthy cup to its dregs? I miss Jane. I want to look at her. Can't we bring her here?

THOMAS. No. Let's wait until the business is more forward.

KING HENRY. No, you are right – she must not be brought here until the air is pure again. Go to her, Thomas – take Jane this... (*A small book.*) It was my wife's – I mean to say, it was poor Katherine's... You can arrest the... her... now. Be close – be discreet.

Scene Twenty-Three

Outside ANNE*'s chamber.* THOMAS *and* RAFE, GUARDS *and* COUNCILLORS.

NORFOLK. Cromwell, this must not bear on me – only the Boleyns. I want her father's titles taken off him – I want him diminished – cast down in all his pride. I warned Henry of her character, but would he listen?

SUFFOLK. I warned him too – I was thrown out of Court.

THOMAS. My Lord, do you have the warrant?

They go in.

ANNE. Cremuel… I created you –

NORFOLK. He created you, madam.

SUFFOLK. And now he repents him of it.

ANNE. Take me to my husband the King. Let them row me up to Whitehall – I would rather not go to the Tower.

No response.

Surely you'll not take me like this I've no necessities – not so much as a change of shift. And my own women must come with me – so I can keep my proper state.

THOMAS. Madam, your household is to be dissolved.

ANNE. Send for Archbishop Cranmer. I will go with him.

NORFOLK. Go with Cranmer, will you? (*Chuckles.*) By God, I'll drag you to the boat with your arse in the air.

RAFE. My Lord!

THOMAS. Madam, be assured – you will be handled as befits your status. Come.

ANNE. Cremuel, you have never forgiven me for Wolsey.

They take her to the boat.

THOMAS. To be turned out of your house and put upon the river – your whole life receding with every stroke of the oars. As it was with him, so it is with her…

SUFFOLK (*dawning horror on his face: if* THOMAS *is seeking revenge for* WOLSEY, *could he be next?*). Cromwell –

THOMAS *turns to him.*

The Cardinal's griefs are forgotten. Let him go. He rests in peace –

THOMAS. But I do not.

SUFFOLK (*to himself, not swearing but praying*). Oh Christ help me…

THOMAS. My Lord, will you step aboard?

They all get aboard.

ANNE. Where are my bishops? They owe their promotion to me. Cranmer will swear I am a good woman.

NORFOLK. Your churchmen will spit on you.

ANNE. I am the Queen – if you do me harm a curse will come on you. No rain will fall till I am released.

SUFFOLK. Witchcraft, is it? Madam, it is such foolish talk of curses and spells that brought you here.

ANNE. Oh? You said I was a false wife? Am I a sorcerer now?

SUFFOLK. None of us raised the subject of curses.

ANNE. I will swear on oath I am true. The King will listen. You can bring no witnesses. You do not even know how to charge me.

NORFOLK. Yes – it would save trouble if we ducked and drowned you here.

They arrive at the Tower. KINGSTON *is waiting with others.* KINGSTON *helps* ANNE *out of the barge.*

ANNE. Is Harry Norris here? Has he cleared my name?

KINGSTON. I fear not, madam. Nor his own.

ANNE (*laughs*). Are you going to put me in your dungeon, Master Kingston?

KINGSTON. No, madam. You shall have the chamber where you lay before your coronation.

ANNE (*collapses*). Jesus have mercy, it is too good for me.

> THOMAS *lifts her – hands her to* KINGSTON. *She is taken away.*

RAFE. What did she mean by it? 'Too good for me'?

THOMAS. She's failed. One thing she set out to do – to get Henry and keep him. She's lost him to Jane Seymour – no court will judge her more harshly than she'll judge herself. Henry made her Queen. If he turns his back, what is she? An imposter. Her rooms are empty. Jane will wear her clothes. She's dead to herself now. All we have to do is bury her.

ACT FIVE

Scene Twenty-Four

The Tower.

THOMAS. Christmas last, Sir Henry, you impersonated a Moor, and Sir William Brereton showed himself half-naked in the guise of a wild man of the woods, in the Queen's chamber.

NORRIS. Oh, for God's sake. You're asking me – in all seriousness – about what we did when costumed for a masque?

THOMAS. I counselled Brereton against exposing his person. Your retort was that the Queen had seen it many a time.

NORRIS. You know what I meant! She's a married woman – a man's… gear is no strange sight to her.

THOMAS. But I don't know what you meant, Harry, I only know what you said. What about Francis Weston? You told me he was going to the Queen.

NORRIS. Well, Weston wasn't naked. He was in a dragon suit.

THOMAS. He was not naked when we saw him. You were jealous of Weston, Harry – you didn't deny it –

NORRIS. Weston's a boy.

WESTON. Does she prefer men? Men like yourself?

NORRIS (*trying to contain the situation*). Cromwell… I… (*Carefully selecting a word.*) I revere the lady – it's no secret – why shouldn't I admit it? But ask yourself – why would I forget my honour? Why would I betray my King? I've been at Henry's side since he was a boy – I love him as a brother.

THOMAS. Ah, these are dark days, Harry. Faith falters and hope grows faint – and even brotherly love is not what it used to be. Look at George Boleyn.

NORRIS. I have no opinon on George Boleyn.

THOMAS. No opinion on incest?

NORRIS. I'll not be drawn. All you have is women's gossip.
You'll get no confessions – so where are you?

THOMAS. Mark Smeaton has confessed. He gave me names.
Some of them surprised me.

NORRIS. What did you do to him?

Silence. THOMAS *looks back at him.*

Smeaton is nobody. He has no friends.

Silence. NORRIS *is unnerved.*

You cannot put a gentleman to the torture.

THOMAS. I could put my thumbs in your eyes here and now,
and you'd sing 'Green Grows the Holly' if I asked you to. You
made a pact with the King's wife, to wed her after his death.

NORRIS. There was no pact.

THOMAS. Hoping for a 'dead man's shoes', Harry. You and
Anne wished the King away. Half the Court heard you.

NORRIS. Never in my life have I entertained one thought, one
thought, which would injure my sovereign lord. Even if I
had – which before God I deny – you cannot make my
thoughts a crime.

THOMAS. Oh, but I can, you see – if your thoughts were
malicious, and expressed in words, and directed against the
King's Majesty.

NORRIS. Then bring us before a jury. They'll laugh at you.
You've no witnesses – no proofs. All you can do is try and
turn one man against the other – cheat and lie and distort our
words – place wilful misconstruction on the law of England –

THOMAS. I wrote the law of England, Harry. I'll bring you a
copy of the Treasons Act, shall I? I'll talk you through it,
clause by clause. Why go to your death ignorant?

NORRIS. I think that you presume –

THOMAS (*cuts him off, laughing at him*). Harry, Harry. Don't tell me your thoughts. You know what I'll do with them.

NORRIS (*harrowed, sees he's trapped*). Do you not fear God's judgement?

THOMAS. Yes, I do. But you'll be meeting Him before I do, Harry – your sins on your head. There is no faith in you gentlemen, is there? No duty, no pity –

NORRIS. Pity –

THOMAS. When Wolsey was disgraced, hounded to his death. You all behaved like savages – like wolves, falling on his estates and possessions. And even then, you couldn't let him rest. Cast your mind back, Norris. Recall an entertainment at Court, in which the late Cardinal was set upon by demons and carried down to Hell.

NORRIS (*gapes*). And… is that why? It was a play! Wolsey was dead – how could it hurt him? And when he was alive, was I not good to him in his trouble? Did I not ride after him with a token from the King's own hand?

THOMAS. And he knelt in the mud, to you. (*Pulls* NORRIS *to the ground.*) Life pays you out, Norris, don't you find? Henry Norris. Chief arse-wiper to the King. Left forepaw.

He goes into BRERETON's *cell.*

William Brereton of Cheshire. A violent man from a violent line.

BRERETON. Cromwell, when the King releases me, my people will take you and hang you.

THOMAS. I'd expect no less, it's their custom. I remember, back in the Cardinal's time, a servant of yours killed a man during a bowls match.

BRERETON. The game can get very heated.

THOMAS. I know. I play myself.

BRERETON (*nasty*). Do you? We'll set up a match then.

THOMAS. What, in here?

BRERETON. Let me out. You know you've no case.

THOMAS (*cheerful*). No, possibly not.

BRERETON. So go on. Whistle for the turn-key.

THOMAS. Why don't you whistle for the King. Tell me about Weston, Will. Do you think he's had the Queen?

BRERETON (*seeing a way out*). Why not? He's always on the scent, isn't he? Tongue out? (*Like a dog panting.*) She may be the Queen but she's only a woman.

THOMAS. And who else, besides Weston?

BRERETON. Wyatt. Your friend Wyatt. Why is he not locked up?

THOMAS. He may be, before long. But as you're already here, William, allow me to put a question to you. Do you remember a man called John ap Eyton? A gentleman of Flintshire?

BRERETON. Who? Eyton? (*Incredulous.*) Is that what this is about? A man of no consequence at all?

THOMAS. Leave aside the matter of your adultery with the Queen – going naked into her chamber – Do not interrupt me, sir – and concentrate first on Eyton. There's a quarrel, one of your household ends up dead. Eyton is tried for murder, and acquitted. But having no respect for law you abduct him, and your servants hang him.

BRERETON. It's how we do things in Cheshire.

THOMAS. You think this is only one man and he doesn't matter. No one remembers him? He does matter, I remember him. Your family think you write the law. You bring the King's justice and the King's name into contempt. You murder for pleasure. You kill men for sport. But that game's finished, Brereton. There are no private kingdoms now. New times. New rules.

BRERETON (*mocking*). Ah. Your rules?

THOMAS. Even though you don't want to learn them, William. As God's my witness, your kinsmen in the north will look at your severed head and learn them fast.

BRERETON. So that's it, is it? Thomas Cromwell, judge, jury and executioner?

THOMAS. It's better justice than Eyton had. William Brereton. Left hindpaw.

He goes into GEORGE'*s cell.*

The Martin Tower, George? How do you like your lodgings?

GEORGE. I suppose I'm accused of concealing my sister's misconduct?

THOMAS. No.

GEORGE. The charge won't stand. There's been no misconduct.

THOMAS. That's not the charge… It's been explained to me how a brother may grow up apart from his sister and hardly know her when she's a child. When he meets her as a grown woman he finds she's like himself. Yet not. One day his brotherly embrace is a little longer than usual. Neither party feels they are doing wrong… until a frontier is crossed. Did it begin before her marriage or after?

GEORGE (*astonished*). You call yourself a Christian and you ask… I refuse to answer – such –

THOMAS. I am accustomed to dealing with those who refuse to answer.

GEORGE. Henry killed his father's Councillors – he struck off the head of Thomas More – one of Europe's greatest scholars – he harried the Cardinal to his death – and now he's scheming to kill his wife. What makes you think it will be any different with you when your time comes?

THOMAS. It ill becomes a Boleyn to evoke the Cardinal's name. Or Thomas More's for that matter. Your sister burned for vengeance – she would say to me 'What! Thomas More? Is he not dead yet?'

GEORGE. Who began this slander against me? (*Pause.*) It's my wife, isn't it? How can you really believe something so monstrous? On the word of one woman?

THOMAS. Think what reason you've given that woman to say such a word.

GEORGE (*he is frightened*). I'll speak to my confessor.

THOMAS. I'm your confessor now, George. What would
absolve you – what might preserve your life – is a full
statement – everything you know about your sister's dealings
with other men.

GEORGE. You ask me for evidence that will kill my sister?

THOMAS. Then you do have such evidence? Evidence that will
kill her? (*Opens his hands.*) Look. I've nothing to offer you.
The King might let you slip abroad. Or he might grant you
mercy as to the manner of your death. Or not. A traitor's death
is a terrible thing, you know, George – shocking… And so
public. Stripped naked – your privy member sliced off – your
stomach slit opened – your false heart torn from your breast…
Such pain – such humiliation! Oh… I see you have witnessed
it. Did you say, in the hearing of others, that the King was
impotent? That he could not get a child on your sister?

GEORGE *slumps at the table, clutching his stomach.*

In saying so you call in question the parentage of the
Princess. Elizabeth is England's heir… You must see –
you've spoken treason?

GEORGE. What I said…

THOMAS. The King believes the true reason he could not get a
son upon your sister is because the marriage was unlawful
and unclean –

GEORGE. Christ! God grants sons to every beggar – he grants
them to the illicit union as well as the blessed – to whores
and to queens! Can the King be so simple?

THOMAS. His is a holy simplicity. He's an anointed King –
and very close to God.

GEORGE *studies* THOMAS*'s face for signs of levity – the
face is a blank. He's puzzled. Then resigned.*

GEORGE. Close to God…

THOMAS *comes out of the cell.*

THOMAS. George Boleyn –

WOLSEY'S GHOST. Right forepaw?

THOMAS *goes in to* WESTON*'s cell.*

WESTON. I taunted you, sir. I belittled you. I'm sorry now I
ever did so. You are the King's servant – it was proper for
me to respect that.

THOMAS. A handsome apology, Francis.

WESTON. You know I am not long married.

THOMAS. But you left your wife at home in the country. Now
we know for whom you left her.

WESTON. I have a son… Not yet a year old. (*Silence.*) I wish
my soul to be prayed for after I'm dead. (*Silence.*) I am in
debt, Master Secretary – I owe a thousand pounds.

THOMAS. Nobody expects a young gentleman to be thrifty.
(*Kindly.*) We know the Queen gave you money.

WESTON. I've been a fool, I have undone myself and you have
stood by and watched it all. I cannot fault your conduct – for
I would have injured you if I could… I know I have not
lived… I have not lived… a good life. I thought I'd have
another twenty years – and then – when I was old, I'd give to
hospitals and endow a chantry. God would see I was sorry.

THOMAS. Well, Francis, we know not the hour, do we?

WESTON. But, Master Secretary, whatever wrong I have done,
I am not guilty in this matter of the Queen. I see by your face
you know it. And all the people will know it too when I am
brought out to die. And the King will know it, and think
about it in his private hours. I shall be remembered as the
innocent are remembered.

THOMAS. Fortune is fickle – every young adventurer knows
that. Resign yourself. Look at Norris – he shows no
bitterness.

WESTON. Norris has no reason for bitterness. Norris deserves
his death. I do not.

THOMAS. You think him well paid-out for meddling with the
Queen?

WESTON. He's never out of her company... They are not discussing the Gospel, Master Secretary, are they? I know... I can tell you that she –

WESTON *is on the verge of the confession* THOMAS *needs.*

THOMAS. Francis... Excuse me.

THOMAS *falters – comes out of the room.*

RAFE. He's confessed?

THOMAS. He says he's innocent. I no longer know what that means. He believes Norris is guilty. I don't know what he means by guilt. Weston is a child. Everything good in life was brought to him on a silver plate when he was christened. He's never striven – never suffered – he can't anticipate pain because he's never felt it. He doesn't know what he's saying. The lambs have begun to slaughter themselves. I don't need to stand by and watch it.

RAFE. You're tired. Shall I do this – shall I go in to him.

THOMAS. No. They all say 'I am innocent...' But none of them says Anne is innocent.

He goes into ANNE*'s room. She is praying – her* AUNTS *sewing.* ANNE *is deflated and bewildered. She has no idea what is happening.*

ANNE. Why is the King still holding me here? Is it to test me? Some stratagem he has devised – yes?

No response.

Will you fetch my father? And my bishops – where are they? I have nourished them – I have protected them. I have furthered the cause of religion... I can't understand why they don't go to the King for me...

THOMAS. Help the King. Unless he is merciful you are lost.

ANNE. No – you're wrong –

THOMAS. You can do nothing for yourself... but you may do something for your child, Elizabeth.

ANNE. No – I'll not be here much longer. The King of France will speak for me.

THOMAS. Humble yourself – make a show of penitence. If you bear the process patiently –

ANNE (*bewildered*). 'The process'? What process?

THOMAS. The form of your trial will be decided when the confessions of the gentlemen –

ANNE. What confessions?

THOMAS. Of their adulteries with you.

ANNE (*shock*). When I am released you'll not speak to me in that way.

THOMAS. By speaking out now – by being open – you could shorten the pain for all concerned. The gentlemen will be tried together. Your peers – since you are ennobled – will try yourself and your brother.

ANNE. There will be no trial. They can't have a trial without evidence – without witnesses. Whatever accusation they make – I can simply say 'no' to it.

THOMAS. When you were at liberty, madam, your ladies were intimidated – forced to lie for you. Now… they are emboldened. There are witnesses.

ANNE. Is Jane Seymour emboldened? Tell her, God sees her tricks.

THOMAS. The King has begun a process to nullify your marriage.

ANNE. Is murdering me not enough? What then will become of Elizabeth? And where is Wyatt? Oh, Wyatt – Thomas Wyatt, I shall soon see you here. Have I ruined you or have you ruined me?

He turns to go.

Cremuel – you don't believe these stories against me? I know in your heart you do not.

THOMAS. I do not know what is in your heart, madam. And sure, you do not know what is in mine.

ANNE. Shall I not have justice? (*Puts her fingers to her throat.*) Then… I have only a little neck. It will be the work of a moment.

Scene Twenty-Five

Court. WYATT *and* SUFFOLK *shouting at each other.*
THOMAS *and his entourage intervene.*

SUFFOLK. You're not going in there, Tom Wyatt. The King's
seeing no one – he won't even see me, so why would you
think… (*Laughs.*) If you're going anywhere, it's to the
Tower. Oh, you tell him, Cromwell. Explain it to him.
(*Goes.*)

THOMAS. Come with me, Tom.

WYATT. Where? People will say I'm arrested – they'll think
you're putting me in the Tower.

THOMAS. You are arrested. I *am* putting you in the Tower.

WYATT. That's the end of me then.

THOMAS. I'm locking you up for safekeeping.

WYATT. As you have Anne? Is she there for safekeeping? What
has she confessed?

THOMAS. She admits she never loved the King.

WYATT. Of course she never loved him! If he thinks she did,
he's a fool… Or perhaps that's treason – is it – to call the
King a fool?

THOMAS. No treason… but perhaps keep it in the heart, Tom.
Picture his shame. He believes she has betrayed him with the
men he trusted most. He thinks she laughs at him.

WYATT. She does.

THOMAS. He laid half the world at her feet, but when she lay
with him, she imagined someone else.

WYATT. Isn't that how marriage works? If fantasy is to be
made treason, half England should be locked up. If feelings
are to be made crimes, then I admit —

THOMAS. Admit nothing. Norris admitted he loved her. He's
in the Tower – he'll not come out. Tom, I need…

He breaks off, considers him.

WYATT. What? What do you need?

THOMAS. Evidence... Against Anne.

WYATT. I knew you had nothing. (*Passionate*.) What are you doing? What, in the name of God, are you doing?

THOMAS. I'm taking a case to trial.

WYATT. Where the verdict is already given? Where the law is what the King wills?

THOMAS. If that were true I wouldn't need your help. In the name of Christ, Tom, I'm trying to keep your head on your shoulders! Listen. You've told me how Anne conducts herself with men. 'Yes, yes, yes, no.' Now... you must add another word of testimony. 'Yes, yes, yes, no, yes.'

WYATT. It was not testimony.

THOMAS. What was it then? I can't split myself in two – one part your friend, the other the King's servant. So – here and now – you must decide. Will you add that one word? Will you write it down for me? If you do, you'll come out of this alive.

Pause. WYATT *gives a slight nod.*

Good.

WYATT. She would not be his mistress, she must be Queen of England. So there is breaking of faith, and making of laws, and the country is set in an uproar. He walked on severed heads to get her. Why would he flinch now? One corpse more, why count them? Let's not deceive ourselves. If you put me in the Tower I'll not come out. I've many enemies – they want me dead.

THOMAS. I want you alive.

WYATT. I wonder, what for?

He starts to leave with the OFFICERS *– then stops and turns. He studies* THOMAS.

THOMAS (*to* OFFICER). Show Sir Thomas every mark of respect.

WYATT. 'I want you alive'... Isn't that what you said to Thomas More?

They take WYATT *away to the Tower.*

Scene Twenty-Six

Westminster Hall. A court assembles, presided over by NORFOLK.

NORFOLK. Bring up the bodies.

> GUARDS *bring in* NORRIS, BRERETON, WESTON *and* MARK. *The three gentlemen shuffle away from* MARK. *The doors close.*

Scene Twenty-Seven

THOMAS*'s office.* THOMAS, GREGORY, CLERKS.

GREGORY. They are offering twenty to one that Weston will get off.

THOMAS. He won't. I wish you'd stayed away, Gregory – I wanted you clear of this sordid business.

GREGORY. Well, I wanted to be with you. They say in the kitchen that if George Boleyn goes free he'll kill you.

THOMAS. George won't go free.

> RAFE *and* EDWARD *burst in.*

At last! Come on! The verdict?

RAFE. Norris, Brereton, Weston and Mark. All guilty – all condemned – though nobody knows if they'll go to Tyburn or not.

THOMAS. I'll move the King to grant them a swifter end.

GREGORY. Mark too?

THOMAS. Mark too. For his confession I offered him mercy. This is all mercy can deliver. How did they bear themselves?

EDWARD. They were steady enough.

RAFE. Resigned. They begged God and the King to forgive them their offences – though only Mark said what his offences were.

GREGORY (*slightly accusingly at his father*). Poor little Weston! Who would have thought you could feel sorry for him?

RAFE. I know the King must be served… but couldn't it have been managed with less bloodshed?

THOMAS. What? You think I could have negotiated *with Anne Boleyn*? Look, Rafe – once you have exhausted the process of negotiation and compromise – once you have fixed on the destruction of your enemy – his destruction must be swift – it must be perfect. Before you even glance in his direction, you should have his name on a warrant, the ports blocked, his wife and friends bought, his heir under your protection, his money in your strongroom, and his dog answering your whistle. And before he wakes in the morning you should have the axe in your hand. Listen, boys. When men say it is I who have condemned these men, tell them that it is the King, and a court of law. Tell them proper formalities have been observed – that no torture has been used – whatever the word is in the city. These men are not dying only because I have a grudge against them. It's beyond grudge. I could not save them if I tried.

GREGORY. I hope you can save Tom Wyatt.

RAFE. I must go back to Court. And you must go back to your sister.

Exeunt RAFE *and* EDWARD.

GREGORY. Are they really guilty – and why so many? Would it not have stood better with the King's honour if they'd named only one adulterer?

THOMAS. It would distinguish that one gentleman too much.

GREGORY. People would say Mark Smeaton has a bigger cock than the King, and he knows better than His Majesty what to do with it?

THOMAS. What a way with words you have, Gregory! The King's no private man – he cannot be secret – so he must take his cuckolding patiently. If he can show the world that the Queen's nature is so bad she cannot control it – if it's proved that so many men have sinned with her, any possible defence is stripped away. That's why these men came to trial first. They are found guilty, so must she be.

GREGORY. I didn't mean, 'Did the court find them guilty?'
Father. I meant, 'Did they do it?'

Pause.

THOMAS. Who knows? Intrigue feeds on itself – conspiracies
have neither mother nor father, and yet they thrive –

GREGORY. So they didn't do it. When will they die?

THOMAS (*studies him*). The Queen and her brother are to be
tried in the Tower on Monday. It must be after that. And
there's still the matter of the annulment – and please, my
dear son, don't ask me why there has to be an annulment.
Just know it's what the King wants.

Scene Twenty-Eight

The Tower, ANNE*'s trial. She stands isolated, as huge crowd
noise almost drowns out* NORFOLK, *who is presiding.*
THOMAS, *impassive, watching.*

NORFOLK. You're found guilty of treason, girl. (*Roaring.*) If
you hinder me from reading the sentence of the court I'll come
down among you and slaughter the whole baying pack of you.

Noise continues. THOMAS *walks forward into the arena. The
noise level fades: to silence. He looks at* ANNE. *The tension is
held. He approaches her. Will he speak to her? Tension held.*
THOMAS *and* ANNE *look into each other's eyes.*

THOMAS. My Lord Norfolk, read your sentence.

NORFOLK. The judgment is this: to be burned here within the
Tower, or else to have your head smitten off – as the King's
pleasure shall be further known.

SUFFOLK. Now do the same for her brother and we can all go
home to dinner.

Scene Twenty-Nine

Outside KING HENRY*'s chamber.* KINGSTON *comes out.*

KINGSTON. Master Secretary, what's to be done? Is she to be burned? Surely the King will not permit it?

THOMAS. We must wait for the King to speak.

KINGSTON. And what of the men? Five to die – all on the same day – five graves to dig – and the next a Queen of England! I'll have the flagstones in the chapel levered up. It's a lot of trouble, you know – it might not even be necessary – if she's burned will there be anything left to bury?

THOMAS. Yes there will. Lever up your flags, Sir William.

KINGSTON. Her brother must go under anyway. He's an Earl, isn't he?

RAFE. A viscount.

KINGSTON. Makes no difference – lords under the chapel flags – commoners outside. Did you ever see a woman burned? It's something I wish never to see, as I trust in God.

KINGSTON *leaves.* CRANMER *arrives.*

THOMAS. How is the Queen? Did she make her confession?

CRANMER. She will – at the last. But she hopes of course…

Looks at THOMAS. *He waits.* THOMAS *meets his eye but says nothing.*

She thinks the King might let her go to France?

Still nothing.

A convent then? She'll agree to anything—sign anything. She asks, does the King want her to say she was married to Harry Percy?

THOMAS. All he wants is to wipe her from his mind.

CRANMER (*absorbing this, broken*). So I may offer her no hope at all? She asked me… 'If I die, shall I be the King's wife?' I said 'No, madam, your marriage is to be annulled.' She said 'But shall I still be Queen?' I didn't know what to say.

THOMAS. Under statute she will. Offer her that. I think it will console her to know she will be Queen of England when… (*Now he can't face saying it either.*) She will be Queen until her last moments… (*More briskly.*) It's what she wanted, isn't it? I must go to the King.

CRANMER *is silent.*

No word for His Majesty?

CRANMER. My duty. My obedience. My prayers.

THOMAS *goes in to* KING HENRY.

KING HENRY. We must look into a glass of truth. I am to blame. What I suspected I would not admit, not even to myself. So much falls into place. So many friends and good servants lost. Wolsey, poor Wolsey. She practised upon him with every weapon of her slyness and malice. Pray. Pray for me. Pray God does not abandon me. What have you brought me?

THOMAS. Death warrants, Majesty. Majesty, there is no gallows at Tower Hill –

KING HENRY. No? Let it be Tyburn then. Though you know… Young Weston… He's very young – easily misled…

THOMAS. I don't think it a good idea to take them to Tyburn – the crowds might be unruly.

KING HENRY. Why would they? The people of London don't love these men – they hardly know them. (*A grunt.*) Very well – let us be merciful. The axeman then.

THOMAS. Mark too? You know, he did confess – freely.

KING HENRY. Has the Frenchman come?

THOMAS. Ah – the man from Calais? Not yet, sir. I wonder… Do you think, Majesty, it was in France – when the Queen was first compromised?

KING HENRY (*considers it*). She was too fond of that nation – Imagined her daughter Elizabeth would one day be Queen of France. You know, I think you are right, Cromwell. She was always pressing on me the advantage of the French. I can't believe it was Harry Percy took her maidenhead. He wouldn't lie, would he? Not on his honour as an English peer. No – it was in the Court of France she was first debauched.

THOMAS. So it was in France. I never thought it was Wyatt.

KING HENRY. No. It was not Wyatt. Not Wyatt.

THOMAS. Majesty.

Puts the warrants in front of KING HENRY. KING HENRY
*glances at them. He takes a pen and signs five of them
straight off, a laborious, slow signature on each. He picks up
the sixth and studies it.*

KING HENRY. You know… young Weston…

*He thinks for a long time. Then he signs it and starts to go,
leaving* THOMAS *to collect the warrants.*

I cannot see how the whole thing occurred. I wish someone
would explain it to me. When I look back over the last ten
years I simply cannot understand myself. It's as if I have
been asleep – dreaming… Bewitched.

Scene Thirty

*Death knell. Cart of bodies enters. The bodies are in shrouds,
knotted over the place where their heads used to be. The heads
are in separate bags. Fresh, wet, scarlet blood. The effect is of a
ghastly altar. They are framed at the centre of the tableau as*
THOMAS, GREGORY, RAFE *and* CHRISTOPHE *cross
themselves and go briefly on one knee, heads bowed.*
KINGSTON *comes in, papers in hand.*

KINGSTON. Master Cromwell, still nobody will tell me, I must
have an answer. When is the Queen to die?

THOMAS. We're waiting for the man from Calais. They say
he'll be here tomorrow.

KINGSTON. Who?

THOMAS. The executioner. (*In answer to* KINGSTON*'s look.*)
The swordsman.

KINGSTON. A sword – Not the fire then? At least it will be…

THOMAS. Quick.

KINGSTON. But…

THOMAS. What is it now?

KINGSTON. If he's to come from Calais...? He'll never get here by tomorrow?

THOMAS. The King sent over there five days ago.

KINGSTON. He didn't even wait for the verdict?

THOMAS. His Majesty's in a hurry to be married.

KINGSTON. God forgive him! What has he become?

THOMAS. Though we've had to wait anyway till Cranmer's court pronounced the marriage null.

> KINGSTON *looks at him.*

It's done. She can die now.

KINGSTON (*snorts*). Jesu!

OFFICER (*near the bodies – calling*). Sir William?

> KINGSTON *wilts under* CROMWELL's *eye, turns away, and goes to the cart of bodies. His conversation with the* OFFICERS *progresses to a mute, gesticulating argument.*

GREGORY. What were the grounds?

THOMAS. Hmmm?

GREGORY. For the annulment?

THOMAS. Oh – witchcraft.

RAFE. Witchcraft!

THOMAS. It was the Duke of Suffolk's suggestion. Nobody could come up with a better idea.

CHRISTOPHE. I told you! I told you! And you said there were no such things as witches! Pah!

GREGORY. So the King will be a widower, or... (*Frowns, trying to think it out.*)

THOMAS. No.

RAFE. No, he'll be a bachelor, Gregory. His marriages – they never really occurred. They were illicit –

GREGORY. What – both of them!

RAFE. Illicit and accursed. He has never been married. Though he has been trying for twenty-five years.

KINGSTON *returns, and is followed by an* OFFICER *with a pile of clothes.* KINGSTON *is hesitant and hideously embarrassed.*

KINGSTON. Master Secretary, it appears… There is some… confusion. Now the corpses are stripped of their clothes, badges of rank… Dear God, I have never in my whole life –

GREGORY. You mean you can't tell which head goes with which body? –

KINGSTON. My men are accustomed to one execution at a time. I've never in my whole life been so humiliated. We have to clean up this mess, God's blood, man, tomorrow we have a Queen of England to behead. It's too much!

CHRISTOPHE. Fetch her down here right now! She should be able to put a cock to a face!

RAFE. Shame on you, Christophe! (*To* KINGSTON*'s* MEN.) Shame on you all!

THOMAS. Open the shrouds, Rafe. Look at their hands. Norris has a scar in his palm, his left palm… You must feel their fingertips. Mark's will be calloused, from the lute strings. Weston bit his nails.

RAFE. George Boleyn, sir?

THOMAS. George is still wearing his wedding ring. They'll be able to slide it off now. And – (*Shrugging.*) the other one's Brereton.

RAFE. Master constable.

THOMAS. Go help him, Gregory.

GREGORY (*appalled*). Me?

THOMAS *nods. Sickened and reluctant,* GREGORY *follows* RAFE. *Turns back. The full horror has just hit him.*

I caught sight of Tom Wyatt looking down from the Bell Tower.

THOMAS *is walking away.*

In the name of God. Don't let the King kill him too.

THOMAS (*walking away*). Tom Wyatt will go free. He's innocent. The King himself told me so.

Scene Thirty-One

A scaffold is erected.

CHRISTOPHE *talking in French to a well-dressed young man. The audience should not realise the young man is the* EXECUTIONER OF CALAIS. THOMAS *enters.*

CHRISTOPHE. *Voici mon maître – il est le Secrétaire du Roi.*

EXECUTIONER. *Oh merde – vous voulez dire Cremuel le boucher?*

CHRISTOPHE. *Oui – c'est lui.*

THOMAS. *J'ai entendu ca.*

EXECUTIONER. You are Cremuel. You are in charge of everything. (*Gives the sword to* THOMAS.) They joke with me. This fellow says if I faint when I see her face – because she is so ugly – Cremuel will pick up the sword himself – and he is such a man he can cut off the head of the Hydra… Which I do not know what the Hydra is.

CHRISTOPHE. *C'est ce que je t'ai dit. C'est un lézard ou un serpent et pour chaque tête que tu coupe, deux autres la remplacent.*

THOMAS. Not in this case. Once the Boleyns are done, they are done. It's heavy.

EXECUTIONER. Of course. Let me show you. One has to practise – like this. (*Whirls it expertly, like a dancer.*) Every day one must handle the weapon. One may be called at any time. We do not kill so many in Calais. But one is called to other towns.

He gives it back to THOMAS *who handles it almost as expertly as the* EXECUTIONER.

CHRISTOPHE. It is a good trade. Let me have a turn.

THOMAS *gives the sword to* CHRISTOPHE *who hacks around wildly.*

EXECUTIONER. They tell me I can speak French to her and she will understand.

THOMAS. Yes, do so. For the love of God, Christophe – be careful with that!

The EXECUTIONER *takes the sword back from* CHRISTOPHE.

Now, young man, show me how this is to be done…

EXECUTIONER *indicates to* CHRISTOPHE *to put a hassock down. The space is for* ANNE*'s phantom body.*

EXECUTIONER. There is no block, she must kneel. Arms down. She must not bow the head. If she is steady it will be the work of a moment. If she moves, she will be cut to pieces.

THOMAS. I can answer for her – she is brave.

EXECUTIONER. She never sees the weapon. I call out 'give me the sword'. Her head turns – (*Mimes his killing stroke.*) Between one beat of the heart and the next, and it is done, she is in eternity.

CHRISTOPHE. They are coming.

Scene Thirty-Two

*Enter a black-veiled lady, with two veiled ladies attending her.
Behind her, a procession with cross. The whole court assembles,
living and dead. The veiled lady kneels on the hassock left by the*
EXECUTIONER. *She raises her veil. It is not* ANNE
BOLEYN, *as we expect, but* JANE SEYMOUR. *The two ladies
attending her raise their veils. They are* KATHERINE OF
ARAGON *and* ANNE BOLEYN, *now ghosts. Over* JANE
SEYMOUR*'s head they exchange a glance, then move aside.*
KING HENRY *approaches* JANE SEYMOUR *and she stands.
They join hands and* CRANMER *marries them. They step over
the* EXECUTIONER*'s hassock, and dance.*

KING HENRY (*cheerful*). What happened to her clothes? Her
headdress?

THOMAS. The people at the Tower have them. It is their
perquisite.

KING HENRY. Buy them back. Burn them – see to it yourself.
I'm making you a baron. Lord Cromwell of Putney.

THOMAS. No… Not Putney, Majesty – I might laugh.

KING HENRY. Wimbledon then. Lord Cromwell of Wimbledon.

KING HENRY *and* JANE SEYMOUR *lead everybody out –
except* THOMAS *and* STEPHEN. GHOSTS *gather.*

STEPHEN. I stand, as if upon a headland, my back to the sea,
and below me a burning plain.

THOMAS. Do you, Stephen? Have a cup of this wine. A good
one – Lord Lisle sends it from France for the King's own
drinking. (*Gives him a cup.*)

STEPHEN. Do you believe there can be peace in England now?

THOMAS. Peace? What was that saying of Thomas More's?

MORE'S GHOST. 'The peace of the hen coop when the fox has
run home'?

STEPHEN. I smell burning buildings. Fallen towers. Indeed
there is nothing but ash. Wreckage.

THOMAS. Wreckage is useful, isn't it? It can be fashioned into
all sorts of new things. Ask any dweller by the shore.

STEPHEN. Why did you let Wyatt go free – other than because he's your friend?

WOLSEY'S GHOST. Perhaps Stephen does not rate friendship as highly as we do.

STEPHEN. Brereton was high-handed and offended many. Harry Norris, Weston, well, there are gaps where they stood and you can put your own friends in the Privy Chamber alongside your man Rafe. And Mark – that squib of a boy with his lute – I grant you the place looks tidier without him. But George Rochford struck down and the rest of the Boleyns scurrying away – the Duke of Norfolk disgraced – now that really is wreckage. It's the end of everything. The Emperor will be delighted.

THOMAS. There are no endings. If you think so you are deceived as to their nature. They are all beginnings. This is one. (*Turns upstage.*)

STEPHEN. But all the players are gone! All those who carried the Cardinal to Hell –

WOLSEY'S GHOST. All of them.

STEPHEN. I am thinking… if this is what Cromwell does to the Cardinal's lesser enemies, what will he do, by and by, to the King himself?

THOMAS, *among the* GHOSTS, *turns slowly and fixes* STEPHEN *with a look that turns him to jelly. He holds him, mesmerised, for moment, then suddenly smiles.*

THOMAS. Drink my health.

STEPHEN, *trembling, does so.*

End.